1 - 11 - 98

ENEMIES OF THE PERMANENT THINGS

❋❋❋❋❋❋❋❋❋❋❋❋❋❋❋❋❋❋❋❋❋❋❋

RUSSELL KIRK

❋❋❋❋❋❋❋❋❋❋❋❋❋❋❋❋❋❋

Enemies

of the Permanent

Things

OBSERVATIONS OF ABNORMITY IN LITERATURE
AND POLITICS

❋❋❋❋❋❋❋❋❋❋❋❋❋❋❋❋❋❋❋❋

ARLINGTON HOUSE   *New Rochelle, New York*

To my father
RUSSELL ANDREW KIRK

Acknowledgements

The germ of this book was my Dancy Lectures on "Norms, Conformity, and Culture" at Alabama College, in 1958. To those lectures I have added here a number of related addresses and lectures at the New School for Social Research, Boston College, St. John's University, the Carnegie Institute of Technology, the University of Oklahoma, the University of Chicago, Eastern Michigan University, the College of William and Mary, Pepperdine College, and Park College.

Other portions of the following chapters have appeared, in different form, in *The Kenyon Review, The Sewanee Review, The Yale Review, The New York Times Magazine, Confluence, Cosmopolitan, The Eleusis, Modern Age, The University of Detroit Law Journal, Christianity Today, Catholic Mind, The Western Humanities Review, Phalanx, National Review, The Critic, The Month, The Dublin Review, Western Politica, Book Week, U.S.A., The University Bookman, Southwest Review, The Annals of the American Academy of Political and Social Science, The New Individualist Review, Catholic World, The Congressional Record, The Intercollegiate Review, Triumph,* and *Religion and Society.*

Finally, some portions—here reworked and integrated—have been printed previously as prefaces, in symposia, or in works of reference: as an introduction to Ehrenberg's *The Thaw* (Regnery); in *The Handbook of World History* (Philosophical Library); in *What Is Conservatism?* (Holt, Rinehart, and Winston); in *A Nation of States* (Rand McNally); and in *Freedom and Serfdom* (Reidel).

The proofs of this book were read, and the index compiled, by Mr. William Odell.

—Russell Kirk
Piety Hill
Mecosta, Michigan

Contents

ENEMIES OF THE PERMANENT THINGS

✻✻✻✻✻✻✻✻✻✻✻✻✻✻✻✻✻✻✻✻✻✻✻

"Four reformers met under a bramble bush. They were all agreed that the world must be changed. 'We must abolish property,' said one.

" 'We must abolish marriage,' said the second.

" 'We must abolish God,' said the third.

" 'I wish we could abolish work,' said the fourth.

" 'Do not let us get beyond practical politics,' said the first. 'The first thing is to reduce men to a common level.'

" 'The first thing,' said the second, 'is to give freedom to the sexes.'

" 'The first thing,' said the third, 'is to find out how to do it.'

" 'The first step,' said the first, 'is to abolish the Bible.'

" 'The first thing,' said the second, 'is to abolish the laws.'

" 'The first thing,' said the third, 'is to abolish mankind.' "

—ROBERT LOUIS STEVENSON, *"The Four Reformers"*

Part One

THE RECOVERY OF NORMS

✽✽✽✽✽✽✽✽✽✽✽✽✽✽✽✽✽✽✽✽✽✽✽

Normative Art and Modern Vices

THE WORD "VICE" ORIGINALLY MEANT ABNORMALITY, DEFORMITY, failing. This is a book about modern vices—that is, modern flaws—and about norms, the standards by which we live. I shall touch upon moral normality, although that subject is too intricate for any thorough discussion in these pages. For the most part, I am concerned here with the modern defiance of enduring standards in literature and politics. Although now and again I shall suggest means for the restoration of true standards, my primary purpose is diagnostic.

The malady of normative decay gnaws at order in the person and at order in the republic. Until we recognize the nature of this affliction, we must sink ever deeper into the disorder of the soul and the disorder of the state. A recovery of norms can be commenced only when we moderns come to understand in what manner we have fallen away from old truths.

Good literature and bad literature exert powerful influences upon private character and upon the polity of the commonwealth. Sound political theory and practice make it possible to maintain and improve private virtue; debased politics must debase human character. If ethical understanding, then, is ignored in modern letters and politics, we are left at the mercy of consuming private appetite and oppressive political power. We end in Darkness.

Rather than a systematic treatise, this book is a series of inquiries. My endeavor is to help to refurbish what Edmund Burke called "the wardrobe of a moral imagination." When the moral imagination is enriched, a people find themselves capable of great things; when it is impoverished, they cannot act effectively even for their own survival, no matter how immense their material resources. I am suggesting in these pages no panacea, then, but am attempting to point the way to first principles. Most of these principles are very old ones, obscured by neglect.

"Art is man's nature," said Burke, playing upon Aristotle's remark that art is the imitation of nature. We are not wholly subject to Fate and Fortune: for the art of the man of letters, and the art of the statist, determine in large part whether we become normal human beings, or are perverted into abnormal creatures. In erring Reason's spite, as Samuel Johnson knew, the will is free. All argument may be against it, but all necessity is for it. Personal and social decadence are not the work of ineluctable forces, but are the consequences of defying normative truth: a failure of right reason, if you will, resulting in abnormality. When we distort the arts of literature and statecraft, we warp our nature before long.

An abnormity, in its Latin root, means a monstrosity, defying the norm, the nature of things. (These words "abnormality" and "abnormity" are interchangeable.) An abnormal generation is a generation of monsters, enslaved by will and appetite. To recover an apprehension of normality, then, is to acquire an understanding of one's real nature. The alternative to such recovery is not a piquant pose of "nonconformity," but monstrosity in the soul and in society. If normative art expires, the people perish. This book is a discussion of the modern temper's inclination toward the abnormal, the enormous, the monstrous—often disguised in the garments of humanitarianism, amusing innovation, or delusive security.

Standardization without Standards

On few subjects has more nonsense been uttered, in our own time, than the meaning of the concept "norm." The confused discussion, these past few years, of convention, conformity, and intellectuality is bound up necessarily with the understanding—or mis-understanding—of this word "norm." I propose here to bring some order into this discussion, and to relate my considerations to the moral imagination.

A norm means an enduring standard. It is a law of nature, which we ignore at our peril. It is a rule of human conduct and a measure of public virtue. The norm does not signify the average, the median, the mean, the mediocre. The norm is not the conduct of the average sensual man. A norm is not simply a measure of average performance within a group. There is law for man, and law for thing; the late Alfred Kinsey notwithstanding, the norm for the wasp and the snake is not the norm for man. A norm exists: though men may ignore or forget a norm, still that norm does not cease to be, nor does it cease to influence men. A man apprehends a norm, or fails to apprehend it; but he does not create or destroy important norms.

We have learnt something, in this century, about the ineluctable character of norms; we have learnt from the disasters of an era in which norms were forgotten or defied—in which ideology did duty for moral standards and principles of justice. We have discovered that were there no norms for man, it would be necessary for us to invent some.

But I do not propose to invent norms. The sanction for obedience to norms must come from a source higher than private speculation: men do not submit long to their own creations. Standards erected out of expediency will be hurled down, soon enough, also out of expediency. Either norms have a reality independent of immediate social utility, or they are mere fictions. If men assume that norms are no better than the pompous fabrications of their ancestors, got up to serve the interests of a faction or an age, then every rising generation will challenge the principles of personal and social order, and will learn wisdom only through agony. For half a century, we have been experiencing the consequences of moral and social neoterism: so, like the generation of Socrates and Thucydides in the fifth century, we begin to perceive that somehow we have acted on false assumptions. No, norms cannot be invented. All that we can do is to reawaken our consciousness to the existence of norms; to confess that there are enduring standards superior to our petty private stock of rationality.

An inhumane view of life speedily leads to an inhumane social order. Men in society must subscribe to some body of principles; and when they have lost sight of norms, they attach themselves in panic to some fanatic set of secular dogmas. For a generation and more, many men have tried to make an ideology serve a normative end; and they have failed.

Indulge me in one anecdote of my undergraduate days. An old friend of mine—agent of a textbook publisher—whom we may call Mr. Stewart, for years went about quizzing people as to their first principles, after the fashion of Socrates. He was interested especially in whether they made any distinction between virtue and vice; or, at least, whether they acknowledged any means for measuring vice and virtue. One day he was in colloquy with a learned professor of languages, whom we may call Dr. Nemo. Mr. Stewart experienced some difficulty in persuading Dr. Nemo to affirm any first principle. Everything, Dr. Nemo implied, is subjective and relative and tentative and—well, ambivalent. Indeed, Dr. Nemo would not affirm positively, on being pressed, that two and two are four.

"Which was the better person, do you think," Mr. Stewart inquired presently, "Jesus or Nero?"

But Dr. Nemo declined to sit in judgment on this vexed question, lest he be judged. We don't have all the facts, he said; and there is Nero's childhood to consider; and the two held different social stations; and, after all, one of these persons held one set of value-preferences, and the other subscribed to a different set. Who could say which was the worthier?

It became clear that Dr. Nemo felt a marked aversion to acknowledging any norm. Dr. Nemo affirmed one thing only: that he was a liberal. Liberals, he explained, know that there exist two sides to every question, and that we ought to sheer away from prejudices, and that we have no right to come to any conclusion until all the facts are available and scientific tests are applied. Morals, besides, are the product of cultural circumstances.

"Who is the better man," Mr. Stewart persisted—this was shortly before the Second World War—"Hitler or Stalin?"

"Let's not reduce matters to absurdity," said Dr. Nemo. "Stalin's the better man, of course."

So, after all, Dr. Nemo did recognize the existence of some

norms. Stalin, he then believed, was a Man of Good Will—however much he might suffer from peccadilloes of taste and temper—a champion of Progress and Equality. Conceivably Dr. Nemo's opinion is modified today. Just here, however, I am not concerned with the relative degrees of iniquity of Hitler and Stalin. My point is that Dr. Nemo and persons like him—persons influenced by what the late Gordon Chalmers called "disintegrated liberalism"—recognize certain norms even at the moment they deny the existence of permanent standards. But their norms have the sanction only of ideological commitment; and that is a perilous sanction, often leading to erroneous judgments of men like Stalin.

Dr. Nemo held rather a friendly opinion of Stalin because he thought Stalin shared his own vague humanitarian value-preferences. Progress and Equality are charismatic terms, god-terms, for Dr. Nemo and his friends. These abstract concepts of his are derived, however remotely, from certain traditional norms. Had Dr. Nemo really discarded norms altogether, he would not have been able to believe even in Progress and Equality. Although he feared that Mr. Stewart might entrap him in some illiberal set of doctrines by obtaining his judgment concerning Jesus and Nero, he could not resist sitting in judgment when his ideological affections were in question.

With a man who maintains that he can discover no real standards for moral judgment of any sort, it is impossible to argue. Even Samuel Johnson, when told of a gentleman who maintained that virtue and vice are indistinguishable, contented himself with observing, "Why, sir, when he leaves our houses let us count our spoons." The most formidable of skeptics, David Hume, in his *Enquiry concerning the Principles of Morals*, put this difficulty with his usual acuteness:

"Disputes with men, pertinaciously obstinate in their principles, are, of all others, the most irksome; except, perhaps, those with persons, entirely disingenuous, who really do not believe the opinions they defend, but engage in the controversy, from affectation, from a spirit of opposition, or from a desire of showing wit and ingenuity, superior to the rest of mankind." It is best to shun their company. "Those who have denied the reality of moral distinctions," Hume continues, "may be ranked among the disingenuous disputants; nor is it conceivable, that any human creature could

ever seriously believe, that all characters and actions were alike
entitled to the affection and regard of everyone. . . . Let a man's
insensibility be ever so great, he must often be touched with the
images of Right and Wrong; and let his prejudices be ever so obstinate, he must observe, that others are susceptible of like impressions. The only way, therefore, of converting an antagonist of this
kind, is to leave him to himself."

So I do not propose to undertake just now a task from which
even the philosopher of Ninewells shrank; I do not intend to try to
refute the nihilist by the methods of pure reason. I do not mean to
survey the whole hoary controversy which has recurred perennially,
over twenty-six centuries, concerning the existence or character of
norms. To awaken an apprehension of norms was the high endeavor of Socrates and Plato; it was the constant theme of the
Christian divines; it weighed on the minds of the rationalists of the
eighteenth century and the positivists of the nineteenth. Nor shall I
attempt a systematic refutation of the positions held by the instru-
mentalists and the logical positivists of our century: that work already has been commenced by a variety of writers.

But I do propose to assist in the rescue of normative consciousness from the clutch of ideology. For it ought to be the moral
imagination which creates political doctrines, and not political doctrines which seduce the moral imagination. Our first task here is the
restoration of a proper vocabulary.

A norm, I have said, is an enduring standard for private and public conduct. It is a canon of human nature. Real progress consists in
the movement of mankind toward the understanding of norms, and
toward conformity to norms. Real decadence consists in the movement of mankind away from the understanding of norms, and away
from obedience to norms. The decay of the Greek civilization in the
fifth and fourth centuries before Christ; the decline of the Roman
order in the four centuries after Christ; the collapse of the medieval world in the fourteenth century; the decline of culture and the
eruption of dark powers in our own twentieth century—these were
times in which norms were forgotten or defied. The disintegration
of moral understanding was at once cause and consequence of confusion in the social order.

One cannot draw up a catalogue of norms as if it were an inven-
tory of goods. Normality inheres in some sensible object, and norms

depend one upon another, like the stones of a cathedral. But it is possible to say that there is a norm of charity; a norm of justice; a norm of freedom; a norm of duty; a norm of fortitude. Most of us perceive these norms clearly only when they are part and parcel of the life of a human being. Aristotle made norms recognizable by describing his "magnanimous man," the upright person and citizen. For the Christian, the norm is made flesh in the person of Christ. Normality is not what the average sensual man ordinarily possesses: it is what he ought to try to possess.

When I write of a "norm," I do not mean a "value" merely. A value is the quality of worth. Many things are worthwhile that are not normative. When most writers nowadays employ the word "value" as a term of philosophy, moreover, they mean "subjective value"—that is, the quality of being worthwhile, of giving pleasure or satisfaction to individuals, without judgment upon the intrinsic, absolute, essential merit of the sensation or action in question; without reference to its objective deserts. In the subjective sense, going to church is a value for some persons, and taking one's ease in a brothel is a value for others. A norm has value, but has more than value. A norm endures in its own right, whether or not it gives pleasure to particular individuals. A norm is the standard against which any alleged value must be measured objectively.

So much, just now, for definition. I am embarked upon a labor thoroughly conservative and thoroughly unpopular. The unabashed defender of traditional norms, and the unregenerate champion of prescriptive institutions—though they may have gained some ground in recent years—remain members of a Remnant. To be conservative is to be a conservator—a guardian of old truths and old rights. This rarely has been a popular office—not with the leaders of the crowd.

Yet for the restoration of normality, the understanding of the problem must extend beyond any narrow circle of intellectuals. The little knots of Stoics, isolated from the Roman masses, could retard the decay of their sprawling society; but they could not renew the vitality of their social order: and it was only in the hour of that order's destruction that inner order in soul and personality was restored by Christian faith—or by that religion which has existed since the beginning of the world, but which now takes the name of Christianity.

Yet Riesman and Viereck at least recognize that defiance of convention and militant nonconformity require some sort of apology. Others among us deny outright—or remain ignorant of the fact—that an intelligent case may be made for a convention in the service of normality and a conformity to enduring principles. These latter cry up a new convention of unconventionality and a new conformity of nonconformity, as if the civil social order had been created only so that we might have the fun of knocking it down again.

To deny for the sake of denial is to live with a sour taste in one's mouth. The sort of person whom Sidney Hook calls the "ritualistic liberal" is intolerant in the cause of toleration, conformist in the championship of nonconformity.

These excesses of the ritualistic liberal, nevertheless, sometimes produce a reaction among well-intentioned men which has its own blindness. "Let's be pragmatic, and forget about abstract theory." Because the ritualistic liberal, captive to ideology, has cried "wolf, wolf!" so shrilly and often so pointlessly, some among us suggest that all this fretting about the state of society is no better than a pathological condition of the critic: that somehow sweet reason and moderation and social legislation will carry us through our time of troubles without any need for discussion of general principles and aims. The complaints of the critic of society, whether he is conservative or liberal, are dismissed "pragmatically" as mere Anxiety.

"Anxiety" means distress of mind produced by prolonged apprehension of impending disaster. In our century, the dominant schools of psychology have arrogated the word as a term of pathology; and when many psychologists employ it, they imply that anxiety is apprehension without real cause: that is, a dread purely subjective, conjured up by the sufferer's mental sickness.

But in truth, anxiety is produced by disorder: disorder in private existence, and disorder in social existence. If the disorder which afflicts the anxious man is purely illusory, the product of his sick fancy, then anxiety falls within the borders of pathology; but if the disorder, internal and external, which the anxious man experiences is the product of a real moral and social confusion in his time, then the cure for anxiety lies not in psychiatric and physiological treatment, but in a stern endeavor to lessen this real disorder—an endeavor best lightened occasionally by letting cheerfulness break in.

A condition of anxiety brought on by a demonstrably real decay of order can be alleviated only by a restoration of order—or, at least, by satisfying work toward such a restoration, both in the order of the soul and in the order of politics. Anxiety results from the collapse of normative belief, the dissolution of standards of private conduct and public justice. Before anxiety may be dissipated, norms must be recognized and obeyed. It is not necessary for the dispelling of anxiety that the norms be wholly triumphant in society at large: no society ever has been wholly submissive to normative precepts. But it is essential that the sufferer from anxiety become aware of the reality of norms, and that he do something to signify his recognition of those standards, at least in his inner life, before he can be relieved from his affliction in any degree. Anxiety battens on fecklessness, impotence, frustration; it shrinks when conformity to norms restores purpose to a man's existence.

Dante knew all the woes to which humanity is heir. Yet Dante was not an Anxious Man, though he lived in a time of violent disorder. He knew that the principles of order abide, and that justice is more than human, and that art is the servant of enduring standards. His vision of eternal happiness and eternal torment was not a vision of disharmony; it was governed by norms; and in the certitude of those standards, all his mundane sorrows found their remedy. He faced Terror unflinchingly, and his achievement was not simply artistic mastery, nor yet remedy of the immediate distresses of his century, but rather the burning renewal of certain ancient moral insights, which he bequeathed as a legacy beyond price to the troubled souls who were to succeed him in time. It is thus that the consummate artist fights his battle against obsessive Anxiety.

Finally, so far as anxiety is bound up with the stress and tension essential to human nature, anxiety never can be abolished; and if it could, great literature would be written no longer. For a body that has ceased to react is a corpse, and an artist who has ceased to dread disorder is a vegetable. Anxiety in the artist and the statesman and the moralist is one of the products of that "fortunate fall," that contradiction which lies at the heart of human life—a contradiction which even the melioristic liberal mind, long dominant among us, now is beginning to make out. "This inner contradiction," as Arnold Toynbee writes in *An Historian's Approach to*

Religion, "means that ordinary life is a tension for which another
name is Suffering." We are not constituted for perfect happiness;
we are meant to struggle; we are Suffering Servants. The world
always is full of genuine reasons for serious anxiety among thinking
men. Our hope, and the mission of the man of letters, the statist,
and the ethical philosopher, is not to sweep away that anxiety—for
such an aspiration would be Gnostic illusion—but to keep anxiety
from usurping the whole of life. Only when man perceives the
norms that regulate inner and outer order is he armed to contend
against anxiety as an obsession.

So the moral and cultural conservative, the guardian of normality, declines to embrace dime-store pragmatism: in rejecting ideology, he does not deny the reality of much anxiety about the state of
the person and the state of the republic. He neither denounces
convention and conformity indiscriminately, nor defends every
popular fashion of the evanescent hour. What he respects is a sound
conformity to abiding principles and a healthy convention which
keeps the knife from our throats. Conformity to enduring moral
truths is not servile. Obedience to the conventions of the just civil
social order is not stupid.

In our time, when the fountains of the great deep are broken up,
conformity and convention of the higher sort deserve the support of
every man who values civilization. Coleridge says that there are
two great elements in any society, its Permanence and its Progression. The Permanence of a state, roughly speaking, is its conservative interest; its Progression, what nowadays we call its liberal interest. There are ages in which intelligent people would do well to ally
themselves with the Progression of their nation, to contend against
stagnation; for a society without the means of renewal is not long
for this world.

But our time is not such an age. We do not live in an ancient
Egyptian or Peruvian culture, where the dead hand of the past
seems to lie mercilessly upon a whole people, and where the only
change is corruption. Our modern peril, rather, is that of vertiginous speed: the traditions of civility may be swallowed up by will
and appetite; with us, the expectation of change is greater than the
expectation of continuity, and generation scarcely links with generation. In the twentieth century, it is our Permanence, not our Progression, which needs the adherence of thinking men and women.

The twentieth-century ideologue—who, as Hawthorne said of the Abolitionist, brandishes his one idea like an iron flail—detests the champions of norms and conventions. To the Gnostic visionary, to the secularist worshipper of Progress and Uniformity, respect for norms and conventions is the mark of the beast. He hopes to sweep away every obstacle to the attainment of his standardized, regulated, mechanized, unified world, purged of faith, variety, and ancient longings. Permanence he cannot abide. He hungers after a state like a tapioca pudding, composed of so many identical globules of other-directed men.

Yet the troubles of our time have worried this zealot for heaven upon earth; he experiences secret misgivings nowadays; and the more he suffers from inner doubts of the perfectibility of man and society, the harder does he flail against the defenders of norm and convention, endeavoring in the heat of his assault to forget the disquieting voice—in Santayana's phrase—of a forlorn and dispossessed orthodoxy that prophesies disaster for men who would be as gods.

Lacking an apprehension of norms, there is no living in society or out of it. Lacking sound conventions, the civil social order dissolves. And lacking variety of life and diversity of institutions, normality succumbs to the tyranny of standardization without standards.

The Shoulders of Giants

"We are dwarfs mounted upon the shoulders of giants," Fulbert of Chartres told his scholars in the eleventh century. The great Schoolman meant that we modern folk—and the people of the eleventh century thought themselves quite as modern as we do— incline toward the opinion that wisdom was born with our generation. In a number of respects, whether in the twelfth century or the twentieth, the living generation knows more than did its grandparents' or great-grandparents' generation. The folk of Fulbert's generation knew more about the principles of architecture, for instance, than the folk of the tenth century had known. We people of the twentieth century, in our turn, know more about physics or chemistry, for example, than did the finest scholars at Chartres.

But for all that, Fulbert argued, we are no better than dwarfs mounted upon the shoulders of giants. We see so far only because of the tremendous stature of those giants, our ancestors, upon whose shoulders we stand. Gothic architecture in the eleventh century could not have existed without its foundations in the ninth and tenth centuries—or, for that matter, in the architecture of ancient Syria. Atomic physics in our sense could not have come into being without the speculative spirit of the seventeenth century—or, for that matter, without the intuitions of the pre-Socratic Greeks. Our civilization is an immense continuity and essence. Fulbert, Bishop of Chartres, was right: if we ignore or disdain those ancestral giants who uphold us in our modern vainglory, we tumble down into the ditch of unreason.

So if it is true that even our scientific knowledge, in considerable part, is a legacy from our forbears, it is still more certain that our moral, our social, and our artistic knowledge is an inheritance from men long dead. G. K. Chesterton coined the phrase "the democracy of the dead." In deciding any important moral or political question, Chesterton writes, we have the obligation to consult the considered opinions of the wise men who have preceded us in time. We owe these dead an immense debt, and their ballots deserve to be counted. Thus we have no right simply to decide any question by what the momentary advantage may be to us privately: we have the duty of respecting the wisdom of our ancestors; and also we have the duty of respecting the rights of posterity, the generations that are to come after us. This complex of duties is what the old Romans called piety: reverence for our nation, our family in the larger sense, our ancestors, in a spirit of religious veneration. A French philosopher of our time, Gabriel Marcel, writes that the only healthy society is the society which respects tradition. We ought to live, Marcel says, in an atmosphere of "diffused gratitude"—of sympathy for the hopes and achievements of our ancestors, from whom we derive our life and our culture, and which we are morally obliged to pass on undiminished, if not enhanced, to our descendants. We are grateful to the giants upon whose shoulders we stand. This feeling or atmosphere of diffused veneration is weakened in our modern age, for many people live only for themselves, ignoring the debt they owe to the past and the responsibility they owe to the future. They are ungrateful; and ingratitude brings on its own punishment.

Normative knowledge, then, is no burden, but instead a rich patrimony. Those who refuse it must be taught by personal experience—a hard master, as Benjamin Franklin says, though fools will have no other. Edmund Burke gave this concept of willing obligation to the dead, the living, and those yet unborn its most moving expression. We all are subject, he wrote, to "the contract of eternal society." This immortal contract is made between God and mankind, and between the generations that have perished from the earth, and the generation that is living now, and the generations that are yet to come. It is a covenant binding upon us all. No man has a right to abridge that contract at will; and if we do break it, we suffer personally and all society suffers; and we are cast out of this civil social order (built by the giants) into an "antagonist world" of total disorder—or, as the New Testament has it, into the outer darkness, where there shall be wailing and gnashing of teeth.

We moderns, Burke continued, tend to be puffed up with a little petty private rationality, thinking ourselves wiser than the prophets and the law-givers, and are disposed to trade upon the trifling bank and capital of our private intelligence. That way lies ruin. But though the individual is foolish, the species is wise; and, given time, the species judges rightly. The moral precepts and the social conventions which we obey represent the considered judgments and filtered experience of many generations of prudent and dutiful human beings—the most sagacious of our species. It is folly to ignore this inherited wisdom in favor of our own arrogant little notions of right and wrong, of profit and loss, of justice and injustice. Burke, though the most prophetic man of his age, never thought himself taller than the giants from whom came his strength.

This is no less true in the twentieth century, and in America. Our normative inheritance in the United States is of European and Asiatic origin: normality does not recognize frontiers.

In *The Revolt of the Masses*, Ortega declared that American civilization could not long endure, were it severed from European culture. Ortega was right: American culture, and the American civil social order, share with modern European civilization a common patrimony. The principal elements in that inheritance are though they may, the ideologues cannot break altogether with the Christian religion.

The second article in our common patrimony is our theory and practice of ordered liberty: our system of law and politics. This is derived from Roman and from medieval sources—and in part, more remotely, from Greek philosophy and historic experience. To the classical and medieval ideas of justice, and to the classical and medieval social experience, there has been added a modern body of theory and practice—although too often we modern folk, including the scholars among us, exaggerate the importance of "liberal" contributions in the eighteenth and nineteenth centuries, some of which latter contributions have not stoutly withstood the severe tests of our twentieth-century time of troubles.

The doctrines of natural law; the concept of a polity, a just and balanced commonwealth; the principle of a government of laws, not of men; the understanding that justice means "to each his own"; the idea of a healthful tension between the claims of order and the claims of freedom—these passed directly from Europe into American theory and institution. More than any other single figure, Cicero influenced the theory of both European and American politics—and through that theory, our political institutions.

To this general heritage, the English added their common law and their prudent, prescriptive politics; and the English patrimony was directly incorporated in the American social order. The founders of the American Republic, especially the lawyers and politicians among them, took for granted this English pattern of politics, modifying it only slightly to conform to colonial usage and to suit the new nation—and even then modifying it not in favor of some newfangled abstract scheme, but rather on the model of the Roman Republic.

The principle of .elaborate restraints upon political power, for instance, is conspicuous in the political theory and practice of Britain and in that of the United States. It has been so since the beginning of American society. John Cotton declared in Massachusetts in the third decade of the seventeenth century: "Let all the world learn to give mortal men no greater power than they are content they shall use—for use it they will. . . . This is one of the strains of nature: it affects boundless liberty, and to run to the utmost extent. Whatever power he hath received, he hath a corrupt nature that will improve it in one thing or other; if he have liberty, he will think why may he not use it. . . . There is a strain in a man's heart that sometime or other runs out to excess, unless the Lord restrain it; but it is not good to venture it."

Yet the third article in this common patrimony is more enduring, perhaps, than even political usage. Great works of literature join us in an intellectual community. And the ethical cast of enduring humane letters, working upon the imagination, is as normative as is religious doctrine or political principle. Humane literature teaches us what it is to be a man. Homer and Hesiod; Herodotus and Thucydides; Sophocles and Plato; Virgil and Horace; Livy and Tacitus; Cicero and Seneca; Epictetus and Marcus Aurelius; Dante, Petrarch, Erasmus, Shakespeare, Cervantes, Goethe, and all the rest—these have formed the mind and character of Americans as well as of Europeans. The best of American literature is part and parcel of the normative continuity of literature, extending back beyond the dawn of history.

In all essential respects, then, Europe and America enjoy a common faith, a common system of law and politics, and a common body of great literature. They make one civilization still. These normative and cultural bonds have outlasted dynasties, empire, and even philosophies; though injured now and again by war or social dissolution, they rise with renewed vigor after every period of violence or decadence. Whether this heritage is to survive the twentieth century must depend, in no small part, upon the reinvigoration of a popular normative consciousness. Although I shall touch only glancingly in this book upon religious faith, the following chapters have to do with particular difficulties of the modern age in politics and in literature—and in education, which is concerned with the whole of our patrimony.

The soul of a civilization may be lost at the very moment of that culture's material triumph. In our time, we run no risk of experiencing too little change; whether we like it or not, we ride the whirlwind of innovation. To give direction to this change, and to insure that generation may link with generation, some of us must undertake the rescue of the moral imagination.

The undisciplined modern mind, thinking it pursues facts, often follows a corpse-candle to the brink of the abyss—and, sometimes, over that brink. "The Devil played at chess with me," wrote Sir

Thomas Browne, "and yielding a Pawn, thought to gain a Queen of me, taking advantage of my honest endeavours; and whilst I laboured to raise the structure of my Reason, he strived to undermine the edifice of my Faith." If a man relies wholly upon his private rational powers, he will lose his faith—and perhaps the world as well, risking his nature at the Devil's chess-game. But if a man fortifies himself with the normative disciplines, he draws upon the imagination and the lessons of the ages, and so is fit to confront even a diabolical adversary.

The Doors of Normative Perception

"How were the giants so wise?" Sincerely or mordantly, this question will be asked. To phrase it another way, what are the sources of the enduring norms? Why should we take them on authority?

The answer, which is not simple, will be touched upon repeatedly in the following chapters. But for the moment, we may indicate three doors of normative perception: revelation, custom or common sense, and the insights of the seer.

For the man of religious convictions—Christian, or Jew, or Moslem—the primary source of knowledge about faith and morals is divine revelation. Yet this will not suffice for the unbeliever or the skeptic; neither will revelation tell us much about political prudence, nor about the standards of art. I am one who embraces the transcendent truth of revelation. In this book, nevertheless, I argue chiefly on the foundation of the other two means of normative perception—both because the discussion of revelation's validity would be too intricate and lengthy for these pages, and because I address myself to doubters, as well as to the converted.

Direct revelation, moreover, has been extremely rare: on most occasions, divine wisdom was expressed through the mouths of very human prophets—who may be categorized, if you wish, under the later classification of "seer." The most important of all direct revelations was simply the sentence that Moses heard from the burning bush: "I am the God of thy father, the God of Abraham, the God of Isaac, and the God of Jacob." (The first phrase, I am told, is more accurately rendered, "I am that am.") And those words were heard not by the Israelite people collectively, but by Moses in solitude; revelation requires its agents, and the man who has penetrated beyond the veil of sense may be able to say only, with Pascal, "Fire, fire, fire!"—the rest being inexpressible in language, and almost unthinkable in thought.

To maintain that *all* normative truth may be found in the Bible, or in any other sacred book, is to fall into the error of what Coleridge called "bibliolatry." Though the Decalogue is the word of God, it is not the sole source of the commandments for mankind. The universality of such moral laws is summed up succinctly by C. S. Lewis, in his *Abolition of Man*; Lewis calls these universal commandments, perceived and expressed variously in every culture, "the Tao." "Honor thy father and thy mother, that thy days may be long in the land," for example, is an injunction of which every people have been made aware. Although in our Father's house are many mansions, they are not all on the same floor, true enough; yet Jewish and Christian dogmas, if the clearest and highest expression of moral normality, nevertheless do not enjoy an exclusive claim to such revelation.

"Orthodoxy is my doxy; heterodoxy is another man's doxy." I subscribe to Samuel Johnson's profession. When the art of worldly wisdom is in question, for all that, the modern opponent of abnormality, if he means to persuade the heterodox, repairs to the arguments of Johnson's "Tory by accident," David Hume. In morals and taste, says Hume, we govern ourselves by custom—that is, by the habits of the human race. The standards of morality are shown to us by study of the story of mankind, and the arbiters of those standards are men of strong sense and delicate sentiment, whose impressions force themselves upon the wills of their fellow-men.

This is another way of saying what I suggested a few paragraphs ago: that for the most part our norms are derived from the experience of the species, the ancient usages of humanity; and from the perceptions of genius, of those rare men who have seen profoundly into the human condition—and whose wisdom soon is accepted by the mass of men, down the generations. I turn first to custom, or what we call common sense.

The good citizen, Virgil remarks, is a law-abiding traditionalist:

that is, a man governing himself by custom, deferring to the habits formed among a people through their painful process of trial and error, their encounters with gods and men over a great many years. Custom is the expression of a people's collective experience, some of it accumulated before that people had a history. "Custom, then, is the great guide of human life," says Hume. "It is that principle alone which renders our experience useful to us, and makes us expect, for the future, a similar train of events with those which have appeared in the past. Without the influence of custom, we should be entirely ignorant of every matter of fact beyond what is immediately present to the memory and senses."

Custom is closely allied with common sense, "those convictions which we receive from nature, which all men possess in common, and by which they test the truth of knowledge and the morality of actions; the practical sense of the greater part of mankind, especially as unaffected by logical subtleties or imagination," as the old *Century Dictionary* puts it. Common sense is "consensus," or general agreement on first principles—a word somewhat tarnished by politicians in recent years. In the vast majority of our normative decisions, we defer to the consensus of mankind—that is, we feel ourselves bound to think and behave as decent men always have thought and behaved. Conformity to custom—call it prejudice, if you will—makes a man's virtue his habit, as Burke expressed this idea. Without the power of custom to control and instruct us, we should be involved perpetually in "agonizing reappraisals," endeavoring to decide every question upon its particular merits and advantages of the moment; we would be unnerved incessantly by doubt and vacillation.

Common sense and custom, then, are the practical expressions of what mankind has learnt in the school of hard knocks. There exists a legitimate presumption in favor of venerable usages; for your or my private experience is brief and confused, but the experience of the race takes into account the consequences suffered or the rewards obtained by multitudes of human beings in circumstances similar to yours and mine. Custom and common sense constitute an immemorial empiricism, with roots so antique and obscure that we can only conjecture the origins of any general habit. One thing we do know: it is dangerous to break with ways that have been intertwined so intricately in human longings and satisfactions. Those who toss the cake of custom into the rubbish-bin may find themselves supperless. And if common sense is discarded—why, it is supplanted not by a universal intellectualism, but by common nonsense.

Yet how did folk-wisdom come into being? It cannot be that a crowd of dullards, merely by the accumulation of numbers and the passage of time, somehow produce a collective sagacity. Penetrating insights guided the Greeks before Homer. "The old Greeks knew everything," a talented friend said to me once. "But how did they know it?"

The answer may be that at the beginnings of anything resembling a true civil social order, individual men possessed of genius—obscure men whose very names have perished—were the discoverers of the truths which we now call custom and common sense. Hume's men of strong sense and delicate sentiment, or their primitive forerunners, presumably existed when man was becoming true man; and their insights were impressed upon their primitive fellows. It is believed that those old-fangled and picturesque garments we now call "folk costumes" once were the dress of a local aristocracy; the peasants adopted these fashions, but have retained them long after the aristocracy has gone on to newer modes—or perhaps has gone on to extinction. So it may be with the practices and beliefs which we call custom and common sense: originally these may have been the intuitions or the empirical conclusions of gifted individuals, who were emulated by the common man; but as the elapse of centuries has hidden the original authorship of folkways and popular convictions, so mankind has come to assume that the multitude itself always apprehended these truths, much as the ant-hill and the hive seem to be governed by a collective consciousness without the direction of commanding intellects.

Such reflections—perhaps impossible to demonstrate or to disprove—lead us to the third principal door to normative understanding: the astounding perceptions of the seer—"the blind man who sees," like Homer. A few men mysteriously endowed with a power of vision denied to the overwhelming majority of us have been the Hammurabis of our moral and political and literary codes. We know their names, although sometimes we know little but their names and some appended scanty legends. (As Mark Twain put it, the Iliad and the Odyssey were written either by Homer or by another man with the same name.) We accept such men of genius as authorities because we recognize, however imperfectly, that they see farther than you or I see.

A typical undergraduate may inquire at this point, "Who made these seers normative authorities?" Why, no one appointed them: their strength of mind and eloquence of expression conquered the mass of men. Their authority in part is vindicated by the immense influence which their words have exerted ever since those words were uttered; and in part by the fact that intelligent men in every age, upon reflection, have assented to the truths exerted by these prophets and poets and philosophers. You and I see as in a glass, darkly—the riddle of a mirror; but those few men of vision saw something of the real nature of things. It is as if they had the eyes of eagles, and we the eyes of moles. (A mole, it is true, knows the eagle only by his talons, when unhappily that mole has ventured above ground.) Presumably the mole cannot even dream of that power of vision which the eagle takes as his birthright.

Moses and Solon were such seers for the Jews and for the Athenians. Through the moral perception of these law-givers, these half-symbolic figures who burst the bounds of pragmatic reasoning, their peoples experienced what Eric Voegelin calls "a leap in being," a new and stronger apprehension of truth. What before had been mere cloudy surmises became norms: the law for man.

Such seers were the unknown author of the book of Job, and the prophet called Isaiah; such were Heraclitus and Democritus, and such Sophocles and Plato. Such, in the Orient, were Confucius and Lao-tse, and Gautama. Such was Virgil for the Romans—and, in some sense, Livy. In the Christian continuity, such seers were St. Paul, St. Augustine, St. Thomas Aquinas, Dante, and Pascal. Yet other seers will appear in our midst, no doubt, unless we make it impossible for them to exist, or unless we close our eyes and ears to the very possibility of the transcendent.

These are the giants, upon whose shoulders we stand. No one knows better than a great scientist the extent of our debt to men of vision who have preceded us in time. "If I have seen farther, it is by standing on the shoulders of giants," said Sir Isaac Newton, echoing Fulbert of Chartres. To overthrow a giant, it is necessary either to be a giant one's self, or else a David favored of the Lord; and few of us are either. Therefore we yield to the seers—the prophets and poets and philosophers of the Great Tradition—as authorities, because without their guidance we would wander hungry in a dark wood. The life of pygmies in the modern world would be poor, nasty, brutish, and short.

We are governed by the normative insights of the giants because we are incapable of inventing better rules for ourselves. A college sophomore once informed me that *he* was ready to work out a complete moral system without reference to the opinions of our ancestors. I inquired whether he thought himself capable of constructing, unaided, an automobile. He confessed that he did not so think. I then suggested that a contraption merely mechanical, like an automobile, is simple when compared with an instrument for controlling the passions of men. Indeed, this student's system of morality would be patched together, at best, from fragments of Christian doctrine and classical philosophy: he might regard our moral order as a junkyard, yet only there would he find his parts.

Karl Marx had some of the qualities of a seer, and he postulated a new normative order. His moral system, nevertheless, was a caricature of Christian doctrine, combined with ideas from Bentham and Hegel (both of whom Marx reviled); and, once tested, Marxism turned out to be hideous, and quite contrary to its inventor's expectations. Many false prophets have gone forth into the world; but by their works may they be known.

By definition, human nature is constant. Because of that constancy, men of vision are able to describe the norms, the rules, for mankind. From revelation, from custom and common sense, and from the intuitive powers of men possessed by genius, we know that there exist law for man and law for thing. Normality is the goal of human striving; abnormity is the descent toward a condition less than human, surrender to vice. With these premises in mind, we may turn to some examination of the struggle between the normal and the abnormal in twentieth-century letters and politics.

Part Two

THE NORMS OF LITERATURE

✿✿✿✿✿✿✿✿✿✿✿✿✿✿✿✿✿✿✿✿

I. THE PURPOSE OF HUMANE LETTERS

Nature Imitating Art

THE AIM OF GREAT BOOKS IS ETHICAL—TO TEACH WHAT IT MEANS to be a man. Every major form of literary art has taken for its deeper themes what T. S. Eliot called "the permanent things"—the norms of human nature. Until very recent years, men took it for granted that literature exists to form the normative consciousness: that is, to teach human beings their true nature, their dignity, and their rightful place in the scheme of things. Such has been the end of poetry— in the largest sense of that word—ever since Job and Homer.

The very phrase "humane letters" implies that literature is meant to teach us the character of human normality. As Irving Babbitt wrote in his *Literature and the American College,* humanism (derived from the Latin *humanitas*) is an ethical discipline, intended to develop the qualities of manliness through the study of important books. The literature of nihilism, of pornography, and of sensationalism, as Albert Salomon suggests in *The Tyranny of Progress,* is a recent development, arising in the eighteenth century (though stronger still in our time) with the decay of the religious understanding of life and with the decline of the Great Tradition in philosophy.

This normative end of letters has been especially powerful in English literature, which never succumbed to the egoism that came to dominate French letters at the end of the eighteenth century. The names of Milton, Bunyan, Dryden, and Johnson—or, in America, of Hawthorne, Emerson, Melville, and Henry Adams—may be sufficient illustrations of the point. The great popular novelists of the nineteenth century—Scott, Dickens, Thackeray, Trollope—all assumed that the writer is under a moral obligation to normality: that is, explicitly or implicitly, bound by certain enduring standards of private and public conduct.

Now I do not mean that the great writer incessantly utters homilies. With Ben Jonson, he may "scourge the naked follies of the time," but he does not often murmur, "Be good, fair maid, and let who will be clever." Rather, the man of letters teaches the norms of our existence through parable, allegory, analogy, and holding up the mirror to nature. Like William Faulkner, the writer may write much more about what is evil than about what is good; and yet, exhibiting the depravity of human nature, he establishes in his reader's mind the awareness that there exist enduring standards from which we fall away; and that fallen nature is an ugly sight. Or the writer may deal chiefly, as did John P. Marquand, with the triviality and emptiness of a smug society that has forgotten norms. Often, in his appeal of a conscience to a conscience, he may row with muffled oars; sometimes he is aware only dimly of his normative function. The better the artist, one almost may say, the more subtle the preacher. Imaginative persuasion, not blunt exhortation, commonly is the method of the literary champion of norms.

So it was that the most influential poet and critic of our century, T. S. Eliot, saw himself as the heir of Virgil and Dante. The poet—and by that word Eliot meant the imaginative and philosophical writer in general—ought not to force his ego upon the public, Eliot maintained; instead, the poet's mission is to transcend the personal and the particular. As he wrote in "Tradition and the Individual Talent" (1917), the poet will find nothing new under the sun:

"It is not in his personal emotions, the emotions provoked by particular events in his life, that the poet is in any way remarkable or interesting. His particular emotions may be very simple, or crude, or flat. The emotion in his poetry will be a very complex thing, but not with the complexity of the emotions of people who have very complex or unusual emotion in life. One error, in fact, of eccentricity in poetry is to seek for new human emotions to express; and in this search for novelty in the wrong place it discovers the perverse. The business of the poet is not to find new emotions, but to use the ordinary ones and, in working them up into poetry, to express feelings which are not in actual emotions at all."

No poet ever seemed more normal than did Eliot himself; yet few poets can have been more interesting, face to face. I used to meet Eliot chiefly in bare little Edinburgh hotel parlors—where nobody could find him and lionize him—or in fusty London clubs, where the traditions of civility had swept emotion under the old Turkey carpet. I marvelled always at his calm *kindness*, and it came into my mind that the kindly man has comparatively little ego in his cosmos. In his private life, as in his poems and his criticism and his plays, Eliot abided by the permanent things; and from that fidelity came his quiet strength. A late Augustan, he was resolved *not* to be a literary show: not to exhibit himself, but to dress old truths in modern clothing, was Eliot's first principle.

This principle prevailed until almost the end of the eighteenth century. Since then, the egoism of one school of the Romantics has obscured the primary purpose of humane letters. And many of the Realists have written of man as if he were brute only—or, at best, brutalized by institutions. In our own time, and especially in America, we have seen the rise to popularity of a school of writers more nihilistic than ever were the Russian nihilists: the literature of *merde,* of disgust and denunciation, sufficiently described in Edmund Fuller's *Man in Modern Fiction.* To the members of this school, the writer is no defender or expositor of standards, for there are no norms to explain or defend: a writer merely registers, unreservedly, his disgust with humanity and with himself—and makes money by it. (This is a world away from Jonathan Swift, who, despite his loathing of most human beings, detested them only because they fell short of what they were meant to be.)

Yet the names of our twentieth-century nihilists will be forgotten in less than a generation, I suspect, while there will endure from our age the works of a few men of letters whose appeal is to the enduring things, and therefore to posterity. I think, for instance, of Gironella's novel *The Cypresses Believe in God.* The gentle novice who trims the hair and washes the bodies of the poorest of the poor in old Gerona, though he dies by Communist bullets, will live a long span in the realm of letters; while the scantily-disguised personalities of our nihilistic authors, swaggering nastily as characters in the best-sellers, will be extinguished the moment when the public's fancy veers to some newer sensation. For as the normative consciousness breathes life into the soul and into the social order, so the normative understanding gives an author lasting fame.

Malcolm Cowley, writing a few years ago about the recent crop of first-novelists, observed that the several writers he had discussed scarcely had heard of the Seven Cardinal Virtues or of the Seven Deadly Sins. To these young novelists, crimes and sins are merely mischances; real love and real hate are absent from their books. To this rising generation of writers, the world seems purposeless, and human actions meaningless. They seek to express nothing but a vagrant ego. (Jacques Barzun, in *The House of Intellect,* has some shrewd things to say about the unjustified pride of these aspiring writers.) And Cowley suggests that these young men and women, introduced to no norms in childhood and youth except the vague attitude that one is entitled to do as one likes, so long as it doesn't injure somebody else, are devoid of spiritual and intellectual discipline—empty, indeed, of real desire for anything.

This sort of aimless and unhappy writer is the product of a time in which the normative function of letters has been badly neglected. Ignorant of his own mission, such a writer tends to think of his occupation as a mere skill, possibly lucrative, sometimes satisfying to one's vanity, but dedicated to no end. Even the "proletarian" writing of the twenties and thirties acknowledged an end; but that has died of disillusion and inanition. If writers are in this plight, in consequence of the prevailing "permissive" climate of opinion, what of their readers? Comparatively few book-readers nowadays seek normative knowledge. They are after amusement, sometimes of a vicariously gross character, or else pursue a vague "awareness" of current affairs and intellectual currents, suitable for cocktail-party conversation.

The young novelists described by Malcolm Cowley are of the number of Eliot's "Hollow Men." And nature abhorring a vacuum, into minds that are vacant of norms must come some force—sometimes a force of diabolical bent.

Literature can corrupt; and it is possible, too, to be corrupted by an ignorance of humane letters, much of our normative knowledge

necessarily being derived from our reading. The person who reads
bad books instead of good may be subtly corrupted; the person who
reads nothing at all may be forever adrift in life, unless he lives in a
community still powerfully influenced by what Gustave Thibon
calls "moral habits" and by oral tradition. And absolute abstinence
from printed matter has become rare. If a small boy does not read
Treasure Island, the odds are that he will read *Mad Ghoul Comics*.

So I think it worthwhile to suggest the outlines of the literary
discipline which induces some understanding of enduring standards. For centuries, such a program of reading—though never
called a program—existed in Western nations. It strongly influenced the minds and actions of the leaders of the infant American
Republic, for instance. If one pokes into what books were read by
the leaders of the Revolution, the framers of the Constitution, and
the principal men of America before 1800, one finds that nearly all
of them were acquainted with a few important books: the King
James version of the Bible, Plutarch's *Lives*, Shakespeare, something of Cicero, something of Virgil. This was a body of literature
highly normative. The founders of the Republic thought of their
new commonwealth as a blending of the Roman Republic with
prescriptive English institutions; and they took for their models in
leadership the prophets and kings and apostles of the Bible, and the
noble Greeks and Romans of Plutarch. Cato's stubborn virtue,
Demosthenes' eloquent vaticinations, Cleomenes' rash reforming
impulse—these were in their minds' eyes; and they tempered their
conduct accordingly. "But nowadays," as Chateaubriand wrote
more than a century ago, "statesmen understand only the stock-
market—and that badly."

Of course it was not by books alone that the normative understanding of the framers of the Constitution, for instance, was
formed. Their apprehension of norms was acquired in family,
church, and school, and in the business of life. But that portion of
their normative consciousness which was obtained from books did
loom large. For we cannot attain very well to enduring standards if
we rely simply on personal experience as a normative mentor. Personal experiment with first principles often is ruinous, and always is
time-consuming; and as Newman wrote, "Life is for action." Therefore we turn to the bank and capital of the ages, the normative
knowledge found in literature, if we seek guidance in morals, poli-

tics, and taste. Ever since the invention of printing, this normative understanding has been expressed increasingly in books, so that nowadays most people form their opinions, in considerable part, from the printed page. This may be regrettable sometimes; it may be what D. H. Lawrence called "chewing the newspapers"; but it is a fact. Deny a fact, and that fact will be your master.

Another fact is this: for some thirty years we have been failing, in America, to develop a normative consciousness in young people through a careful plan of reading important literature. We have talked about "education for life" and "training for life-adjustment"; but many of us seem to have forgotten that literary disciplines are a principal means for learning to accept the conditions of existence. Moreover, unless the life to which we are urged to adjust ourselves is governed by norms, it must be a bad life for everyone.

One of the faults of the typical "life-adjustment" or "permissive" curriculum in the schools—paralleled, commonly, by similarly indulgent attitudes in the family—has been the substitution of "real-life situation" reading for the study of truly imaginative literature. This tendency has been especially noticeable in the lower grades of school, but it extends upward in some degree through high school. The "Dick and Jane" and "run, Spot, run" school of letters does not stir the imagination, and it imparts small apprehension of norms. Apologists for this aspect of life-adjustment schooling believe that they are inculcating respect for values by prescribing simple readings that commend tolerant, kindly, co-operative behavior. Yet this is no effective way to impart a knowledge of norms: direct moral didacticism, whether of the Victorian or of the twentieth-century variety, usually awakens resistance in the recipient, particularly if he has some natural intellectual power.

The fulsome praise of goodness can alienate; it can whet the appetite for the cookie-jar on the top shelf. In Saki's "The Story-Teller," a mischievous bachelor tells three children on a train the tale of a wondrously good little girl, awarded medals for her propriety. But she met a wolf in the park; and hard though she ran, the jangling of her medals led the wolf straight to her, so that she was devoured utterly. Although the children are delighted by this unconventional narration, their aunt protests: "A most improper story to tell to young children!" "Unfortunate woman!" the departing bachelor reflects. "For the next six months or so those children will assail her in public with demands for an improper story!"

Well, Greek and Norse myths, for instance, sometimes are not very proper; yet, stirring the moral imagination, they do more to bring about an early apprehension of standards than do any number of dull and interminable doings of Dick and Jane. The story of Pandora, or of Thor's adventure with the old woman and her cat, gives any child an insight into the conditions of existence—dimly grasped at the moment, perhaps, but gaining in power as the years pass—that no utilitarian "real-life situation" fiction can match. Because they are eternally valid, Hesiod and the saga-singers are modern. And the versions of Hawthorne or of Andrew Lang are infinitely better prose than the quasi-basic English thrust upon young people in most twentieth-century textbooks. That illative sense described by John Henry Newman—that valid if complex means of normative judgment produced by the conjunction of a great variety of little proofs, illustrations, and inferences—is developed early in life, in no small part, by the wisdom latent in traditional fantasy.

At a higher level of learning a young teacher of English tells me that her tenth-grade pupils do not take to the stories of virtuous basketball players, dutiful student nurses, and other "real-life" idols which are thrust upon them. Those students turn, instead, to what they may procure at the corner drugstore: Ian Fleming, Mickey Spillane, or worse. If we starve young people for imagination, adventure, and some heroism, they are not likely to embrace Good Approved Real-Life Tales for Good Approved Real-Life Boys and Girls; on the contrary, they will resort to the dregs of letters, rather than be bored altogether. And the consequences will be felt not merely in their failure of taste, but in their misapprehension of human nature, lifelong; and, eventually, in the whole temper of a nation.

In one of his Causeries, Sainte-Beuve tells of a playwright, standing at a friend's window to watch a frantic Parisian mob pouring through the street: "See my pageant passing!" the complacent dramatist says. Again, art is man's nature; and it is true enough, as Oscar Wilde said whimsically, that nature imitates art. Our private and public actions, in mature years, have been determined by the

opinions and tastes we acquired in youth. Great books do influence
societies for the better, and bad books do drag down the general
level of personal and social conduct. Having seen the pageant, the
mob proceeds to behave as a playwright thinks it should. I suppose
that a public which goes often enough to the plays of Tennessee
Williams may begin to behave as Williams thinks Americans behave already. We become what others, in a voice of authority, tell
us we are or ought to be.

So I think that in the teaching of literature, some of the theories
of the life-adjustment and permissive schools have done considerable mischief. Nowadays the advocates of life-adjustment education
give a little ground here and there, sullenly, before their critics. The
intellectual ancestor of their doctrines is Rousseau. Though I am no
warm admirer of the ideas of Rousseau, I like still less the doctrines
of Gradgrind, in *Hard Times*; so I hope that life-adjustment methods of teaching literature will not be supplanted by something yet
worse conceived. After all, *real* adjustment to the conditions of
human existence is adjustment to norms. Even an ineffectual endeavor to teach standards is better than ignoring or denying all
models. A mistaken zeal for utilitarian, vocational training in place
of normative instruction; an emphasis upon the physical and biological sciences that would push literature into a dusty corner of the
curriculum; an attempt to secure spoken competence in foreign
languages at the expense of the great works of our own language—
these might be changes in education as hostile to the imparting of
norms through literature as anything which the life-adjustment and
permissive people have done.

Literary Approaches to Normative Consciousness

Therefore I venture to set down here, in scanty fashion, the
means of forming a normative consciousness through the study of
humane letters. What I have to say ought to be commonplace; but
these ideas seem to have been forgotten in many quarters. This
normative endeavor ought to be the joint work of family and

school. As the art of reading often is better taught by parents than it can be taught in a large class in school, so a knowledge of good books comes from the home at least as frequently as from the classroom. My own taste for books grew from both sources: my grandfather's and my mother's bookshelves, and from a good little gradeschool library. And if a school is failing to impart a taste for good books, often this can be remedied by discreet guidance in the family.

Tentatively, I distinguish four levels of literature by which a normative consciousness is developed. The upper levels do not supplant the earlier, but instead supplement and blend with them; and the process of becoming familiar with these four levels or bodies of normative knowledge extends from the age of three or four to the studies of college and university. We may call these levels fantasy; narrative history and biography; reflective prose and poetic fiction; and philosophy and theology.

(1) Fantasy. The fantastic and the fey, far from being unhealthy for small children, are precisely what a healthy child needs; under such stimulus a child's moral imagination quickens. Out of the early tales of wonder comes a sense of awe—and the beginning of philosophy. All things begin and end in mystery. For that matter, a normative consciousness may be aroused by themes less striking than the Arthurian legends or the folktales of the brothers Grimm. The second book I had read to me was *Little Black Sambo.* Learning it by heart then, I can recite it still. (One symptom of the growing silliness of our time is the demand that *Little Black Sambo* be banned as "racist"—an epithet itself drawn from the jargon of the quarter-literate.) Though I risk falling into bathos, I cannot resist remarking that even *Little Black Sambo* touches upon norms. What child fails to reflect upon the *hubris* of the tigers, or the cheerful prudence of Sambo?

If children are to begin to understand themselves, and to understand other people, and to know the laws that govern our nature, they ought to be encouraged to read Andersen, and the *Arabian Nights,* and all the rest; and presently the better romancers for young people, like Blackmore and Howard Pyle. Even the Bible, in the beginning, is fantasy for the young. The allegory of Jonah and the whale is accepted, initially, as a tale of the marvelous, and so sticks in the memory. Only in later years does one recognize the story as the symbol of the Jews' exile in Babylon, and of how faith may preserve men and nations through the most terrible of trials.

(2) Narrative history and biography. My grandfather and I, during the long walks that we used to take when I was six or seven years old, would talk of the character of Richard III, and of Puritan domestic life, and of the ferocity of the Assyrians. This intellectual partnership of an imaginative man of sixty and an inquisitive boy of seven is an edifying thing. My preparation for those conversations came from books in my grandfather's library: Dickens' *Child's History of England,* Hawthorne's *Grandfather's Chair,* Ridpath's four-volume illustrated *History of the World.* Later my grandfather gave me H. G. Wells' *Outline of History.* In the fullness of time, I came to disagree with Dickens' and Wells' interpretations of history; but that was all to the good, for it stimulated my critical faculties and led me to the proper study of mankind—and to the great historians, Herodotus, Thucydides, Xenophon, Polybius, Livy, Tacitus, and all the rest; to the great biographies, also, like Plutarch's, and Boswell's *Johnson,* and Lockhart's *Scott.* Reading of grand lives does something to form decent lives.

(3) Reflective prose and poetic fiction. When I was seven, my mother gave me a set of Fenimore Cooper's novels; and about the same time I inherited from a great-uncle my set of Hawthorne. That launched me upon novel-reading, so that by the time I was ten I had read all of Hugo, Dickens, and Mark Twain. Fiction is truer than fact: I mean that in accomplished fiction we obtain the distilled wisdom of men of genius, understandings of human nature which we could attain—if at all—unaided by books, only at the end of life, after numberless painful experiences. I began to read Sir Walter Scott when I was twelve or thirteen; and I think I learnt from the Waverley novels, and from Shakespeare, more of the varieties of character than ever I have got since from the manuals of psychology.

Such miscellaneous browsing in the realm of fiction rarely does harm. When I was eleven or twelve, I was much influenced by Twain's *Mysterious Stranger,* an atheist tract delightfully disguised as a romance of medieval Austria. It did not turn me into a juvenile atheist; but it set me to inquiring after first causes—and in time, paradoxically, it led me to Dante, my mainstay ever since. In certain ways, the great novel and the great poem can teach more of norms than can philosophy and theology.

(4) Philosophy and theology. For the crown of normative literary studies, we turn, about the age of nineteen or twenty, to abstraction and generalization, chastened by logic. It simply is not true that

> One impulse from a vernal wood
>> May teach you more of man,
> Of moral evil and of good,
>> Than all the sages can.

It is not from vegetal nature that one acquires some knowledge of human passions and longings. There exist, in Emerson's phrase, law for man and law for thing. The law for man we learn from Plato, Aristotle, Cicero, Seneca, Marcus Aurelius, Epictetus; from St. Augustine, St. Thomas Aquinas, Sir Thomas More, Pascal, Burke, Newman; from Isaiah, the Apostles, and the Schoolmen.

"Scientific" truth, or what is popularly taken to be scientific truth, alters from year to year—with accelerating speed, indeed, in our day. But poetic and moral truth changes little with the elapse of the centuries; and the norms of politics are fairly constant. Although virtue and wisdom are not identical, humane letters give to the imagination and the reason a moral bent.

T. S. Eliot's Permanent Things

In every age, the dominant man of letters has been a champion of normality, with only here and there a national or a temporary exception. Frequently he has swum against the strong intellectual and social currents of his time. So it was even with Homer, before classical history began: the *Iliad* is a noble appeal to divine justice and order, against the violence of a brutal epoch and the confused passions of its masters. Homer's strong and subtle portrait of Achilles in his wrath, delivered up to *ate* (folly and guilt), is an epitome of the impious errors of a people and an age.

In the twentieth century, T. S. Eliot became the principal poet and critic in this ethical continuity. Like Samuel Johnson in the eighteenth century, Eliot held in contempt the climate of "progressive" opinion in which he found himself. He was as much amused as vexed at those intellectuals who mistook Eliot's analysis of the modern temper for assent to the modern temper, with its weariness and futility. At length the reviewers perceived what way Eliot was rowing—and grew indignant. As Eliot remarks in "Thoughts after Lambeth" (1931):

"When . . . I brought out a small book of essays, several years ago, called *For Lancelot Andrewes*, the anonymous reviewer in the *Times Literary Supplement* made it the occasion for what I can only describe as a flattering obituary notice. In words of great seriousness and manifest sincerity, he pointed out that I had suddenly arrested my progress—whither he had supposed me to be moving I do not know—and that to his distress I was unmistakably making off in the wrong direction. Somehow I had failed, and had admitted my failure; if not a lost leader, at least a lost sheep; what is more, I was a kind of traitor; and those who were to find their way to the promised land beyond the waste, might drop a tear at my absence from the roll-call of the new saints."

In fact, from the beginning it had been Eliot's purpose to attack this new inverted orthodoxy of "progressivism." He meant to defend "lost" causes, because he knew that no cause worth upholding ever is lost altogether. He had sworn fealty to what he called "the permanent things," and he understood that these permanent things were the creations of an intention and a wisdom more than natural, more than private, more than human.

Any attentive reader may discern without difficulty this dedication in *The Waste Land* and *The Cocktail Party*. It is no less strong in Eliot's later writings. I attended the first performance, at the Edinburgh Festival, of Eliot's comedy *The Confidential Clerk,* and soon after published a criticism of that play. When next we met, Eliot told me that I had understood him better than had anyone else who had ventured to write about *The Confidential Clerk* before that comedy was printed; and, indeed, when the British and American editions of the play appeared, I was surprised to find that some of my own remarks had been chosen to appear on the jackets of both editions, in pride of place. This approbation from a gentleman who almost invariably refrained, on principle, from comment upon interpretations of his writings may be sufficient excuse for examining here *The Confidential Clerk* as a less-known model of Eliot's normative undertaking, which ran through almost everything he wrote.

The sinister suggestions latent in the title of this play are not realized: for Eliot's clerk is simply a man of business, and all the characters are people ordinary enough, with the partial exception of Colby, the new clerk. Their ordinariness, indeed, is the cause of their unhappiness, and provides the play with its principal theme: the prison of Self.

Sir Claude Mulhammer the financier, and his flighty wife Lady Elizabeth, and his protégés Lucasta Angel and Colby, and B. Kaghan the rising young broker, do not understand one another, or themselves, or even from whence they came. The younger people know that they were born out of wedlock, but apprehend little else about their world. Sir Claude, in the first act, declares that his principle of action is always to assume that he understands nothing about any man he meets; yet to assume that the other man understands *him* thoroughly. Yet even this premise betrays Mulhammer in the end, until he cries, with his eyes shut, "Is Colby coming back?"—knowing now that even the presumed existence of his own son had been an illusion for twenty-five years.

These people, the wrack of broken families, specimens of a generation without certitudes and deprived of continuity with the past, are involved in the very oldest of dramatic plots—mistaken identity, the missing son, and the classical comedy of errors. Eliot revives these devices ingeniously, doubtless with some pleasure in his anachronisms; and, perhaps consciously, he writes whole speeches that could have been Shaw's, and others that could have been the work of Wilde, and others Ibsen's. Lady Elizabeth with her "mind study," her Swiss clinics, and her intuitions, would have done credit to Wilde; the bond between Lucasta and Colby, broken by Colby's discovery that they may be brother and sister, has a Shavian touch; while through all three acts, somberly, the ghost of *The Wild Duck* whispers that the truth we ween about ourselves may be our undoing. When all is over, Colby and Lucasta and Kaghan, at least, do know who they are, and in some degree realize their end in life, but they accept the discovery of their true nature with resignation, not with relief. Upon them all, though most heavily upon Mulhammer, descends a consciousness of the vanity of human wishes.

Everyone in the play (except, possibly, for old Eggerson, the retiring clerk, with his wife and garden and simple virtues) is haunted by a terrifying loneliness and a regret for talents frustrated. Even accomplishment in the arts (Mulhammer would have liked to be a praiseworthy potter, and Colby a talented organist and composer) is baffled by the spirit of our age, Eliot seems to suggest. These people are what Burke called the flies of a summer, unable to link with dead generations or those yet unborn, lacking memories or high hope. They seek for continuity, status, faith; and, beyond all these (though only Colby, probably, knows this) they seek for some assurance that their lives *matter,* and that the barriers which separate every man from his fellows are transcended by a Reality more than fleshly.

In structure, *The Confidential Clerk* is close to *The Importance of Being Earnest,* even to the revelations in the final act by the old nurse (or rather, here, Mrs. Guzzard, the foster-mother); and it is possible to laugh at certain lines and certain characters. Yet the man who sees *The Confidential Clerk* laughs only after the fashion of Democritus, at the pathos of all evanescent things; for in its essence this play is sad, profoundly sad, as sad as *The Waste Land.* In the second part, especially, occur lines of high tenderness and pathos, as when Lucasta comes to believe that she understands Colby and herself, and is on the brink of self-realization—and then this is overwhelmed, the next instant, by disillusion, or rather by illusion of a different sort. Throughout the play, Eliot treats his people with mercy and sympathy; they become lovable, indeed, all of them. From Sir Claude to Mrs. Guzzard, they are men and women of kindly natures, honest inclinations, and generous hearts. But, being human and modern, they are heir to all the imperfections of the spirit and the flesh; thus they cannot escape the rootlessness of their time, nor the sense of talents run to waste, nor the prison of Self. They do not know themselves, nor the nature of being.

Lucasta thinks that Colby is different from the rest of them, for he can withdraw from their midst into his garden of the imagination, a sanctuary from the desolated material world. But Colby himself knows better: his garden of mind is as lonely as the real world without. If Colby were endowed with conviction of an abiding reality that surpassed the Waste Land—why, then indeed he never would be solitary in his domain of fancy, for "God would walk in my garden." Wanting this faith, however, the man is left melancholy and unnerved, deprived of love, and scarcely caring to know the identity of his parents. We see him, near the end of the third act, groping toward a churchly vocation; yet only Eggerson, the practical old clerk, has come close to understanding Colby. Lucasta, turning back to Kaghan for some sense of affection and belonging, thinks that Colby needs no human company, being secure in the citadel of self-knowledge. She does not understand how like a citadel is to a prison.

Although successful enough as a dramatic production, *The Confidential Clerk* will be remembered more for its occasional lines of twilight beauty and its penetration into the recesses of Self than as a neat and close-knit comedy. Few consider it one of Eliot's principal works. Yet I am not sure of this judgment; for this is a play which touches most movingly upon the sources of longing and the need for enduring love, and so bears the mark of a man of genius.

Now the permanent things for which Eliot stands, in this comedy and in all his writing, are not difficult to make out. First, he is governed by what Unamuno called "the tragic sense of life," the Christian knowledge that men never will be as gods; that we all are imperfectible creatures, necessarily discontented even in our sensate triumphs. Were it not for the hope that man is made for eternity, we should be the most miserable of creatures; but that hope is compensation for all our mishaps here below, and it sets the Christian world high above the gloomy classical world.

Second, Eliot abides by the wisdom of our ancestors: the Christian and Judaic and classical patrimony, incorporated in tradition. As Eliot expressed this in his essay "Tradition and the Individual Talent" (1917), "Some one said: 'The dead writers are remote from us because we *know* so much more than they did.' Precisely, and they are that which we know." Here are Fulbert's giants again. As Virgil, in his Fourth Eclogue, seems to have prophesied the coming of Christ, so the writer of vision may foresee and describe what he does not wholly understand himself. In this vein, Eliot wrote in "Virgil and the Christian World" (1951):

"A poet may believe that he is expressing only his private experience; his lines may be for him only a means of talking about himself without giving himself away; yet for his readers what he has written may come to be the expression both of their own secret feelings and of the exultation or despair of a generation. He need not know what his poetry will come to mean to others; and a prophet need not understand the meaning of his private utterance."

Because the poet lives in a tradition, he may become a prophet; the great mysterious incorporation of the human race speaks through him, so that he says more than he comprehends. Tradition is not mere purblind stumbling in the track of yesterday's common men; and Eliot makes this point clear in "Tradition and the Individual Talent":

"Yet if the only form of tradition, of handing down, consisted in following the ways of the immediate generation before us in a blind or timid adherence to its ways, 'tradition' should positively be discouraged. We have seen many such simple currents soon lost in the sand; and novelty is better than repetition. Tradition is a matter of much wider significance. It cannot be inherited, and if you want it you must obtain it by great labour. It involves, in the first place, the historical sense, which we may call nearly indispensable to any one who would continue to be a poet beyond his twenty-fifth year; and the historical sense involves a perception, not only of the pastness of the past, but of its presence; the historical sense compels a man to write not merely with his own generation in his bones, but with a feeling that the whole of the literature of Europe from Homer and within it the whole of the literature of his country has a simultaneous existence and composes a simultaneous order. This historical sense, which is a sense of the timeless as well as of the temporal and of the timeless and temporal together, is what makes a writer traditional. And it is at the same time what makes a writer most acutely conscious of his place in time, of his own contemporaneity."

Third, Eliot seeks to recover the idea of a Christian society, in which order and justice and freedom obtain their fullest possible expression in a world irremediably flawed. As he wrote in 1939:

"So long . . . as we consider finance, industry, trade, agriculture merely as competing interests to be reconciled from time to time as best they may, so long as we consider 'education' as a good in itself of which everyone has a right to the utmost, without any ideal of the good life for society or for the individual, we shall move from one uneasy compromise to another. To the quick and simple organization of society for ends which, being only material and worldly, must be as ephemeral as worldly success, there is only one alternative. As political philosophy derives its sanction from ethics, and ethics from the truth of religion, it is only by returning to the eternal source of truth that we can hope for any social organization which will not, to its ultimate destruction, ignore some essential aspect of reality. The term 'democracy,' as I have said again and again, does not contain enough positive content to stand alone against the forces that you dislike—it can easily be transformed by them. If you will not have God (and He is a jealous God) you should pay your respects to Hitler or Stalin."

Only a civil social order, that is, which retains some understanding of consecration, ordination, and reverence can withstand fanatic ideologues and squalid oligarchs. It is not a theocracy that Eliot desires, but a commonwealth in which the leaders and the people alike acknowledge their mystical brotherhood in Christ, with the social consequences which arise from that community of spirit.

These standards—the tragic view of life, the adherence to real tradition, the Christian community expressed in the political order —are Eliot's fundamentals. We cannot retain or regain normative principles, he reasons, without an authoritative source of knowledge. And that fountain of authority, for Eliot, is the revelation— from prophets and from poets—which we possess already. As I mentioned earlier, David Hume maintains that we are governed by "impressions," or innate ideas, the source of which is unknowable. Basil Willey, in *The Eighteenth Century Background,* paraphrases Hume's argument: "Religion is irrational, theism is permissible only in utter attenuation: oh for a revelation! but not, if you please, the one we are supposed to have had already."

Such skepticism is a far cry from Eliot's premises. "Impressions," Eliot says, are perilous guides, in private affairs as in public; nor will Irving Babbitt's "inner check" upon appetite suffice. John Middleton Murry had declared that an impressionistic "inner voice"— of what?—is quite enough, and preferable far to obeying tradition. Eliot replied in his essay "The Function of Criticism" (1923):

"Those of us who find ourselves supporting what Mr. Murry calls Classicism believe that men cannot get on without giving allegiance to something outside themselves. 'The English writer, the English divine, the English statesman, inherit no rules from their forebears; they inherit only this: a sense that in the last resort they must depend upon the inner voice.' This statement does, I admit, appear to cover certain cases; it throws a flood of light upon Mr. Lloyd George. But why *in the last resort*? Do they, then, avoid the dictates of the inner voice up to the last extremity? My belief is that those who possess this inner voice are ready enough to hearken to it, and will hear no other. The inner voice, in fact, sounds remarkably like an old principle which has been formulated by an elder critic in the now familiar phrase of 'doing as one likes.' The possessors of the inner voice ride ten in a compartment to a football match at Swansea, listening to the inner voice, which breathes the eternal message of vanity, fear, and lust."

So Eliot submits himself to Authority, as described by Cardinal Newman: "Conscience is an authority; the Bible is an authority; such is the Church; such is Antiquity; such are the words of the wise, such are hereditary memories, such are legal saws and state maxims; such are proverbs; such are sentiments, presages, and prepossessions." The inner voice speaks often of desires, but seldom of norms; and only from Authority may we learn normality.

Accordingly, genuine education is the conveying of normative wisdom, through study of authorities. The liberals, says Eliot, have gone astray in education by their assumption that we learn chiefly through personal experience. Having declared this (in "Religion and Literature," 1934), Eliot struck out at the liberals' fallacies:

"At this point I anticipate a rejoinder from the liberal-minded, from all those who are convinced that if everybody says what he thinks, things will somehow, by some automatic compensation and adjustment, come right in the end. 'Let everything be tried,' they say, 'and if it is a mistake, then we shall learn by experience.' This argument might have some value, if we were always the same generation upon earth; or if, as we know to be not the case, people ever learned much from the experience of their elders. The liberals are convinced that only by what is called unrestrained individualism, will truth ever emerge. Ideas, views of life, they think, issue distinct from independent heads, and in consequence of their knocking violently against each other, the fittest survives, and truth rises triumphant. Anyone who dissents from this view must be either a medievalist, wishful only to set back the clock, or else a fascist, and probably both."

But wisdom is not got through shouting-matches within one generation. Culture is the creation of a talented little minority, over centuries; what we call "mass culture" either is the emulation by the crowd of the culture conferred—even imposed—by Fulbert's giants, or else it is a popular degradation and caricature of a dying genuine culture. In *Notes towards the Definition of Culture* (1948), Eliot describes the destruction of civilization by educationists' "mass culture":

"And yet the culture of Europe has deteriorated visibly within the memory of many of us who are by no means the oldest among us. And we know, that whether education can foster and improve culture or not, it can surely adulterate and degrade it. For there is no doubt that in our headlong rush to educate everybody, we are lowering our standards, and more and more abandoning the study of those subjects by which the essentials of our culture—of that part of it which is transmissible by education—are transmitted; destroying our ancient edifices to make ready the ground upon which the barbarian nomads of the future will encamp in their mechanized caravans."

The Church is the great repository of authoritative wisdom; so real education necessarily is religious; "secularized" instruction undoes itself. "As only the Catholic and the communist know," Eliot wrote in 1933, "*all* education must be ultimately religious education. I do not mean that education should be confined to postulants for the priesthood or for the higher ranks of Soviet bureaucracy; I mean that the hierarchy of education should be a religious hierarchy."

The rationalist liberal will protest promptly that we must no longer be suckled in a creed outworn. Yet Eliot replies in "The *Pensées* of Pascal" (1933) that Christianity is not merely a credible body of belief, but the only source of certitude:

"The Christian thinker—and I mean the man who is trying consciously and conscientiously to explain to himself the sequence which culminates in faith, rather than the public apologist—proceeds by rejection and elimination. He finds the world to be so and so; he finds its character inexplicable by any non-religious theory; among religions he finds Christianity, and Catholic Christianity, to account most satisfactorily for the world, and especially for the world within; and thus, by what Newman calls 'powerful and concurrent' reasons, he finds himself inexorably committed to the dogma of the Incarnation. To the unbeliever, this method seems disingenuous and perverse: for the unbeliever is, as a rule, not so greatly troubled to explain the world to himself, nor so greatly distressed by its disorder; nor is he generally concerned (in modern terms) to 'preserve values.' He does not consider that if certain emotional states, certain development of character, and what in the highest sense can be called 'saintliness' are inherently and by inspection known to be good, then the satisfactory explanation of the world must be an explanation which will admit the 'reality' of those values."

If men reject authority and reject all the inferences which we draw from religious doctrine, then they are left with no better ethics than the moral system of Thomas Hobbes. As Eliot writes in his essay on John Bramhall (1927), the modern notion that value resides "entirely in the degree of organization of natural impulses" is close akin to Hobbes' assumptions. Eliot proceeds to quote a passage from I. A. Richards' *Principles of Literary Criticism,* by way of illustrating the narrow naturalism of the liberal who will not accept authority, tradition, and the illative sense:

"Anything is valuable which will satisfy an appetency without involving the frustration of some equal or more important appetency; in other words, the only reason which can be given for not satisfying a desire is that more important desires will thereby be thwarted. Thus morals become purely prudential, and ethical codes merely the expression of the most general schemes of expediency to which an individual or a race has attained."

These "values" of I. A. Richards or Bertrand Russell, it appears, are no better than the satisfaction of appetites upon a Benthamite moral calculus. For ethical codes which are simply "general schemes of expediency," Eliot had no respect. What revelation, tradition, and normative insight dictate often is highly inexpedient for a particular person at a particular time, or indeed for certain communities; yet those commands must be obeyed. In the intricate and unending calculation of appetite-preferences, every man must be bewildered all his life, and so must any society that tries to govern itself expediently by a perpetual measuring of relative frustrations. We cling to the permanent things, the norms of our being, because all other grounds are quicksand.

Only by the recovery of normative truths, Eliot argued decade after decade, can we save ourselves from the forces of disintegration. Perhaps he put this best in "Thoughts after Lambeth":

"I do not mean that our times are particularly corrupt; all times are corrupt. I mean that Christianity, in spite of certain local appearances, is not, and cannot be within measurable time, 'official.' The World is trying the experiment of attempting to form a civilized but non-Christian mentality. The experiment will fail; but we must be very patient in awaiting its collapse; meanwhile redeeming the time: so that the Faith may be preserved alive through the dark ages before us; to renew and rebuild civilization, and save the World from suicide."

To those chilled by the foggy climate of opinion in which we dwell now, it should be some comfort and encouragement that the greatest man of letters of this century, with his penetrating critical intellect (which did not spare certain insufficiencies in important Christian writers), set his face unflinchingly against the enemies of the permanent things. In the long run, it is the man of vision who prevails, not the eager little knot of intellectuals hot after novelties. We speak, long later, of an "Age of Milton," an "Age of Dryden," an "Age of Johnson"—not an age of this or that neoterist. The little dogs and all, Tray, Blanch, and Sweet-heart, will bark at Eliot; he is feared and disliked by those "intellectualists" disparaged by Francis Bacon (after Heraclitus) as cloudy speculators "which are, notwithstanding, commonly taken for the most sublime and divine philosophers." The modern ideologue is such an intellectualist, and the modern ideologue detests Eliot—precisely because Eliot is so persuasive and so difficult to refute. Yet in the fullness of time, if indeed not tomorrow, the greater part of the twentieth century will be known, in letters, as the Age of Eliot.

In the chapters which immediately follow, I shall discuss normality and abnormality in literature by the light of the normative purpose that I have just tried to suggest. Although sometimes I may employ the method of Hume, I confess to writing in the spirit of Eliot. I shall deal consecutively with the relationship between literature and tolerable social order; with humane letters under in-humane dominations; with the essayist-sage as prophet; with the author of fantasy as moralist; with the struggle between the ideo-logue and the humanist in the republic of letters. These are vignettes and excursions, but they may hearten some folk of like mind—and occasionally may wake some salutary misgivings even among the neoterists.

II. LITERATURE AND THE CONTRACT
OF ETERNAL SOCIETY

An Ochiltree Parable

BOOKS OFTEN REFLECT THE SPIRIT OF THE AGE; BUT ALSO BOOKS can conjure up the spirit of the age. Good literature alters the climate of opinion, and the shape of society, for the better; while the literature of decadence, or the decay of literary tradition, can undermine the commonwealth.

Some years ago, I walked across the braes from Old Cumnock, in Ayrshire, to the village of Ochiltree. Now Ochiltree is the "Barbie" of George Douglas Brown's grim realistic novel *The House with the Green Shutters*. And the Scottish village of Ochiltree is dying.

Brown described the changes that began to destroy little Barbie in the last century: trade drained away by the building of railroads in Ayrshire, cattle expelled by coal, the carter sinking to his ruin, and the shadow of the noose upon the House with the Green Shutters. The white-harled cottage in which George Douglas Brown was born still stands in Ochiltree, and its shutters are green still; but the rest of old Ochiltree is not long for this world.

Of the shops of a century ago, there survive only two meagre little cubbyholes (reminding one of the shop kept by an old Sheep, as Tenniel draws it in *Through the Looking Glass*); for the vans of the omnipresent Co-operative come from Cumnock to supply miners' families at their doorsteps. Ochiltree is a market-town no longer, having sunk to the estate of a mere dormitory-village to accommodate some of the miners at the pits near Auchinleck. The tidy stone cottages are sagging to their ruin, their rents having been fixed by act of Parliament ever since 1914, which means that their owners cannot afford to mend the roofs; and at the back of them, higher up the hill down which the single long street of Ochiltree runs, loom the hideous barracks-like rows of county council houses, built out of state funds to serve the ends of the state—in this instance, to lodge the Coal Board's miners.

The church, I think, is derelict; the hotel, the Black Bull, though there is a charm to its facade still, is become nothing more than a decayed ale-house; the only cheerful spot is another public-house, opposite, where the publican, one of the last men in the village to retain some affection for the place, told us how life has been drained out of Ochiltree. In the evening, the miners and their families queue for the buses to Ayr, fifteen miles away, where they can go to one of the cinemas; most of them wish they lived in Ayr, instead of here in this green countryside. Some coats of arms carved above doorways in the road that leads to Cumnock are the last traces of the old families of the place—these, and Ochiltree House, which (when last I was in Ochiltree) lay at the foot of the long street, set in a desolated garden, with a fine high dyke running round it.

But Ochiltree House—a long, severe, crow-step-gabled building of the seventeenth century, with some good interiors, once—has been swept away since I was in Ochiltree. It had stood empty most of the time for the past hundred years; troops had been quartered there in both wars, and had made kindling of the paneling and staircases; and to escape from taxes, the proprietor took the roof off not long ago, and sold the stone of the walls. The village is left forever without a focus, now, and whatever remained of a sense of community and a sense of continuity has vanished. In Ochiltree House, Graham of Claverhouse was married, long before he appealed to men beyond Stirling and lands beyond Forth. In the older Ochiltree House which stood on this spot during the sixteenth century, old John Knox was married to the heiress of Ochiltree, a girl of sixteen. These things will be forgotten wholly now, in Ochiltree, and the daily labor at the pit, and the evening cinema in Ayr, will be the whole of existence for the people in the village.

A mile and a half to the north of Ochiltree, across Lugar Water, is Auchinleck House. The Boswells hold Auchinleck still; the splendid square ashlar house that Lord Auchinleck, James Boswell's father, built in the middle of the eighteenth century is grand still, and the lands of Auchinleck stretch green and prosperous round it, with the ruined old castle overlooking the den of the Lugar—that castle in which, said Dr. Johnson, he and Bozzy would lodge when they came to Auchinleck. This is one of the few landed properties in all Scotland maintained in its old state; and, death duties being what they are, it is highly improbable that the beauty and tranquility of Auchinleck can last out this present generation. A few years ago, the ancient town-house of the Boswells, in Ayr, was demolished; the splendid country house must follow, unless it is an exception to the general rule in modern Britain.

The fountains of the great deep seem to be broken up in our time. Institutions that have endured for a millennium are awash, and the surly question before us is whether the whole fabric of civilization can survive the present rate of economic and social alteration. Material forces have had a large part in this transformation of life; but more and more, I think, we are coming to understand, in our decade, that certain powerful tendencies of the intellect have been quite as active in the destruction of what I like to call—with Cicero and with Burke—"the unbought grace of life." It is time we began to examine the part that a general decay of interest in great literature has had in this corrosive process.

Even in a quiet corner like Ayrshire, the revolution of our times seems to have been as much a consequence of ideas as of material influences. It is quite true that the coming of rapid transportation, the need for coal, and the displacement of traditional popular interests by mass-amusement devices have altered the whole face of life in Ayrshire. It is also quite true that the decay of the old literary culture of Ayrshire and of Scotland generally has prepared the way for a disintegration of everything long established.

The popular literary culture of the little Scottish towns used to consist of Bible-reading and of sermon-listening, which imparted a solemn and sometimes eloquent character to the Scottish people—

dour, often enough, but strong and even heroic. And the literary culture of Auchinleck House and Ochiltree House used to consist of the lively rational curiosity and the speculative interests of Hume and Boswell and Monboddo, persisting little altered down to 1914.

The dwindling of religious convictions has brought about the ruin of the popular culture; taxation and a sea of troubles virtually have put an end to the civilizing influences of the old-fashioned laird. Leisure indeed is the basis of culture; and it is one of the paradoxes of our age that while we boast of our time-saving machines, neither the villager nor the laird has half the time to think that once he had. So Tellie-culture supplants the old Scots life of the mind; in Ochiltree or in Glasgow, men are content to be the passive recipients of commercial television or of the British Broadcasting Company. And social community decays proportionately: decisions, like entertainment, are manufactured in London. What need to read, to write, or to take any active part in public matters?

I have described Ochiltree as a microcosm of our modern culture: impoverished in spirit and community by an alleged material progress, enervated by the decay of religious and literary tradition. When the spirit has departed, the material fabric crumbles. I might give fifty other examples of such decay, in Britain or in America. When the old religious and literary culture trickles away, there is left a dreary vacuum, in little towns or in the biggest cities. In that vacuum, civic vigor expires. And presently some new system of compulsions is devised to substitute for the old voluntary commonwealth and the old loyalties of heart and mind.

Here I am emphasizing the necessity of an elevated and uninterrupted literary tradition to sustain civilized existence. We must pay increasing attention, during the rest of this decade and a great while after, to what is called the social significance of literature. I ask you not to be alarmed by this presumptuous and tawdry phrase: what I have in mind is not the superficial idea of the function of literature entertained by the positivist or the Marxist or the literary "social realist." I am not referring to that school of social naturalists in fiction whose system, as defined by Ambrose Bierce in The Devil's Dictionary, is "the art of depicting nature as seen by toads."

I am thinking, rather, of the high language that Burke uses in describing the condition of a society which forsakes or forgets the principle of continuity: "No part of life," he says, "would retain its acquisitions; barbarism with regard to science and literature, unskilfulness with regard to arts and manufacturers, would infallibly succeed to the want of a steady education and settled principle; and thus the commonwealth itself would, in a few generations, crumble away, be disconnected into the dust and powder of individuality, and at length dispersed to all the winds of heaven."

In this great duty of ensuring a continuity of the mind among men, the man of letters and the teacher of literature have a principal responsibility. I do not hesitate to say that theirs is a sacred function; they are keepers of the Word. It is they who, more than the statesman, remind us of what Burke calls "the great primaeval contract of eternal society, linking the lower with the higher natures, connecting the visible and invisible world, according to a fixed compact sanctioned by the inviolable oath which holds all physical and all moral natures, each in their appointed place." It is they who guard this contract of those who are dead, and those who are living, and those who are to be born. If this contract, this law of continuity, is broken, Burke continues, "nature is disobeyed, and the rebellious are outlawed, cast forth, and exiled, from this world of reason, and order, and peace, and virtue, and fruitful penitence, into the antagonist world of madness, discord, vice, confusion, and unavailing sorrow."

Just this is the punishment of our rebel generation, which has thrown away the literary heritage of the past quite as it has broken with the moral and social prescriptions of traditional civil social existence. In some measure, the guardians of our literature have been overwhelmed by the deluge of industrialism, mass schooling, and physical alteration of society. But probably it is true that no dominant class in society ever is overthrown simply by a force from below; what undoes the masters of the state is a failure of nerve, a disease of their confidence. And probably it is true, similarly, that no set or school of men who stand for an ancient cultural inheritance ever is broken simply by the blow of an innovating system of thought; when the old order of civilization reels and falls, it is because the keepers of the Word no longer are confident in their truth. I am inclined to think that humane learning has been terribly injured in our time because the people who are entrusted with the conservation of humane letters have forgotten the true meaning of humanism; and I believe that English literature has been treated with contempt in our schools and our colleges because of what a friend of mine calls "the treason of the English teacher."

The Social Significance of Literature

Lacking two influences, generation could not link with generation. Those influences are religious tradition and the continuity of literature. For literature is the breath of society, transmitting to successive rising generations, century upon century, a body of ethical principles and critical standards and imaginative creations that constitutes a kind of collective intellect of humanity, the formalized wisdom of our ancestors.

This is the sense in which we need to remind ourselves that men of letters and teachers of literature are entrusted with a social responsibility; they have no right to be nihilists or fantastic or neoterists, because the terms on which they hold their trust are conservative. Whatever the immediate political opinions of the guardian of the Word, his first duty is conservative in the larger sense of that adjective: his work, his end, is to shelter and promulgate an inherited body of learning and myth. The man of letters and the teacher of literature have no right to be irresponsible dilettantes or reckless iconoclasts; they are placed in their high dignity so that they may preserve the ideas which make all men one, not so that they may indulge an appetite for denigration and a taste for anarchic cleverness. In a time like ours, when the political and religious institutions which kept some continuity in civilization are weakened or broken, the responsibility of the writer and the teacher of literature is greater than ever; it is possible that the only tie with the past which will survive our century may be a literary continuity, just as in the ages which followed the collapse of the Roman state. That is what I mean when I use the phrase "the social significance of literature."

But there exists another meaning for this phrase, baser and more popular: the sense in which it is employed by the social positivist and the sentimental humanitarian (as distinguished from the humanist). This latter body of opinion looks upon education in general, and literary education in particular, as an instrument for compelling the rising generation to "adjust to society"—that is, to submit to those social principles which the positivist, the pragmatist, and the sentimental humanitarian endorse. They propose, in short, to make the teaching of literature an arm of social indoctrination.

As Gordon Chalmers observes in *The Republic and the Person,* "Education as a social technique is thus preoccupied with group behavior. It seeks not human values but political or economic or institutional ones, applicable to men because they are collected together. It is based on the sentimental belief that the individual can best be served by neglect of his character and by attention to the circumstances which surround him. By contrast, the ethical and liberal theory of education holds that he can best be served by intensive study of the nature of men and their character as persons, undertaken *before* a direct study of social problems, which, while of immense importance, is an advanced and less central study than the great humane one."

Now the professor of English literature, almost without exception, has not been deluded by this sociological notion of the function of letters. He does not labor under the illusion that it is his duty to persuade young people to "conform to the group," nor that he ought to devote his lectures to the repetition of arid humanitarian abstractions. The teacher of humane literature remains a humanist, in defiance of the great blind and dumb tendency of our times; as Irving Babbitt wrote nearly fifty years ago, in *Literature and the American College,* "The humanist, then, as opposed to the humanitarian, is interested in the perfecting of the individual rather than in schemes for the elevation of mankind as a whole." The professor of English literature has held out with fortitude against powerful endeavors to convert his discipline into an apparatus for social indoctrination. Sometimes, it is true, he has fallen victim to the whim of the season or the decade, and has taught literature on Marxist principles, or on Freudian principles, or on nationalistic principles; but this fall from grace has been exceptional; the majority of teachers of literature have recognized and have fulfilled their obligation to declare the truth and beauty of humane letters, without subjugation to the popular appetite of the hour; they have understood that their function is to lift up the imagination of man, not to dictate his social arrangements.

No, it is not in this respect that the guardians of the World have failed. It is true that their constancy has cost them dear. I know of one institution of higher learning in America in which the budget of the social scientists exceeds the budget of the humane scholars by the ratio of forty to one. The Benthamite charlatan, the counter of noses, has been willing to pander to the modern affection for quantitative judgments, which everyone can understand precisely because they contain no real meaning; while the humane scholar, who looks upon men as persons, not units, and upon knowledge as imagination, not mensuration, has been starved for funds and cheated of his students. The sociologist, the engineer, and the technician have been pampered at the expense of the intellectual and ethical instruction of our rising generation, and I am afraid that society is going to have to pay the price of that error for the rest of this century.

Five decades ago, in his essay called "Academic Leadership," printed in *Aristocracy and Justice,* Paul Elmer More warned us that we ought to "distrust the present huge overgrowth of courses in government and sociology, which send men into the world skilled in the machinery of statecraft and with minds sharpened to the immediate demands of special groups, but with no genuine training of the imagination and no understanding of the longer problems of humanity." The dominance of such studies, More added, "is one of the causes that men leave our colleges with no hold on the past, with nothing, as Burke said, 'amidst so vast a fluctuation of passions and opinions, to concentrate their thoughts, to ballast their conduct, to preserve them from being blown about by every wind of fashionable doctrine.' "

That overgrowth is far worse today; and it is doubtful whether the social scientists succeed any longer even in imparting genuine skills to their students, or in sharpening their minds; they are content simply to convert them into an inferior order of statisticians. Against this current of degradation, the teachers of literature have contended with resolution; and though, by and large, they have been beaten, theirs has been an honorable defeat. They have not surrendered, and in time they may come into their own once more;

for, in the long run, intelligence and integrity usually tell, even within a college faculty.

Yet those compulsions intended to make the teacher of literature a servant to some evanescent concept of social welfare are growing in intensity just now, rather than diminishing. We hear already the energumen's cry that the writer and the professor ought to teach "the American way of life" or "Americanism." I hope that no honest teacher of literature ever will teach Americanism. I do not know what Americanism is; and I suspect that no one else knows. If that clumsy word means anything, it signifies what Tocqueville calls "democratic despotism," a sullen levelling envy, the determination that mediocrity shall be enforced without exception, the aspiration of the publicist and the demagogue to trample through underfoot. The teacher of literature may, indeed, have a great deal to say about American minds and hearts. He may describe the brooding New England imagination of Hawthorne, or the pragmatic Western skepticism of Mark Twain, or the homely strength of Robert Frost. But he cannot in conscience reduce the proliferating variety of American letters to a lying social abstraction called "Americanism." The honest teacher of literature is the conservator of ethics and of taste—though in either function he succeeds by indirection, not by preaching; if he sets out to force his students into some currently popular mode of social conformity, he is living a lie.

The responsibility of the teacher of literature in maintaining the contract of eternal society is not that of a preacher of doctrines nor an agent of government. His duty is far loftier than this. Paul Elmer More describes the real function of the humane scholar as "a disciplining of the higher faculty of the imagination to the end that the student may behold, as it were in one sublime vision, the whole scale of being in its range from the lowest to the highest under the divine decree of order and subordination, without losing sight of the immutable veracity at the heart of all development, which 'is only the praise and surname of virtue.'" In this elevated sense, the humanist truly is the conservator of society.

Yet I referred earlier to the treason of the English teacher. What I mean was described with passion at the beginning of this century, by Irving Babbitt. Art and literature, he says, fulfilling the prophecy of Herbert Spencer, have become content to be the humble handmaids of what is called science.

All too often, the teacher of literature has succumbed to a failure of nerve, aping the methods of the victorious scientist, endeavoring to develop a scientism of literature, and forgetting the very ends of his own high discipline. He has resisted the positivist and the sociologist and the educationist and the pragmatist, but too often he has resisted ineffectually and halfheartedly, doubting the righteousness of his own cause, almost ready to take the voice of popular folly for the voice of eternal wisdom.

As Irving Babbitt foresaw, in many quarters the study of literature has declined on the one hand into mere philology (worthy though that discipline is in its way), or on the other hand into dilettantism. The ethical purpose of humane letters, ordering the soul and so—though indirectly—ordering the commonwealth, increasingly is obscured. Why, large grants are awarded by foundations for research into the noble question of how computers and business-machines best may be applied to literary studies! And that largesse is gratefully received by professors of English whose most passionate interest is the frequency with which certain words and phrases occur in the writings of great authors. A gulf is fixed between such a notion of literature and the spirit of a principal poet of our age, Roy Campbell; one recalls the concluding lines of Campbell's "To The Survivors":

"For none save those are worthy birth
Who neither life nor death will shun:
And we plow deepest in the Earth
Who ride the nearest to the Sun."

For literature is not merely a slag-heap from which obscure doctoral dissertations may be extracted, as old mine-workings are sifted for mercury. Literature is meant to rouse and fortify the living, to renew the contract of eternal society. And the scholar who treats literature as a mound of ashes—mildly profitable ashes—is false to his discipline and his age.

Until the humane scholar reminds himself that his study and his life are part of a grand continuity and essence, we will continue to behold high-school departments of English literature ludicrously combined with departments of social science, out of a fallacious apprehension of the social function of letters; and what is worse still, we will see this confounding of humane studies with social indoctrination extended to our colleges and our universities. While those of us who know the humane disciplines stand irresolute, this devastation continues with increasing speed; but if we remind ourselves that we are guardians of the Word, then we may carry the war into Africa. Like Merlin locked in the oak, literature seems bewitched today. Yet its power is not extinguished. Unless it is waked in our time, more may fall than the roofs of Ochiltree and Auchinleck.

The creative writer, the critic, and the teacher of literature are heirs to an ancient civilized order. If they fail in their normative duty, or if they betray their culture to the ideologue, they do not get off scot-free. They pay with their lives, sometimes, for their dereliction; always they pay through the loss of their freedom. An inhumane social domination, treating literary men as servile propagandists—or as enemies who must be extirpated—succeeds to the order of the permanent things.

✼✼✼✼✼✼✼✼✼✼✼✼✼✼✼✼✼✼✼✼✼✼✼

III. THE DEATH OF ART: HUMANE LETTERS UNDER INHUMANE DOMINATIONS

Ehrenberg as Deviationist

FIFTY YEARS AFTER THE BOLSHEVIK REVOLUTION, IT IS POSSIBLE to make some analysis of what happens when literature is severed from normative principle, and when totalist ideology is substituted for the permanent things. The career of the late Ilya Ehrenberg is instructive.

Never having felt much appetite for the ideological novel, now and again I re-read Stephen Leacock's burlesque called "Spoof: a Russian Novel." I relish particularly the episode in which a priest promises to teach the youthful hero to read. The boy reaches for a scroll with the alphabet upon it; but the priest says, "Gently—not all of it at once," and tears off a part of the alphabet for his pupil's perusal.

Well, the whole society out of which arose the sober-sided revolutionary novel is swept away into Tophet, now, and the regime that has succeeded to the old order is far more difficult either to criticize safely or to burlesque without a snarl. The total state disapproves of both tears and laughter.

It must be clear now to almost everyone that the Soviet state, for instance, whatever major changes of leadership or minor changes of policy it may experience, cannot possibly tolerate the liberties of the literary mind. This is more than a matter of a particular oligarch's temper. Stalin passes; yet Pasternak dies in a dreadful isolation, compelled to reject the Nobel Prize, denounced and kept under surveillance by the regime. Khrushchev passes; but Tarsis takes refuge in London, while Sinyavsky and Daniel go to concentration camps.

Literature in a totalist society is better judged, nevertheless, by examining the work of those writers who have submitted, rather than that of those who have fled or have been suppressed. If sufficiently obsequious, or sufficiently supple, a man of letters in the Soviet Union may grow very affluent indeed. But his hands are fettered by what the exiled Narakov calls "the chains of fear"; and he must abide by the immutable dogmas of "socialist realism."

Czeslaw Milosz, once an enthusiast of the "New Faith," describes in his preface to *The Captive Mind* the real character of the writer's servitude under the inverted religion of communism, no less abject in Poland than in Russia. "Socialist realism," Milosz says, "is not, as some think, merely an aesthetic theory to which the writer, the musician, the painter, or the theatrical producer is obliged to adhere. On the contrary, it involves by implication the whole Leninist-Stalinist doctrine. If writers and painters are not forced to become members of the Party, that is because such a step is unnecessary. . . . 'Socialist realism' is much more than a matter of taste, of preference for one style of painting or music rather than another. It is concerned with the beliefs which lie at the foundation of human existence. In the field of literature it forbids what has in every age been the writer's essential task—to look at the world from his own independent viewpoint, to tell the truth as he sees it, and so to keep watch and ward in the interest of society as a whole. It preaches a proper attitude of doubt in regard to a merely formal system of ethics but itself makes all judgment of values dependent upon the interest of the dictatorship. Human sufferings are drowned in the trumpet-blare: the orchestra in the concentration camp . . ."

What this "New Faith" does to the man of letters who submits—with whatever private reservations—to ideological orthodoxy may be illustrated sufficiently by the career of Ilya Ehrenberg, the most successful of Soviet writers. Ehrenberg enjoyed the rare privilege of being permitted to travel abroad when he chose: the body may be unconfined, when the mind is captive.

In 1954, Ehrenberg tried to express in fiction the mildest of criticisms and the faintest hint of ridicule of the hierarchs of the New Faith. But he and his novel, *The Thaw*, came off badly within a very few months, being denounced late that summer by the Union of Soviet Writers. With Pomerantsev and other critics, poets, and novelists, Ehrenberg had implied that something long had been wrong with Soviet letters; Pomerantsev went so far as to say that sincerity and honesty, rather than submissive propagandizing, are the marks of the true artist. Such liberties were tolerated only while the masters of the state, following Stalin's death, felt uncertain of their ability to crush criticism effectively; once they were sure of the army and police, Stalin's successors gave the word for a general denunciation of literary deviationists, and from this followed the dismissal of certain editors, the expulsion of certain writers from the Union of Writers, and a fresh searching of consciences. Constantin Simonov, a pillar of Soviet orthodoxy, was appointed to the vacated editorship of *Novy Mir*, the chief literary journal.

In the last days of 1954, there met the Second Congress of Soviet Writers—the first Congress had been held in the thirties—assembled to put down literary heresies and to "systematically combat any deviations from the principle of Socialist Realism." Soviet literature, the Congress was directed to ensure, must be concerned principally with "topical questions of the policy of the Party and the Soviet State"; and there must be no indulgence of "any attempt to substitute a moral criterion unrelated to any specific society or time for the ideological, class-social judgments universally recognized in our literature . . . which can have no other interests but those of the people, the interest of the Soviet state."

The Second Congress forcefully enjoined the deviationists to repent in haste. Recanting, Ehrenberg expressed his contrition at having strayed from the paths of revolutionary righteousness into the labyrinthine ways of bourgeois decadence; and only such obdurate souls as Pasternak and Tarsis failed to take his words to heart. The proletarian heroes of Soviet fiction were restored to their pristine blamelessness, and Soviet writers reminded themselves that their function is to popularize the policy of State and Party, not to form or criticize the policy—or to meddle with any "moral criterion." Upon the delusory spring of post-Stalin letters, the brightest flower of which was Ehrenberg's *Thaw*, fell the icy terror of a Siberian February.

Probably the first impression of many readers of *The Thaw* in its English translation was that they had been well and thoroughly spoofed. The novel is so dull and formless, so flatly and falteringly written, so deficient in analysis and description of its characters, that it seems like one subtle burlesque of letters in modern Russia. Were this really so, Leacock could not hold a candle to Ehrenberg as a satirist. But Ehrenberg writes in earnest, except for occasional morsels of ridicule of certain Soviet peccadilloes. He did his best to write a naturalistic study of life and its discontents among what may be called the middle classes of a provincial town in Soviet Russia. To this book, then, the reader needs to apply that standard of criticism which Dr. Johnson charitably employed when he heard of women preaching or of dogs walking on their hinder legs: "It is not done well; but you are surprised to find it done at all."

For, obedient to the Marxist dogma that the function of literature is to reflect the class struggle and that the mission of the virtuous writer is to advance the cause of proletarian revolution and material advancement, Soviet novelists—with the poisoning of Gorki to encourage them—for many years had devoted their talents almost exclusively to the service of the state propaganda and the Communist Party's interests. The idealization of industrial production, the triumph of the stainless Young Communist over the saboteur, the exposure of Western bourgeois decadence, the portrayal of the Bad Old Days, and recently the resuscitation of Russian patriotism in the face of the German invasion—these themes, together with interminable glorification of the October Revolution, were all the Soviet writer knew, or needed to know.

Early in 1954, an eminent Soviet geologist, V. A. Obruchev, in the magazine *Knowledge is Strength*, described the goals toward which Dialectical Materialism is making its way; and these, the Second Congress of Soviet Writers affirmed, should be the concern of the pure-hearted Soviet author. There are seven of these goals: (1) to lengthen the life of man to 150-200 years on the average; (2) to put at the service of man all the forces of Nature; (3) to foretell and finally render harmless natural calamities; (4 to produce in factories all substances found on the earth, including most complex proteins, and also substances not found in nature; (5) to develop new breeds of livestock and plants; (6) to reduce and master the wastelands; (7) to learn to control the weather. These labors accomplished, men will be as gods. Nothing is said about the human person here; and the dangerous deviationist proclivity of certain writers toward treating of human beings was roundly denounced by the Union of Writers.

Even excursions into the realm of fantasy, like the re-telling of Russian folk-tales, have been tolerated only as so many exercises in dialectical materialism, calculated to obliterate the Past by making the Past merely the reflection of the omnipotent Present, and converting peasant wisdom and peasant prejudice into clumsy allegories of Expropriator and Expropriated. Into this frozen realm of letters, then, where Romance and Criticism and Satire and Verse slumbered like so many of Barbarossa's barons under the Kyffhäusser, free neither to live nor to die, drifted the timid zephyr of *The Thaw*.

Now Ilya Ehrenberg scarcely was the man to wake the dead—or, having waked them, to lead them up to the world of flesh and blood. Like the intruder into the magic mountain, he found upon a rock in this sepulchral realm a sword and a horn; and of the two, he chose the horn; and so a frightful wind blew him back to the Union of Soviet Writers, an assemblage not much given to flights of fancy or to the impulse to make dry bones speak.

"Cursed the craven that ever he was born,
Who did not draw the sword before he blew the horn."

Ehrenberg's motive seems to have been prudential, rather than heroic. His writings long had reflected faithfully the Soviet policy of the hour; and he had been rewarded accordingly by Party and State. With the death of Stalin, nevertheless, Ilya Ehrenberg—like many others—seems to have felt that a new era of good feeling was at hand; the new regime might be inclined to reward the literary reflection of milder political policies; some degree of criticism of Party discipline and State administration might be tolerated, and even smiled upon. That incorrigible longing of a man of letters to lead public opinion seems to have combined with the temper of the early months of 1954 to induce Ehrenberg to write and publish his little novel.

The consequent tempest in a samovar seems surprising, until one recalls to mind the canons of Soviet literary orthodoxy, and the peculiar political circumstances of Russia at the moment. After all, this is a mousy little book, innocent of any high invocations, mildly ironical concerning a painter with an eye to the main chance, placidly describing the worries and neuroses of some members of the administrative and artistic classes. *Riceyman Steps* is grand tragedy and merciless social criticism, by the side of *The Thaw*. The most bigoted functionary of the Old Regime, in either France or Russia, never would have thought of suppressing so timorous and ineffectual a work of fiction. The book has no villains: even Juravliov, the factory director, is merely a little stupid and a little malicious, his principal fault a fatuous optimism. Ehrenberg hedges discreetly, so that when Koroteyev the engineer ventures upon some praise of Americans ("They've any amount of education there, I can tell from their scientific journals") he promptly adds, "But just read what they do to Negroes and see how it depresses you—sheer savagery." This, the Russian's rejoinder in a well-worn joke about subway trains not running in Moscow, appears sufficiently orthodox to satisfy any test of Soviet dialectic.

Yet the Union of Soviet Writers, doubtless in part obeying instructions from on high, but also out of sheer force of habit, plodded through this story for evidences of deviationism, came up with the stale old charges of lusting after bourgeois decadence, and extracted from Ehrenberg a half-hearted *mea culpa*. A writer so long in favor, and so well known to the Western world, stood in no grave peril of suffering extreme penalties—not for sins so minor as Ehrenberg's. The novel still can be read in Russia, and Ehrenberg did not recant totally.

Now Ehrenberg seems to have got himself into these difficulties by a series of miscalculations. First of all, he appears to have overestimated the strength of the influences urging moderation, shortly after the death of Stalin. But the uneasy ascendancy of the moderates was of very brief duration—indeed, the political moderates may not have existed at all, their apparent mildness having been no more than prudent groping by hard men for the reins of power before issuing decrees. When the influence of Malenkov's coterie, at any rate, began to fade before a new coalition of commissars and marshals, the thaw was over, and *The Thaw* out of favor. Second,

Ehrenberg seems to have underestimated the painful sensitivity of the Party leaders and the bureaucracy to criticism even of the feeblest description. Unaccustomed to protest from men of letters, the masters of the State—especially at this uncomfortable juncture —received his book with suspicion and anger. A writer is the Party's and the State's servant; so the dissenter, however eminent, must be disciplined instanter. Third, Ehrenberg seems to have slipped forgetfully into the role of his own character the anonymous young novelist, in the first chapter of *The Thaw*, who impudently ventures to write of Soviet comrades as if they were subject to the infirmities of ordinary mortals—when Ehrenberg's own success had been founded, in no small part, upon his zealous detection of ideological infirmity.

In such a body as the Union of Soviet Writers, the innovator is feared and detested. The members of such an association have prospered precisely because, from the inception of their careers. they have conformed ungrudgingly to Marxist dogma and have recited the slogans and formulas of that creed until those phrases have acquired, by dint of repetition, the power of magical incantation. Their peace of mind, their reputations, their salaries depend upon the permanence of the line they have followed undeviatingly. Now there starts up among them an energumen who would challenge, however modestly, some of the minor articles of their New Faith. How can they help but hate him? Thinking is a painful form of labor; he would make them think; and they have become affluent and privileged not through thinking, but through conforming. Once, then, it became clear to these authors that Ehrenberg, far from being backed by Party and State, had contrived to cast his lot with a sinking coterie, they proceeded to drub the innovator. "Surely," says Koroteyev, hypocritically, in *The Thaw*, "our Soviet people are more honest and more responsible than he has made them out to be." Thus spoke the Union of Soviet Writers concerning Ehrenberg himself, and would not be denied.

"You read novels where everything is in its place," Ehrenberg remarked in his own defense before the Congress of Soviet Writers, "every detail of the machines and of production meetings is properly described . . . but where's the human soul?" The grim history of Soviet letters considered, these were bold words. Possibly Ehrenberg thought some show of sincere opposition safer than abject confession and professed contrition; certainly he came off with nothing worse than a reprimand. With the precise policies of the new regime at Moscow still to be enunciated, Simonov and his colleagues may have thought it the part of discretion to rest content with Ehrenberg's imperfect apology.

For neither Ehrenberg nor Simonov can have forgotten the late Russian Association of Proletarian Writers, which flourished between 1928 and 1932, hounding "non-Communist" writers into the grave. Of a sudden, in 1932, Stalin struck down the Russian Association of Proletarian Writers, on suspicion of deviationism among the inquisitors themselves, and the leader of the Association, Averbakh, was blotted out along with his brother-in-law, the terrible Yagoda. The Union of Soviet Writers succeeded to the powers of the RAPW—and succeeded to its peril. Once the masters of such an organization have crushed their opposition, they themselves, tipsy with power, tend to form a new opposition, critical of the bureaucracy. Thus Ehrenberg, once so zealous for orthodoxy, had drifted into his "Soviet humanism"; and thus Simonov, zealous for conformity, dealt very hardly with lesser writers and dealt with Ehrenberg as hardly as he dared.

I have called this somewhat comical affair a tempest in a samovar. It may become the subject of a footnote in some future history of Russian literature, provided any histories of any literature are published in the age that is dawning. Not by virtue of this squabble, nor yet by virtue of its own literary qualities, does *The Thaw* come to deserve international attention. By the standards of Russian literature before 1918, this is a sorry little book, superficial and boring. To say that it is better than much published in Russia nowadays is to damn it with faint praise. Yet it is an important book; to resort to an ambiguous word much in vogue among reviewers, it is a significant book. What does it signify? I think that it tells us, for one thing, much about the frame of mind and temper at present dominant among the administrative and intellectual orders in Soviet Russia—and gives us some understanding of the motives and prospects of that society. I think also that it unintentionally reveals the ruinous condition of serious literature under a totalist state. I propose to say a little here about these two aspects of *The Thaw*.

Icicles in the Thaw

Realism, Bierce says, emphasizes "the charm suffusing a land-scape painted by a mole, or a story written by a measuring-worm." *The Thaw* is a genuinely realistic novel—and something of an escape from "socialist realism"—but it has little enough in common with the "realism" of Zola, say, or of James T. Farrell. It is much closer to the realistic novel written by the garret-scholar in Gissing's *New Grub Street*, who trails a butcher and his wife about London so as to miss no dull detail of their conversation. What Ehrenberg has endeavored to accomplish is to examine candidly the decent drabness of existence among very ordinary and obscure middle-class Russians of the new order. These people know no tremendous passions or overweening aspirations. Ehrenberg is no mole; but the analogy of the measuring-worm is apt enough.

I repeat that the society of *The Thaw* is restricted middle-class society. Nothing to come out of Soviet Russia since the triumph of Stalin—except, possibly, for two or three films, and those inadvertently—better establishes the fact that the classless society is only a phrase in the Soviet Union. The characters in this novel—characters ineptly drawn, and possessed of little living personality, but nevertheless bearing the stamp of authenticity—are reasonably well off, secure, and even smug, displaying many of the virtues commonly called bourgeois, and few of the vices. They go to the theatre and the opera; they slip into love rather languidly, and slip out of it again. They know next to nothing of the political oligarchy which governs them—only an occasional dreaded reprimand or summons from Moscow disturbs the placid round of domestic duties and factory production and lectures and amusements. And the life of the laboring classes is nearly as remote from them as is the life of the upper ranks of Party and bureaucracy. The Secretary of the Town Committee speaks to the Factory Director about "the dilapidated hovels and hutments of the workers . . . a disgrace"; but the Factory Director has seen worse in Moscow. About the folk who dwell in these hovels and hutments, *The Thaw* tells us little.

The managerial class, with its literary and artistic appendages, is what interests Ehrenberg. There occur some brief conventional glimpses of a *kolkhoz* presided over by a matriarch; yet of how life really is lived in such a collective, we are given few hints. White collar and business suit appear to be the marks of a distinct status even more in this Russian town than they are in Birmingham or Chicago.

Ehrenberg writes, then, of the pillars of society, of the people who read books and form local policy and keep the production-system of the Soviets reasonably efficient. Almost all of them are well-meaning little people, civil and decent, the people who buy Ehrenberg's books. They must have been surprised and gratified, after a literary diet of Socialist Realism, to find themselves represented without distortion in *The Thaw*. That they are not the real masters of Russia, the fate of this novel demonstrates; yet probably we find here a truthful description of the bulk of the intellectual and administrative classes which have settled down into a tolerable routine fifty years after the triumph of the Bolsheviks. These are not Bolsheviks; they do not think of world dominion, nor of the future terrestrial paradise; their own round of small duties, and their private problems, loom much larger than do the old catch-phrases of the class struggle. None of these characters means to lead a crusade. Some of them resent the dull production-obsession of the Factory Director; Savchenko the engineer has a somewhat vague attachment to the doctrine of Progress, which seems to amount principally to "lots and lots of corn"; Saburov the painter actually dares to experiment moderately in his art. But all this is bathos when set beside the October Revolution, for which most of them retain an amorphous admiration; it is the beginning of history for them, and it has become as remote as the battle of the Olympians and the Titans.

Out of the disjointed conversations of this novel comes the impression—never clearly expressed by Ehrenberg himself—that all these people are on the verge of asking themselves, "What are we here for?" And some of them are almost as close to asking themselves a question yet more significant, "Is life worth living?" Are these petty intrigues, these flirtations, these arguments about housing versus the new precision-casting bay, these worries about promotion or demotion, these small headaches and anxieties, the whole end and aim of being? Is this the New Order for which millions of lives were expended? In this book are symptoms of a deep-seated disillusion: the triumph over the Germans, for instance, lingers as scarcely more than an unpleasant business in which some of these people lost friends or lovers. These are not men and women who seek a revolution or a restoration. They are looking, instead, for some clue to the meaning of life; but, cut off from the Past, they find it difficult and sometimes dangerous to carry their curiosity far.

It is not fear, however, that these people commonly suffer from: it is boredom. Now and then some gargoyle face grimaces out of Ehrenberg's pages, as when a tenth-grade girl is expelled from the Komsomol on vague charges, or when Juravliov is removed by the Head Office. ("Where was Juravliov? What had become of him? Not a living soul remembers. A storm comes, gives a lot of trouble and passes over; who remembers when it stopped roaring?") There occurs no mention of the secret police or of the Siberian camps. Yet probably we would fall into error if we were to treat Ehenberg's picture of an administrative class comparatively secure and placid as mere sham. It has been more than three decades since the end of the Russian Revolution; and fanaticism, with its spies and purges, weakens in that length of time, in defiance of all the endeavors of a ministry of propaganda. Any quasi-reasonable political regime, once effectual opposition has been eliminated, will endeavor to rule by custom and persuasion, not by terror. The heartless struggle for power, with its conspiracies and betrayals, will continue among the people who lust after power, in the upper reaches of Party and Army and Bureaucracy and Police; yet to the shallows of provincial towns and conveyor-belt factories will return some considerable measure of peace and toleration, lacking which even a Marxist society cannot get its day's work done. The people in *The Thaw* are somewhat nervous: the possibility of a reprimand from central authority, a transfer to unknown regions, an irremediable blight to a career, a denunciation by a committee, never is quite thrust out of consciousness; but they may expect, by and large, to get on in their world, if they conform to the slogans of the hour and do not trouble themselves with speculation. Volodya the painter knows how to walk discreetly and how to execute portraits of factory-directors likely to succeed. Writers aren't paid to have ideas, he says. "All that happens to you with ideas is that you break your neck. What you're meant to look for in a book is ideology. If it's there what more d'you want? It's lunatics that have ideas." The Second Congress of Writers echoed him.

Ideas abjured, these middle-class comrades may slumber reasonably sound. Escape from less tangible anxieties, all the same, remains difficult. Those vexatious questions, "What are we here for?" and "Is life worth living?" have a way of creeping back into the consciousness of the most orthodox Communist. They plague especially the administrative and artistic classes which Ehrenberg describes, possessed of just enough leisure to make them inquire whether comfort and leisure are all that life ever can afford. By the triumph of revolutionary doctrines from which none of them ventures to dissent, these people have been deprived of nearly all the old motives to integrity which have governed mankind since men entered upon their civil social state, and of nearly all the old rewards. These people are fed; they are housed; they enjoy a fair amount of idleness; but that is all.

Though theirs is not a society in which love lies dead, still love is very sick. In its traditional meaning, love is something intensely private. The Soviet state, like all totalist states, is inimical to privacy. Ehrenberg hints at the conflict between personal loyalty and the demands made by this production-consumption society, in which everyone (as in *Brave New World*) belongs to everyone else. Not that the lovers of *The Thaw* are promiscuous: with one or two exceptions, they are positively Victorian in their proprieties, the erotic emancipation of the first years of the New Order having burnt itself out. At the back of these lovers' difficulties, instead, seems to exist a feeling that something is wrong with tenderness—perhaps it is anti-social. Everything in life is supposed to contribute to the material betterment of the masses: well, what is love good for, and what is marriage good for? In this Soviet society, marriage is simply a union for physical satisfaction and procreation. Lacking any spiritual sanction, or any aspiration toward continuity and immortality in the classical and Christian tradition of family, love is really blind in this New Faith. These people do not defy the State by secret indulgence in lust, as do the rebels in Orwell's *1984;* lust of any description is no strong factor in their lives; they merely ask about love, as about most other phenomena in life, "What is the meaning of all this?" And no one gives them an answer—certainly not Ilya Ehrenberg.

If the sense of meaning in life that comes with enduring love is difficult to attain in this modern Russian society, the sense of meaning that comes with lasting achievement is in worse plight: for under the cloak of collective benevolence, this society has been atomized, and that delicate growth which constitutes genuine community has been destroyed. The provincial town in *The Thaw* resembles an aggregation of barracks and impermanent flats, in which men and women exist after the fashion of what Burke called "the flies of a summer," generation scarcely linking with generation, family reduced to the most tenuous of bonds between husband and wife or mother and son, state disciplines and decrees substituting for that complex of affection and common interest which made the old Russian family—even at its worst, in Gorki's novels—a great power for good. The instinct of the stronger and better natures has been thwarted in obedience to Marxist teaching. Even the successful intriguer cannot spend his money in any way wholly satisfactory to himself. Volodya, musing on how he will use the fat fee from his latest politic portrait, says to himself, "Shall I buy a 'Victory'? Nice to speed on the road, everything flickers past, you haven't time to notice anything. Not worth it, perhaps, better give half to Mother. . . ." Everything flickers past. After three decades and more, the Revolutionary Utopia has faded to this boredom with the present and this indifference to the future. Half a century ago, Graham Wallas, in his *Human Nature in Politics,* while confessing it possible that a desire for property might be ineradicable in human nature, speculated as to just how little and how abstract this property might be made without outraging the instinct. The society which Ehrenberg describes passed that limit of discretion long ago. The salaried administrator and the kept intellectual enjoy many comforts and even luxuries; but they have been deprived of the possibility of enduring accomplishment, either in the sense of material possessions or of family continuity. Thus they languish in an apathy which dismays Ehrenberg himself.

Tanechka the actress, thinking of the approaching summer with a sodden resignation, expresses the whole mood of futility, somehow more depressing than anything in Gogol or Dostoievski: "She would apply to go to Zelenino, that suited her purse. But she could see it all in advance: conversation at lunch on the benefits of steamed cutlets for those who were taking the cure; picking worm-eaten mushrooms in the afternoon; somebody getting drunk at dinner and making a scene which everybody else would go on chewing over; then the crossword from the *Ogoniok*, with twenty people torturing themselves over a mineral of six letters starting with B."

Although boredom of this description is not peculiar to Soviet Russia, one of the oppressive and significant revelations of this disturbing novel is the fact that little *except* this boredom remains for active natures under communism. Those at the very top, it is true, may console themselves with the vast and terrible game of power, what Orwell called "stamping forever on a human face"; the rest find even lively conversation beyond their abilities, because the principal topics of interesting talks are either dangerous or else accepted as having been forever settled by official Soviet philosophy.

The Old Bolsheviks believed they were opening up illimitable vistas to humanity; in fact, they were sealing every avenue of escape from a technological prison. *The Thaw* constitutes a confession that no radical political or economic device can succeed in liberating mankind from the ills to which flesh is heir. John Adams, in the midst of a Gallic and European revolution inspired by similar delusions of social perfectibility, foresaw the consequences of a fatuous optimism: "Amid all their exultations, Americans and Frenchmen should remember that the perfectibility of man is only human and terrestrial perfectibility. Cold will still freeze, and fire will never cease to burn; disease and vice will continue to disorder, and death to terrify mankind. Emulation next to self-preservation will forever be the great spring of human actions, and the balance of a well-ordered government will alone be able to prevent that emulation from degenerating into dangerous ambition, irregular rivalries, destructive factions, wasting seditions, and bloody brutal wars." Only now, after fifty years of hacking brutally at the Past, are thinking men in Russia beginning to listen furtively to such vaticinations.

No counter-revolutionary shows his face in Ehrenberg's portrait-gallery. Yet the very ennui that disheartens the better men and women in *The Thaw* may give some promise of a Russian regeneration. Smugness, far more than oppression, is a common cause of the fall of tyrannies. No regime ever was more smug than the Soviet political power, or more inimical to a liberal understanding. Boredom with the featureless uniformity of Russian life may penetrate even to the ruthless little knots of men who play the grisly game of power, so that they may grow weary of the whole undertaking. And there is this, at least, to be learnt from *The Thaw:* the heart seems to be gone out of the party of proletarian revolution; so conceivably —supposing the Western world can hold its lines against the present physical power of Russia—the forces of "the Great Tradition" in politics and morality may hope to win the battle against a fanatic ideology, an armed doctrine, already sinking into decadence.

Efficacious   Intolerance

Better than a century ago, Turgenev, just returned from his exile at Orel, was the dominant figure in Russian letters. Like Ehrenberg fifteen years ago, he had offended the state censors; and, not being the man to apologize, Turgenev had spent three years in retirement. The gulf between Turgenev and Ehrenberg is sufficient to refute the whole idea of Progress. The year 1917 did not merely bring a change to Russian literature; it put an end to Russian literature, except for such isolated survivors in literary tradition as Boris Pasternak. If one contracts the strength and variety of Russian writing in the nineteenth century with the present outpourings of the writer-bureaucrats, he is struck most forcibly by the swiftness with which Russian civilization has fallen into a slough. About the middle of the nineteenth century, it seemed to many critics that Russian literature was destined to succeed to the ascendancy which English and French had maintained for centuries. Though frequently gloomy and eccentric, Russian writing was marked by an intellectual penetration and a power of style that the older European literatures no longer matched. This Russian literature continued to grow in influence during the latter half of the nineteenth century, the work of Dostoievski, Chekhov, and Tolstoi presaging a future Russian domination of imaginative and critical writing. The Revolution put an end to all that.

Is there anyone left nowadays simple enough to maintain that the devastation of Russian culture has been merely the work of Wicked Men in the Kremlin? This was the theory of the Trotskyites, who are virtually extinct: the notion that, despite Evil being no more than a consequence of social conditions, somehow the Revolution had slipped into the hands of Wicked Men, Stalinists, who perverted the pure doctrines of Marx and Lenin. Until quite recently, some people in the West clung to the hope that a particular faction of beneficent Communists might yet occupy the seats of the mighty in the Kremlin, bringing sweetness and light unto the masses. But these vagrant dreams are dissipated nearly everywhere now, and it is increasingly clear, even to the men and women who for a long while were the most ardent of fellow-travellers, that the evil lies in the very system of thought called Marxism. The ghastly decay of Russian literature is produced directly by Marxism, and cannot be arrested so long as the Marxist ideology prevails.

My argument is not that the orthodox Marxist is merely intolerant. Taken by itself, intolerance is no insurmountable obstacle to high achievement in letters. As Erik von Kuehnelt-Leddihn observed to me once, a certain degree of intolerance, censorship, and state surveillance is a positive stimulus to poet, novelist, critic, and painter. The creative mind, thus challenged, exercises its ingenuity to baffle the obscurants—sometimes through satire, sometimes through outright defiance, sometimes through dissimulation, sometimes by converting the obscurants themselves. So it was in Imperial Russia: the repressive inclination of the State actually helped to nourish the richness and vitality of nineteenth-century Russian writing. Official frowns augmented, rather than crushed, a literature of protest. Even if banished to the provinces, or compelled to take sanctuary abroad, the author retained a devoted following in Russia and (like the *philosophes* of the Old Regime in France) ordinarily had friends at court. Censorship only increased the desire of the rising generation to read the prohibited books.

But this is true only of *limited* intolerance. Imperial Russia was not efficaciously intolerant in any thoroughgoing way. The man of letters was respected, even if he was feared; the influence of Christian morality, however much diluted or debased, forbade the political authority to be wholly ruthless in the repression of opinions; court and bureaucracy were sprinkled with friends of liberal ideas; and the despotism of the Czars was not nimble enough to crush the literary rebel out of existence. Therefore the opposition of the political regime was more stimulating to freedom of thought and power of literary expression than any benevolent program of grants-in-aid to impecunious authors might have been.

But the intolerance of Soviet Russia is unlimited. Before 1917, the rebellious writer was confronted only by the power of government; now he is a rebel not simply against government, but against the State, against society, almost against humanity. Leaving no sanctuaries for the dissident, the State is become all in all. At Orel, Turgenev could live in comfort and safety, his principal privation being separation from the life of the capital—a banishment like that of Ovid to the pleasant shores of the Euxine. A country gentleman of large private means, Turgenev could live in Baden-Baden and Paris, when he chose, for as long as he chose. Now the situation of Ehrenberg was vastly different. Far from being a rebel against the political order, Ehrenberg was a part of the State, a species of bureaucrat, a socialist functionary. His only alternative to intellectual servitude was flight. In his earlier years, at least, he could not have subsisted if his works had been disapproved, even if immunity from positive punishment had been guaranteed to him. In modern Russia, the writer eats only if he makes himself an instrument of ideological propaganda. The private patron has been liquidated; the State is the only publisher; other State servants are the only readers. Ehrenberg was a deputy to the Supreme Soviet and a member of the Soviet commission on foreign affairs: to rebel would have been not simply to destroy himself, but to deny himself. So have the Soviets passed beyond intolerance by leaving no one in a position to ask for toleration.

In 1967 (the fiftieth anniversary of the Bolshevik Revolution and the year of Ehrenberg's death), some stirrings of protest were visible below the surface of the Fourth Congress of the Soviet Writers' Union. Alexander Solzhenitsyn circulated there a letter in which he declared that more than six hundred Soviet writers had been handed over by the Writers' Union to the masters of the state for imprisonment—or, in the Siberian camps, worse than imprisonment. No delegate to the Congress was sufficiently foolhardy to request that Solzhenitsyn's accusation be read into the official proceedings.

I do not imply that the career of writer or artist or scholar was a cheerful one in Imperial Russia. When Razumov, in Conrad's *Under Western Eyes*, announces that he intends "to retire—simply to retire," Councillor Mikulin says to him, quietly and sufficiently, "Where to?" There remained no spot in Russia for Razumov to lie hid from the whirlwind of politics. But what was difficult half a century ago now has become impossible: Ehrenberg would not have dared to think of retiring. Intolerance no longer contents itself with suppressing active opposition, but insists upon obtaining active endorsement. And that works the death of literature, as we have known it for seven or eight centuries, and the death of all art. Through Juravliov, in *The Thaw,* the typical commissar speaks: "Koroteyev was quite right in attacking novelists—we are living in historical times, decent people have no time for intrigues." The task for the writer, under the intolerant regime of the New Faith, is to stimulate production, to induce conformity among the masses, to popularize the decisions of the masters of the State. No time will remain for bothering with the intricacies of human nature and the secrets of human longing.

Artful Dodging

Yet a lucrative and conspicuous place remained for Ilya Ehrenberg in the Soviet structure. Adequately supple and thick-skinned enough to survive all the vicissitudes and humiliations and perils of literary men in Russia from the revolutionary years to the present junta, Ehrenberg lived to be seventy-six years old. He published his reminiscences in several parts, of which the volume *People and Life, 1891-1921,* forms the first two sections.

Tombstones, many of them rising from the graves of Ehrenberg's friends, overshadow these autobiographical pages. The Communist domination being fatal to art, some Russian writers and scholars fled into exile, and others fell silent altogether. But the fate of many Russian men of letters was more violent. Of those mentioned by Ehrenberg in *People and Life* (though he rarely touches upon how they went down to dusty death), Gorki was poisoned by the secret police; Fadeyev killed himself after Khrushchev denounced the dead Stalin; Gumilev was shot by the Bolsheviks; Mandelstam died in a Soviet concentration camp; Markish was executed with other Jewish writers, under Stalin; Mayakovski destroyed himself after being bullied by the Association of Proletarian Writers; Meyerhold vanished in the prison camps; Tairov was put to death in a purge; Yashvili committed suicide; so did Yessenin, when he saw the Communists destroying peasant existence.

So the most remarkable thing about Ehrenberg—a serious journalist and propagandist rather than an imaginative or truly critical writer, and rather a small fish in the Russian literary pond, compared with some who died or fled—is that he lived to be seventy-six years old, and yet did not descend into *total* literary servitude. In contrast with his friend Alexei Tolstoi, whose artful dodging made him the richest Soviet citizen, Ehrenberg stood up now and again, however equivocally, for the freedom of the Soviet intellectual. Still, he was sedulous never to swim perversely against what seemed to be the wave of the Soviet literary future.

A literary man with some international reputation for protest— but whose protest scarcely rose above hint and whisper, and who did not fall into the indiscretion of mentioning how his friends perished—was not without his uses to the masters of the Soviet system. He travelled to Paris, to London, to New York: behold, can the men in the Kremlin be so tyrannical? Most of the time he was able to walk over new-fallen snow without leaving tracks. In his autobiography, his misgivings about Soviet society are no more forthright than they are in *The Thaw,* although in an occasional parenthesis he ventures upon remonstrance, as in this passage:

"(Speaking of the shortcomings of our way of life, people sometimes say that they are 'remnants of capitalism.' Sometimes this is true and sometimes it is not. A bright light casts dark shadows, and good things may have bad consequences. Let me take the most obvious example: that of bureaucracy. Lenin wrote about it and our newspapers are still talking about it today, forty years later. Can anyone really believe that this paper dropsy, this hypertrophy of those who record, discuss, check, file is nothing but a 'remnant'? Is not this disease—which, in the last analysis, can and must disappear—part of the development of organization, accounting, production control, all of which are progressive and useful?)

"I recall a young country girl who worked as a cleaner at the

Military Chemical Academy. She sang a ditty that went like this: 'I'll be in trouble, that I know. I'm going to the privy with no pass to show. I'll be happy to get one, but, alas, there's no one around to issue a pass.' When I first heard it, I laughed. Then it made me stop to think."

And Ehrenberg hints at his own disillusionment with Communist enthusiasm by quoting from a fervent article he wrote at the age of sixteen, crying up Socialism and exhorting students to become "the trumpeters and drummers of the great class," the leaders of the proletariat. Then he comments wryly, "I have quoted my first literary exercise in full, not, of course, because it strikes me as successful; I want to show how words get inflated and change their meaning. In 1907 I longed to become a trumpeter and drummer so that in 1957 I might write: 'An orchestra isn't all trumpets and drums. . . .'"

For those writers who were more bold in their opposition to the total political domination of the works of the mind, Ehrenberg had some kind words. "I am convinced that it was not Pasternak's intention to hurt our country. His guilt consisted only of the fact that he was Pasternak. . . . He did not suspect that his book would create a vile political sensation and that the blow would inevitably be followed by a counterblow."

To "our country," Russia, indeed, Pasternak was more lovingly attached than Ehrenberg—and the religious roots of Pasternak's thought provided that strong writer with a basis for resistance to totalism which Ehrenberg never knew. Pasternak was a Russian: Ehrenberg, a cosmopolitan, happy in bohemian Paris before 1918, "born into a bourgeois Jewish family." His cosmopolitanism went deeper than his Marxism. A certain dispassionate quality—despite his decades as a Soviet propagandist—runs through his memoirs, which offer many interesting glimpses of revolutionary anarchy in the Ukraine and Georgia, for instance, and insights into the Russian intellectual ferment, with its Gallic tinge, that virtually ended in 1917.

Cold-eyed and sardonic in Picasso's drawing of him, Ehrenberg was something of a twentieth-century Talleyrand, though never invested with real political authority. The fatigue which sighs from his pages is like the last gasp of the old liberal rationalism expiring under the weight of Marxism.

The Slums of Literature

Ehrenberg's trumpet was prudently muted. Suppose, neverthe-less, that somehow the Soviet regime should be transmogrified into an association of persons liberal of intellect and intent upon restor-ing the vitality of Russian literature: what then? Suppose that the Supreme Soviet should come around to the way of thinking of the late deputy Ehrenberg, and should perceive, with Ehrenberg's cre-ation Koroteyev, the urgent necessity for something to wake mind and conscience: what then? Koroteyev says, "We have taken a lot of trouble over one half of the human being, but the other half is neglected. The result is that one half of the house is a slum. I remember that article of Gorki's I read long ago, while I was still at school; he said we needed our own Soviet humanism. That word has been forgotten, the task is still to be done. In those days it was only a presentiment, now it's time we tackled it."

A Soviet humanism? Who will be the Soviet Erasmus? Human-ism, true humanism, drew its vigor from the conviction that man was something more than merely flesh, that there existed law for man and law for thing, and that the disciplinary arts of *humanitas* taught a man his rights, his duties, and his station as a truly human person. Humanism and Marxism—to employ another word from *The Devil's Dictionary*—are incompossible. One may conceive of Russian humanism, but not of Soviet humanism. And this distinc-tion is not purely one of toleration and good intentions. For the Marxist ideology destroys the very situations and themes that in-spire humane letters. "This novel touches on a raw spot," Sav-chenko says of the young writer's work in *The Thaw*. "The public is longing for such books." Even a generation of dialectical material-ism has not rooted up utterly the taste for humane letters, appar-ently; yet it may have put an end to the possibility of satisfying that longing.

For I suggest here that four principal themes have inspired our chief works of imaginative literature, from the great age of Greece to our own Wasteland. The first of these is religion: the description of the order that is more than human and more than natural, as in Hesiod's *Theogony* or in Dante's *Divine Comedy* or in Bunyan's *Pilgrim's Progress*. The second of these is love: the devotion of a truly human person to a truly human person, as in the medieval romances or in the major Victorian novels. The third of these is heroism: the triumph of honor, duty, and fortitude, as in the *Aeneid* or in Mallory. The fourth of these is private fortune: the adventures of human individuals within the labyrinth of a diversified society of classes and orders, as in *Don Quixote* or in *Tom Jones*.

Now none of these themes or sources of inspiration is available to the Marxist writer. Religion has become the opiate of the masses: it is forbidden. Love has become the gratification of physical impulse: it is tolerated only. Heroism has become service to the production-consumption State: it is servile. Private fortune, with the abolition of class and order and social diversity, has grown subversive: it is anathema. Just what subjects and sources remain to humane letters? Only, it appears, those endless romances of production-goals in a tractor-factory which bored Ilya Ehrenberg out of countenance, and those fulminations against the Wicked American Capitalism which now ring false even to the provincial middle-class intellectuals of *The Thaw*. I do not believe that humane letters owe allegiance to any particular political program, or any especial economic scheme; yet there are social systems which mean the death of art, dominations under which humanism is inconceivable; and Marxism is such a system or domination carried to its logical extreme.

In *The Liberal Imagination,* Lionel Trilling suggests that imaginative literature, along with most of the prescriptive values of Western civilization, virtually is worn out: "It is not then unreasonable to suppose that we are at the close of a cultural cycle, that the historical circumstances which called forth the particular intellectual effort in which we once lived and moved and had our being is now at an end, and that the novel as part of that effort is as deciduous as the rest."

Professor Trilling does not elevate this speculation to the condition of a dogma; indeed, he proposes alternatives. But he does trace with some pains the connection between the decay of traditional society and the decay of imaginative literature. As the old faith in religion, love, heroism, and personal achievement has decayed, and even more as a society of class and variety—a society in which it is possible to fall and to rise, and in which there exist innumerable human persons quite different one from another—has been eroded to the dry plain of egalitarian uniformity, so have the confidence and courage and inspiration of the humane writer sunk down to a spiritless naturalism or a grubby nihilism. This has been the progress from Turgenev to Ehrenberg—or, to make the contrast greater even at the peril of bathos, from Shakespeare to Ehrenberg. I think it will be unavailing merely to whisper, with Ehrenberg, that literature ought to be something better than State propaganda. No other sort of literature is conceivable in a condition of totalist collectivism.

Savchenko, the romantic engineer, near the end of *The Thaw*, bursts into a timorous gaiety: "Our factory is wonderful. I like seeing it all as in a picture-book; first our conveyor-belt—that's easy, I see that every day; then another factory where our machines are making tractors, then huge tractors rushing out into the steppe, then corn, lots and lots of corn, and the country growing richer, stronger, and then Communism. . . . Anybody would feel happy in such a factory. And there are other things: there's *Hamlet*."

Yes: there's *Hamlet*. There's Communism, an abstraction somewhere in the remote future, after everybody has plenty of corn; and there's *Hamlet*. Communism may be universal long after *Hamlet* has been forgotten—but not until. "Man is a pliable animal," Dostoievski says, "a being who gets accustomed to everything." I continue to hope that this generalization has its bounds.

☯ ☯

IV. A MAN OF VISION IN OUR TIME

Max Picard's World of Silence

NOT ALL MINDS ARE CAPTIVE. THE SERVICE OF GOD BEING perfect freedom, the philosopher and the writer who do not live under totalist dominations, and who do not shut their eyes to a reality which transcends the ordinary senses, are able to enjoy even in our century a liberty far removed from license. I have known some such men of letters and thought; and one of the wiser among them was Max Picard.

He was such a man of vision—a seer, a sage—as perceives the permanent things with a clarity unknown to most of us. With wonderful simplicity, Picard—who was born a Jew, became a Christian, and on his deathbed returned to the faith of his fathers—wrote of our blindness in the modern era; and hope never forsook him, and abnormality never touched him. A few more Picards, and twentieth-century letters would be redeemed.

Cribbed in institutions, battening on linguistic analysis, twentieth-century philosophy—which, today, might better be called philodoxy—seems afflicted with a death-wish. Logical positivism, dominant in American and British universities, is suicidally bent upon establishing the impossibility of knowing anything. (As Wyndham Lewis suggested in *Self Condemned*, the neo-positivist pedant reduces himself to a mosquito, able to wound, nearly invulnerable to counter-assault—but only an insect, not a man.)

Much as the red squirrel retreats before the merciless gray squirrel, so the philosopher, lover of wisdom, has retired from the stricken field; today we know the conquering philodoxer, the lover of opinion or arid doctrine. The sage has succumbed to the ideologue or the "scientific" nihilist. Yet here or there endures a wise man of the stamp of Pascal or Samuel Johnson, abiding in a tradition, still employing the power of the Word to scourge the follies of the time. Such a man was Max Picard, who lived upon a mountain high above Lugano. There in his Ticino village he was nearly as poor in the world's goods as Diogenes, but a better man and a happier man than Diogenes.

In his devotion to the poetic and the intuitive as paths to wisdom, Picard was almost a pre-Socratic. His books are slim, evocative, and unforgettable. Several of them have been done into English: *The Flight from God, The World of Silence, Man and Language, Hitler in Our Selves, The Disintegration of Forms in Modern Art, The Atomizing of the Person.* Picard set his face not only against logical positivism, but against pragmatism, rationalism, and skepticism. Though his every reflection has for its premise the existence of God and a transcendent order, in his temper and style one encounters no suggestion of neo-Thomism. His simplicity and directness, studded with aphorisms, make him one of the few recent writers on first principles who may be read with pleasure and quick apprehension. Yet Picard never beckoned to the vulgar.

He was a hard hater of noise and an ardent lover of silence. But noise, with a diabolical power, followed Picard up from modernity, even to his little Alpine chalet. For the automobile, that mechanical Jacobin, now pants its way up the wooded slopes of the mountains; and trucks shift gears ferociously as they round the bends of the road across the valley from Picard's house, their squeal and screech and grate echoing to the cool terrace where he used to sit. As Picard wrote, modern noise was bent upon the utter conquest of silence in all its forms—the silence which has nurtured contemplation, and even the silence of God.

As eulogist of silent dignity, Picard admired old Spain. In his chapter "History and Silence," in *The World of Silence,* one finds this passage:

"There are nations that seem to slumber in silence for long centuries: such are the Spaniards during the last three centuries. The silence in which they live is not an emptiness, nor is it a symptom of sterility. It is rather a sign of the importance and value of silence for the Spaniards. Spain has been considered backward and old-fashioned because it did not join in the universal noise and mobility of the modern age by industrializing its economy. But Spain is no more backward than a child that wants to stay with its mother, or that comes back to its mother, and to silence."

It was well for Picard, nevertheless, that he—who rarely travelled—did not visit Spain in his later years. For Zurich, a city which Picard despised as the apotheosis of modern avarice and innovation, is quiet and restrained in comparison with modern Madrid, where the blare of radios with their flamenco or pseudo-flamenco wails, the blast of motorcycle exhausts, and all the din of a modern proletarian cosmopolis have tortured silence to death. Once noise breaks in triumphantly upon an ancient citadel of silence, it gives no quarter. Even Toledo, once famous for its almost deathly stillness, now is a place where one has difficulty sleeping o' nights: the nocturnal Spaniard, given electric lights and mechanical noise-makers, goes at the destruction of silence more enthusiastically than the Swiss. In ruinous and impoverished Avila, true enough, the spirits of Saint Teresa and of Saint John of the Cross still brood over the town within the walls, and silence has a respite from torment; there Soledad, Solitude, that beautiful woman's name, is not forgotten.

Modern relish for clatter and jabber, however, has done its work in Spain wherever prosperity has reared its head. Once I lunched in the hills of Mallorca, at an inn set upon the lip of a gorge. On the ridge opposite our windows I saw a big monastic-like building amid the mist, and I asked my friends what it was. "That's the headquarters of the Spanish League of Silence," my friends told me. "Many Spaniards gather there to talk at great length about the virtues of silence."

At this moment, there burst into the inn a well-dressed man who sat himself down and cried to the landlord, "Do you have a radio here? I don't have one at my place." Indeed there was a radio, which the gentleman tuned in, full blast, and proceeded to enjoy by tapping time with his feet.

"That gentlemen is the head of the Spanish League of Silence," my friends remarked. Presently he was joined by two colleagues, and the three of them, ordering lunch, proceeded to talk at the top of their lungs about the wonders of silence. "Silence! That's what we need in Spain! More silence, more silence!"

As frequently occurs in Latin lands, their conversation soon turned to politics. In Palma lives my friend Camilo Cela, who (with Gironella) is one of the two best living Spanish writers. The head of the League of Silence did not like Cela.

"That Cela! He pretends to be against the regime, but he fought for Franco last time, and when the test comes, he'll be on that side again. But then it will be *our* turn; and bam bam bam bam bam bam bam!" The members of the League of Silence simulated the rattle of a machine gun. Don Quixote does forever ride a dusty road in Castile; yet now, as then, he is one of a forlorn and proscribed minority. The world belongs to the vulgar—including the vulgar intellectuals.

Picard detested the radio as much as he did the machine gun. "Radio has occupied the whole space of silence," he wrote. "There is no silence any longer. Even when the radio is turned off, the radio-noise is so amorphous that it seems to have no beginning and no end; it is limitless. And the type of man formed by the constant influence of this noise is the same: formless, undecided inwardly and externally, with no definite limits and no standards."

He knew that nature takes vengeance upon her violators; so it seemed altogether possible that modernity, having obliterated noble silence, may find itself self-condemned to one vast ear-splitting explosion—and then the silence, universal and irrevocable, of extinction. The staccato music of the machine gun is a prelude to that last trump.

The discontinuity of modern existence—from which men turn to noise as an anodyne—provokes the machine gun and the men who command it. So Picard writes in *Hitler in Our Selves:*

"Only in a world of total discontinuity could a nullity such as Hitler become Fuehrer, because only where everything is disjointed has comparison fallen into disuse. There was only Hitler, the nullity, before everybody's eyes, and in this instable world wherein everything was changing at every moment one was glad that at least the one nullity, Hitler, remained stable before one's eyes. An orderly world, a hierarchy, would automatically have placed the nullity, Hitler, into nothingness; he could not have been noticed. Hitler was the excrement of a diabolical world; a world of truth in its order would have pushed him aside. . . .

"There is no permanence in this world of discontinuity. The ego exists only in the moment and for the moment. The individual, therefore, can have no evolution in the dimension of *time*. Everything has to be done in far too little time; hence, the individual gets restless and nervous. In discontinuity the individual also lacks context with his own personal history; he is lacking in the possibility of joining an experience with the context of previous experiences. Since life is lived solely in the moment and for the moment, the moment must carry all the burden; if the experience of a moment is grave, the individual is hit all the harder because the burden cannot be distributed through context with other things. That is what aggravates, exhausts, and unnerves the individual. The ego cries out loud; unable to expand in the dimension of time, the ego in its crying need explodes itself into the dimension of space. Then Hitler came and took over the job of crying into space for all the others, and because his was the loudest cry, he was accepted by all."

At good discourse, Picard was accomplished. Language, divinely implanted, he loved; it was "verbal noise" he condemned. He could talk easily with almost anyone; and when he was in Zurich, his favorite occupation was to converse with market-vendors in the streets. Children understood him readily. In a letter to an American friend, a few years ago, Picard described his visit to a Swiss secondary school:

"A boy stood up and said, 'What are our poets and thinkers for? The statesmen don't bother about them, but behave as though there were no poets and philosophers.'

"I answered that I wouldn't like it, and would be suspicious, if Chancellor Adenauer, for example, should read Sartre or Max Picard. The statesman must derive the practice of his profession from the truth of his profession. I explained to them that at the time of Goethe, the baker and the shoemaker had a more intense relationship to Goethe's poetry, although they never read it, than today when radio and the school stuff Goethe's poetry into everybody. In a real community, as it still existed in Goethe's time, that sort of thing was not necessary. The community joined the individual to everything without his noticing it, and without remark when it happened. All this, strange to say, the students understood."

Such insights the better pupil may grasp from Picard—while the "professional" philosopher might deride them for their very lucidity, much as certain pedants detest Santayana for his felicity of style. To Dr. Dryasdust, now and again Picard will seem platitudinous; but that is because platitudes are true. Though Picard wrote in German, he remained innocent of the ponderous abstraction and obscurity which characterize much of Germanic philosophical discourse. Picard's was more nearly a Latin mind; and, living within sight of Italy, he made cheerful expeditions southward whenever he might.

Though he spoke scarcely more English than I speak German, Picard wrote to me—before we met—that this should be small impediment to our fellowship, for understanding can transcend speech. So, indeed, we found it as we drank wine together on his Alpine terrace. The succinctness of his books was produced by a character that, revering the Word, abhorred wordiness.

"The certainty of self-identification, which man formerly received from his free embrace of language," Picard wrote in *Man and Language*, "is replaced by the merely external duration of verbal noise. The inner, spiritual continuity is replaced by a purely external continuity. Man switches on the radio to make certain that he is still an identifiable person; even the certainty of self-identification is mechanized.

"The language of verbal noise is pervious to everything. 'The earth gives man more self knowledge than all the books, because it offers resistance to him and it is only in conflict with forces outside himself that man finds the way to himself,' writes Antoine de Saint Exupéry. Language is no longer a resisting force. It is pervious to everything, far too pervious. Man is pervious too: he absorbs Negro sculpture and the animal and plant forms of the ninth-century Irish Codex Cenanensis, Toulouse Lautrec and Bavarian folk art, Carpaccio and the moderns, all mixed up together. Man absorbs everything because he has no spiritual continuity. He is no longer committed by anything that comes to him. Everything merely appears and disappears in the verbal noise."

Such loss of intellectual and verbal continuity impoverishes the soul—and destroys the fabric of the civil social order. Words decay into signals for violence. "The word degenerates into the shriek of the moment; by that, it already has sunk to the level of the Hitler shriek." When heart and tongue fall shrieking into disorder, humor perishes.

The ideologue, mistaking abstractions for realities, filled with wrath, forgets how to laugh. In a letter to Henry Regnery, Picard told of an encounter with a gloomy fanatic:

"About fifty years ago, I had a debate on the subject of Communism, with the Communist Frick.

"The Communist: 'In the Communist society, everyone and everything will be equal, everyone will receive the same wage and the same meals, and whoever doesn't work will get neither wages nor anything to eat.'

"I: 'Very well, but what will you do with such people as I, who are completely helpless and impractical? Would I have to go hungry?'

"The Communist: "No, you will receive wages and something to eat, so that you won't get in the way of others who work!'

"The Communist said this with an even more solemn and sour face than previously, and with no trace of humor. I understood even then that Communism is completely without any human quality, because it has no humor.

"Western capitalism doesn't have any humor either, today, and that comes from the fact that the West has lost its faith. A sense of humor can exist only in a world of faith. For in humor is a trace of the smile with which God observes the mistakes of man. That trace of God's smile, in man, is our sense of humor."

Picard had been a physician early in his life, but he turned to the contemplation of divine wisdom. Therefore he prospered almost as little under capitalism as he would have prospered under Communism; but at least he was left in peace. An admirer had given him his little house; otherwise, at his end in a hospital bed, Picard was penniless. But the trace of God's smile did not depart from him.

Without humor, Picard would have sunk into despair. He saw just and beautiful rhetoric supplanted by slogan and cant, the dignity of meditation and of silence subjugated by jabber and mechanical noise. The divine, he declared, has been overwhelmed in our time by the demonic, and the demonic never is more powerful than when it appears trivial, as in the discontinuity and banality of the radio. "God, the eternally Continuous," Picard writes in *The World of Silence,* "has been deposed, and continuous radio-noise has been installed in His place. And the fact that although it is a discovery of man, it nevertheless seems to be independent of him, gives it an appearance of twilight mysticism."

Yet we only think that God has been dethroned. Actually, we flee from God, and do not perceive Him because we have turned our backs upon Him. Ours is the world of the Flight.

The Flight from God

In all ages, Picard writes in his book by this title, man is in flight from God; but in our time, the objective world of Faith has been ruined, and the flight immerses nearly everyone. Formerly, man had to separate himself from the world of Faith by an act of decision; today, it is from the Flight that a man must decide to part himself. The Flight has become an organized thing—almost a conscious thing. It shapes its own pseudo-religion, its own economics, its own language, its own art; it destroys nature and community.

Yet amid the terror of the Flight, Picard reminds us that One pursues. The clash of positivism and technology against tradition and moral insight, the upsurge of the demonic disguised as progress, are the principal matters of Picard's meditations. He was a "visionary" not in the sense of a man imprisoned in illusion or ideology, but instead a philosopher whose vision penetrated beyond the ephemeral to a truth which no quantity of "scientific research" could reveal.

"What a mobility of contrivances for endowing man with mobility for the Flight, to hide man and to cause him to vanish!" So Picard writes in his chapter "The Organization of the Flight." "What is terrible is this: it seems that whenever a man or a thing vanishes, God vanishes too. God must be very great, to be present continually, even though he vanishes continually. Once a man paused in the Flight and his heart, too, stopped when he came to understand that God can show himself again as often as he vanishes and that he can show himself everywhere.

"It is love that holds man back from rendering himself mobile for the Flight. A man who loves another, or a thing, contemplates what he loves with care and for a long time, careful to discover in his contemplation if there is a part he has so far neglected to love; and love is long-suffering, waiting until the beloved grows into love. But all this, in the Flight where one must be for ever *en route*, demands too much time. And so the world is being systematically emptied of love. All the relationships within which love can exist—marriage, the family, friendship—are being brought to destruction by the men of the Flight."

In the Flight there are no memories, and manufacture replaces creation. The love, kindness, and fidelity which one finds in the Flight are brummagem products, easily discarded on impulse or from convenience: they merely simulate true love, kindness, and fidelity. The Flight itself is a sham-god, and most men mistake the Flight for divinity.

"What the Flight wants is this: to be primal, original, creative, as God is. The category of revolution is used to bring about the original and creative situation. The point of revolutionizing things is not that they may be rendered different, but that they may be returned once again to the beginning. Whatever is primitive is emphasized in culture, in art, in history. Man wants to be present at every beginning, imitating the Creator who is present at every beginning. The Chthonic, that which springs out of the earth, and, in general, whatever is dark, these are popular. Darkness exists before the light of the created; it is the moment prior to creation. Best of all, one would like to enclose the entire Flight in the darkness existing before creation, so that over all there may brood the atmosphere of the beginning, for then, at the beginning, there can be no one but God who creates everything. And so it is, for a world devoid of everything feels itself akin to the beginning where as yet nothing exists. In the world of Faith man could not tolerate being so near the true beginning. He not only needs the beginning, even more he needs history, that which follows the beginning, so that there may be a visible gap between himself and the divine beginning."

The Flight, that is, amounts to an inversion of Faith, much as Communism is an inversion of Christianity; it seeks to destroy the past, so that the Flight will seem creator and self-created. The Flight destroys true language and literature, substituting jargon and slogan—after the fashion of Newspeak, to borrow a word from a writer who will be discussed later in this book. For nobility in language is a gift from God, the Pursuer, and therefore cannot be tolerated:

"Whenever in the language of the Flight one reads a sentence, it is as though one leaped across the debris of the word from one part to another, the parts separated by craters. It is no longer as in the world of Faith where the subject is like a pillar from which the sentence begins, passing through the predicate to the object, itself like a pillar. The pillar of the subject is cast down—in the syntax of the Flight one likes to substitute for the massive pillar of the subject some light pronoun; and though in the world of Faith, too, the subject may be replaced by a pronoun, this does not happen so frequently and then with hesitation, for here one feels there is something miraculous about one thing standing for another, the lesser for the greater—the pillar of the subject is cast down and so, too, is the pillar of the object, and both, along with the predicate, lie side by side, the whole a heap of ruins. The erect pillars would arrest the Flight, would stand like a barrier; but now everything lies horizontally, following the line of the Flight."

Thus the Flight from God destroys humane letters. From the Primal Word came our power of language; but we moderns will not acknowledge the Primal Word; therefore we are uncertain, aimlessly wandering, and look upon words as mere counters:

"Those writers who are (in the world of the Flight) judged to be good worry over a word, wondering whether it will keep the meaning they have assigned to it. In thus regarding the word they resemble not a mother looking at her child with love and confidence, but rather a governess whose anxiety, nervousness, and mistrust spring from her profession. In the world of the Flight the poets lose all their strength in patching together the bodies of words as they fall apart and in placing one body of a word beside another and in watching over it lest it should slip away once more. How could anyone still have strength enough to give soul and spirit to the body of the word? In the world of Faith the word has not only an intact body endowed with soul and spirit; it also has a world to live in, the world, that is, of Faith. The poet need not begin by creating a world fit for the word; everything is ready, and the poet can use all his strength in being a poet; and this means letting the word strive with the world, that, more clearly than the world itself, the word may declare the name of the Creator."

Sexual powers, and marriage, are distorted in the world of the Flight. Art, too, dies the death: its forms disintegrate. The pseudo-art of the Flight is paraded as a denial of the existence of God. "Man has deliberately isolated Art in such a way that its otherness is manifest. It is as though those in Flight had appointed a few men to fabricate Art in caverns remote from the main road, and then, all of a sudden (that they may give the impression that Art springs from another world), to hold it high above those who are in flight, as though it were a light shining into the world of the Flight from another world." Art exists not for God's sake, but for Art's sake.

So it is with literature, which also is converted into a sham "otherness." Like the Flight's art, the Flight's literature really is produced by the Flight itself, but it is supposed by nearly everybody to have an origin separate from both God and the Flight. It is converted into an instrument of delusion; and the object of this outpouring of books is to destroy Faith by a Babel of opinions.

"In the art and literature of the Flight, things are put out of shape, stunted, crushed, destroyed. One wants only to accustom oneself to the spectacle of annihilation, so one puts that which has been destroyed into the pictures and into literature. . . . This de-struction—this extravagance of destruction—this state of being hacked into pieces, this prostration of things in pictures and in literature—all these are, as it were, *final*. It resembles a judgment in that for the man of the Flight it is a substitute for the finality of divine judgment. Once one has beheld the destruction of all things in pictures and in literature, one no longer fears a Last Judgment. One knows that everything that can happen has already happened. What God ought to destroy, man has himself destroyed."

In the Flight, even the faces of men take on a vacant cast; Faith, which animated them, is forgotten. The men of the Flight build cities which are monstrous, and which become the Flight's centers. "The streets resemble pipes into which men are sucked; and a few trees have been dragged along with the men into the city. These stand fearfully on the edge of the street. They no longer know their way back into the countryside, and they try slowly to grow down-ward through the asphalt and to disappear."

But, all this said, there remains the Pursuer, who says, "You have not chosen Me; I have chosen you." Everything which flees belongs, after all, to God. One still can fling himself back upon the

Pursuer, and the Pursuer can arrest and redeem the whole Flight, if He so chooses. The danger is that God may cease to pursue, and those in Flight might circle round him for all eternity, like dead moons. And then comes Picard's final illuminating vision:

"It is unnecessary to doubt when one thinks of God: all doubt is within the Flight. It is unnecessary to fall away from God; it is comic, like a copy—though a clumsy one—of the most monstrous apostasy contained within the Flight. The Flight is designed to be an enormous machine of doubt and apostasy; all doubt, all apostasy, all terror of God, are within the Flight, and one's own morsel of doubt, apostasy, terror, is being torn from one by the machinery of the Flight. Doubts, terrors, uncertainties, are no longer scattered, they are concentrated; one can no longer come across them upon Faith's path; they have been driven together and together they roll onward within the enormous machine of the Flight. There remains only God in his full radiance, his utter clarity; and over against him is the Flight into which all dimness and all ambiguity have been driven. The more the structure of the Flight and the more desperately it plunges onward, the more plainly stands before us the one who is alone: God."

So Max Picard was not dismayed, even though "All that is possible is within the Flight. All that is real is without." Such is the literature of vision, allied to the paintings of William Blake. That these words still may be published in our time, and may be read at least by a few, attests the survival of normality. And, as Isaiah discovered to his surprise, the few may be more numerous than one ever had guessed. The best-seller lists will be crammed with salacity and triviality, no doubt, until television extinguishes altogether the books of the Flight. But the literature of the permanent things, submerged though it may be today, retains a power which defies chthonian darkness.

V. REDISCOVERING NORMS
THROUGH FANTASY

The Truth of Myth, Fable, Allegory, and Parable

IF IMAGINATIVE LITERATURE HAS EXPIRED UNDER TOTALIST
dominations, it is sick enough, generally considered, in the "free
world." Some of the most talented writers of our century have died
within a few seasons, as if carried off by a plague: T. S. Eliot,
Robert Frost, Aldous Huxley, C. S. Lewis, William Faulkner,
Wyndham Lewis, Roy Campbell. Their places have not been filled.

Fiction obsessed by the morbid, the perverse, and the senselessly
violent is applauded by the reviewers today. The death of art at the
hands of triumphant ideology, in the Communist states, is paralleled by decadence, or the death-wish, in what we vaguely call "the
West." In literature, naturalism is quite worn out; in philosophy,
logical positivism makes a very thin ghost; in politics, liberal rationalism is at the end of its tether. Among modern men, the imagination is no less fatigued than the fabric of society. We seem close
to fulfilling the predictions made by Robert Graves in his fantasy
Seven Days in New Crete.

In that most readable romance of the future, we are told that by
the close of the "Late Christian epoch" the world will have fallen
altogether under a collectivistic domination, a variant of Communism. Religion, the moral imagination, and nearly everything which
makes life worth living will have been virtually extirpated by ideol-

ogy and atomic war. A system of thought and government called Logicalism, "pantisocratic economics divorced from any religious or nationalistic theory," rules the world—for a brief time.

"Logicalism, hinged on international science, ushered in a gloomy and anti-poetic age. It lasted only a generation or two and ended with a grand defeatism, a sense of perfect futility, that slowly crept over the directors and managers of the régime. The common man had triumphed over his spiritual betters at last, but what was to follow? To what could he look forward with either hope or fear? By the abolition of sovereign states and the disarming of even the police forces, war had become impossible. No one who cherished any religious beliefs whatever, or was interested in sport, poetry, or the arts was allowed to hold a position of public responsibility: 'ice-cold logic' was the most valued civic quality, and those who could not pretend to it were held of no account. Science continued laboriously to expand its over-large corpus of information, and the subjects of research grew more and more beautifully remote and abstract; yet the scientific obsession, so strong at the beginning of the third millennium A. D., was on the wane. Logicalist officials who were neither defeatist nor secretly religious and who kept their noses to the grindstone from a sense of duty, fell a prey to colabromania, a mental disturbance which sent them dancing like dervishes down the corridors of their all-glass laboratories, foaming at the mouth and tearing in pieces any dog, cat, or child that crossed their path. They all suffered from the same hallucination: of a white-faced, hawk-nosed, golden-haired woman who whipped them round and round as if they were tops and urged them to acts of insane violence. No cure could be found by the psychiatrists, who were themselves peculiarly subject to this new form of insanity: all who caught it had to be 'lethalized.' "

The deepest longings of humanity have been outraged, that is, and the soul and the State stagger on the verge of Darkness. Then "an Israeli Sophocrat" writes a book called *A Critique of Utopias,* in which he examines seventy Utopian writings, from Plato to Aldous Huxley. "We must retrace our steps," he concludes, "or perish." Only by the resurrection of religion, the Sophocrats discover, can mankind be kept from total destruction; and that religion, as Graves describes it in his romance, springs from the primitive soil of myth and symbol.

If the moral imagination is denied or suppressed, the person and the republic are bewildered. The decadent "Logicalism" of our century, reflected in much of our literature, is death to the moral imagination, so that we must retrace our steps, or perish. Unless humane literature is returned to its normative purpose, telling us what it is to be truly human, the degradation of the human condition may not be long delayed.

Yet that work of recovering normality in letters has commenced, here and there. Its progress is most hopeful in the branch of literature of which *Seven Days in New Crete* is a healthy specimen: the reviving art of moral fantasy, the ancient and persistent power of myth, fable, allegory, and parable.

I have in mind here such recent or living writers as C. S. Lewis, Charles Williams, J. R. R. Tolkien, Jacquetta Hawkes, Gerald Heard, and John Collier. Their progenitors in the previous age were William Morris, George Macdonald, and Rudyard Kipling. Lewis and Tolkien, at least, have received considerable critical examination. I shall deal at length here with a writer neglected by most serious critics of imaginative literature, although he is the best American artist in fantasy since Nathaniel Hawthorne: a man of insight injudiciously publicized as "the world's greatest living science-fiction writer," Ray Bradbury. But before I turn to Bradbury, I need to describe the general characteristics of this type of humane letters, which has its roots in the myths and parables of the Old Testament, the folklore of many peoples, the legends and allegories of the early Greeks, and the illustrative fictions of Plato.

Myth, fable, allegory, and parable are not falsehoods; on the contrary, they are means for penetrating to the truth by appealing to the moral imagination. Borrowing in part from C. S. Lewis, I suggest here the distinctions among these forms of fantasy.

A myth is a poetic representation of hidden reality. The teller of a myth assumes that he is relating historical occurrences, and does not believe that he is creating a fiction; he explains the operations of natural forces and the events of history as the work of supernatural or living beings—the personifications of dominations and powers, if you will. Myth is religious in origin and purpose.

A fable is a "supposal," as Lewis puts it: an expression of truth through analogy. The fable-teller deliberately creates a fiction, to impart a moral. The Greek root of this term means "to give light."

The fabulist, that is, illuminates the nature of things through a tale which both he and his auditors know to be an ingenious analogical invention.

An allegory is not a "supposal," but a description of one thing under the image of another; commonly it is a narrative outwardly dealing with material things, but intended to expound spiritual truths. "By an allegory," Lewis wrote, "I mean a composition (whether pictorial or literary) in which immaterial realities are represented by feigned physical objects: *e.g.*, a pictured Cupid allegorically represents erotic love (which in reality is an experience, not an object occupying a given area of space), or, in Bunyan, a giant represents despair."

A parable is a comparison, a similitude, an apologue of sorts. It describes events which *might* have occurred, though the particular events in this narration are fictitious. It is seeing as in a glass, darkly—or, as another translation has it, "looking into the riddle of a mirror." Sometimes the parable is employed as a prudent device to express unpopular and perilous truths. "I will open my mouth in a parable; I will utter dark sayings of old."

Now the modern masters of fantasy are not myth-makers, for that power expires with the childhood of the race. But fable, allegory, and parable are coming into their own once more; and as it was in the beginning, their purpose is ethical, rousing the moral imagination of a people long ensnared by idols.

"Fantasy" or "fancy" originally signified the enlightening imagination. In fantasy, things are represented strangely, so as to rouse our wonder; yet the shock of the fantastic is intended to wake us from dullness and complacency. That is precisely what the modern creators of fable, allegory, and parable are doing with some success. They show us the norms for man and society through conjuring up fanciful episodes in which our virtues and vices glimmer as in a looking glass. Were it not for the mirrored reflection, we should not take thought.

In the long run, men are moved more by fantasy than by tractarian polemics. Probably the most powerful allegory of the past three centuries and more has been Bunyan's *Pilgrim's Progress*; and that book is not yet spent. Once, travelling through the autonomous Bantu territory of the Transkei, within South Africa, I saw children trotting to school with their slates and books; and I asked the Xhosa minister of education what these children studied. Their primary manuals, he replied, were the King James version and *Pilgrim's Progress*. (The former of these is virtually forbidden in American public schools by our Logicalist Supreme Court, and the latter is ignored; so the Xhosa children are privileged.) So long as Bantu children know the Bible and Bunyan's allegory, they may escape the fell clutch of ideology.

Of course fantasy may take on an ideological mode; in the nineteenth century, some fables were meant to inculcate socialist doctrine, from the beauty of Morris' *News from Nowhere* to the smug utilitarian collectivism of Bellamy's *Looking Backward* and to the proletarian violence of London's *Iron Heel*. But more often the fabulist is a conservative reformer, on the model of Plato or Thomas More. Such is the bent of Kipling's "The Mother Hive" and of Jacquetta Hawkes' "The City of the Cats."

Logicalism and fantasy were combined successfully only by H. G. Wells. Today, however, Wells' fantasy wears thin; it wore thin with Wells himself, indeed, for at the end of his life he wrote, in despair, *The World at the End of its Tether*. The world declined to be governed by ice-cold logic; so Wells threw out reality together with Utopia.

Although political significance may be read into some of the more influential fantasies of our century, it is notable how successfully our fabulists have sheered away from ideology in an age of political religions. Some critics may identify the evil power in Tolkien's *Lord of the Rings* with Nazi or Communist dominations; yet Tolkien himself does not intend to be bound by yesterday's or today's ideological encounters. His three volumes are a picture of the perpetual struggle between good and evil; his concern is the corrupting intoxication of power. The tremendous popularity of his fable—which, like other enduring fantasies, began as a boys' story but grew into something grander—suggests that the moral imagination of our rising generation, starved though it has been by dominant Logicalism and flabby Sociability in our education system, still may be waked.

And in a time when professors in seminaries inform us that God has expired, and that we must be utterly demythologized, disenchanted, desacralized, and deconsecrated—why, these learned doctors are undone by the Christian fables and allegories of Clive Staples Lewis. What George Macdonald accomplished a century ago with *Phantastes, Lilith,* and (more importantly) his Christian fables for children, Lewis revived in defiance of the spirit of the age. In the Perelandra trilogy, science-fiction is turned against the Logicalists' science; in the chronicles of Narnia, children learn far more of Christian imagery and doctrine than ever they could acquire in Sunday school. In *Pilgrim's Progress,* Bunyan is resurrected to do battle manfully with the modern temper; in *Till We Have Faces,* the meaning of love is set against modern appetites; in *The Great Divorce,* we are reminded that most folk prefer hell to heaven. How shocking to Dr. Harvey Cox and the dwellers in the Secular City! For our fabulists will not permit us to become disenchanted, desacralized, and deconsecrated. Imagination, given time, does rule the world; as Disraeli said, even Mormon counts more votaries than Bentham; and for every doctrinaire secularist who swears by Cox, a hundred young people will have read of Aslan, the lion-Christ of Narnia.

Yes, somewhat tardily the ethical fantasy is working upon us. Thomas Carlyle essayed this task a hundred and forty years ago, in *Sartor Resartus;* but he was hopelessly in advance of his time. Few remember that the great Victorian novelist and historian also was the most ingenious experimental novelist of his age—for *Sartor Resartus,* though it has but two characters of any importance, is a fantastic novel, as curiously devised as the avant-garde novels of our generation.

"Love is not Pleasure; love God. This is the Everlasting Yea, wherein all contradiction is solved; wherein whoso walks and works, it is well with him." So Carlyle. An acute critic, Georg Tennyson, points out that Carlyle's didactic novel is patterned upon the German *Märchen,* the traditionary or folk romances which Carlyle expected to become the vehicle for a new literature, a new and true Age of Reason. Possibly this True Age of Reason, with *Märchen*-figures pointing the way, opens before us long after Carlyle wrote. For today's fabulists say in effect, with Carlyle, "The Universe is not dead and demoniacal, a charnel-house with spectres; but godlike, and my Father's!"

Despite his concern with society, all his life Carlyle sought primarily the order of the soul; only when the soul should be disciplined might men live tolerable with one another. Georg Tennyson sets *Sartor* in its theological matrix:

"Augustine named the turning away from God to the beast the *experimentum medietatis,* the trial of the center. It results from the substitution of one's own ego for God, the desire to relish one's own power. For a time one's own ego becomes the center, the mean, but the assertion of the ego is short-lived. Overburdened by its own weight, the soul loses its holiness and sinks toward evil. The trial of the center is an act of *superbia* that cannot be maintained."

Sartor Resartus owes something to St. Augustine. After his own mystical experience in Leith Walk, Thomas Carlyle marched triumphant, if grim, from the Center of Indifference toward resignation, work, and wonder. The man unable to wonder, says Carlyle, "is but a Pair of Spectacles behind which is no Eye. . . . A Dilettante and sand-blind Pedant!" Carlyle's whole argument, indeed, is directed against the unwondering "secular city" mentality of gentlemen like Dr. Harvey Cox.

Through acknowledging Wonder, Carlyle wins that Reason which is beyond the Understanding—precisely the way in which the folk tale, the fable, the allegory, the parable work upon the consciousness. From living in a tower on Dream Lane, in the town of Know-not-Where, Carlyle's Teufelsdröckh makes his way to London. That is the progress of Lewis and Tolkien and other writers of moral imagination, in our day.

The twentieth-century fabulist may or may not be orthodox in religious convictions. (Carlyle was not.) But he loves the permanent things. If we are arrested in our march toward Logicalism and its inhumane universalism, our rescuers may be the authors of true tales of wonder, not the theologians of our schools. To make myself clearer, I present to you Mr. Ray Bradbury, of Hollywood, a person in most matters very unlike Carlyle or Macdonald, yet a man who overthrows idols by the power of imagery.

The World of Ray Bradbury

To commence as a writer for the pulp-magazines is no advantage; nor is writing screen-plays in Hollywood, decade after decade, generally to be recommended for those who would be men of letters. Such was Ray Bradbury's background. He had the advantage, however, of never attending college—which salutary neglect preserved him from many winds of doctrine, insured that his talents would not be spoilt by Creative Writing 201, and gave him leisure and appetite to read good books innumerable, the love of which suffuses Bradbury story after Bradbury story.

Hollywood writer though he is, Bradbury has had only one of his stories made into a film, and that in England: *Fahrenheit 451*, a passionate and tender and terrifying description of a democratic despotism not necessarily very far distant in the future, in which all books are burnt because they are disturbing influences in an egalitarian and sensate culture. It is something of a pity that Bradbury did not write the screen-play himself, for he is as good a dramatist as he is a writer of stories. His three short plays, under the general title *The World of Ray Bradbury*, ran for nearly a year in Los Angeles—but closed after a few days in Manhattan.

The rising generation in Los Angeles (of whom Bradbury is the chief hero) loved those three plays—*The Veldt, To the Chicago Abyss,* and *The Pedestrians.* Yet the New York play-reviewers were more ferocious with Ray Bradbury than with any other man of mark in my memory, and they succeeded promptly in preventing anyone in New York from perceiving those truths which are best revealed by fable and parable. The rising generation of Manhattan was left with such plays as *The Toilet* for ethical instruction.

Bradbury (who thinks of himself, so far as he has any politics, as something of a revolutionary) was assailed by the New York critics as a "romantic reactionary." Charitably, Bradbury later remarked to me that perhaps the Manhattan critics merely had been waiting to gun him down once he should ride out of his western fastness. But there was more than that to their vituperative detestation. They perceived that Bradbury is a moralist, which they could not abide; that he has no truck with the obscene, which omission they found unpardonable; that he is no complacent liberal, because he knows the Spirit of the Age to be monstrous—for which let him be anathema; that he is one of the last surviving masters of eloquence and glowing description, which ought to be prohibited; that, with Pascal, he understands how the Heart has reasons which the Reason cannot know—so to the Logicalist lamp-post with him.

Thus the champions of decadence and deliquescence, the enemies of the permanent things, accurately discerned in Ray Bradbury a man of moral imagination, who must be put down promptly. For like Lewis, like Tolkien, like other talented fabulists, Ray Bradbury has drawn the sword against the dreary and corrupting materialism of this˙ century; against society as producer-and-consumer equation, against the hideousness in modern life, against mindless power, against sexual obsession, against sham intellectuality, against the perversion of right reason into the mentality of the television-viewer. His Martians, spectres, and witches are not diverting entertainment only: they become, in their eerie manner, the defenders of truth and beauty.

Consider those three short plays attacked by the Manhattan reviewers. *The Veldt* is a story of children abandoned by modern parents to the desolation of the Screen—and of how thwarted imagination takes its vengeance, the predators of the mind growing literally red in tooth and claw. *To the Chicago Abyss* is a picture of the evocative power of tender trifles, restoring the rudiments of order after the Bomb has fallen. *The Pedestrians* has to do with two men flung into prison for preferring nocturnal strolls to the compulsive TV screen. Alive with pity and terror, such plays cannot be tolerated by any Logicalist.

Some librarians, too, have taken alarm. Bradbury's s⁺ories are *disturbing!* No disturbances can be permitted in this perfect American culture of ours. In error, a company which distributes educational books included among a consignment of books for children one copy of *Fahrenheit 451*. A female librarian detected this work of heresy, and fired off a letter of furious protest to the wholesaler. How dared they send such a dreadful book? "I took it right out in back and burned it." Tomorrow is already here.

Some paragraphs ago, I mentioned that Bradbury has been injudiciously described as the world's greatest living science-fiction writer. Now he does, indeed, look forward to man's exploration of the planets, although not to the gloating "conquest" of space. But for science and technology, *per se,* he has no more taste than did C. S. Lewis. H. G. Wells expected man to become godlike through applied science; yet Wells' interior world was dry, unloving, and egotistical. Bradbury (who never drives, never flies in planes if he can help it, and detests most gadgets) thinks it more probable that man may spoil everything, in this planet and in others, by the misapplication of science to avaricious ends—the Baconian and Hobbesian employment of science as power. And Bradbury's interior world is fertile, illuminated by love for the permanent things, warm with generous impulse.

That man may replenish the universe for the greater glory of God, Bradbury would have man fling himself to the most distant worlds. But this is an ambition far different from the arrogance of Wells and his kind—who, in the phrases of Robert Jungk, aspire to the throne of God, and who exhort man "to occupy God's place, to recreate and organize a man-made cosmos according to man-made laws of reason, foresight, and efficiency."

Through nearly all of Bradbury's "science-fiction" tales run forebodings like those of Jungk. Bradbury knows of modern technology, in the phrase of Henry Adams, that we are "monkeys monkeying with a loaded shell." He is interested not in the precise mechanism of rockets, but in the mentality and the morals of fallible human beings who make and use rockets. He is a man of fable and parable.

Every one of us, Bradbury says in a letter to me, has "a private keep somewhere in the upper part of the head where, from time to time, of midnights, the beast can be heard raving. To control that, to the end of life, to stay contemplative, sane, good-humored, is our entire work, in the midst of cities that tempt us to inhumanity, and passions that threaten to drive through the skin with invisible spikes." The author of three hundred tales of the fantastic knows the permanent things as well as did the poet of the Waste Land.

Bradbury is not writing about the gadgets of conquest; his real concerns are the soul and the moral imagination. When the boy-hero of *Dandelion Wine,* in an abrupt mystical experience, is seized almost bodily by the glowing consciousness that he is really *alive,* we glimpse that mystery the soul. When, in *Something Wicked This*

Way Comes, the lightning-rod salesman is reduced magically to an idiot dwarf because all his life he had fled from perilous responsibility, we know the moral imagination.

"Soul," a word much out of fashion nowadays, signifies a man's animating entity. That flaming spark the soul is the real space-traveller of Bradbury's stories. "I'm alive!"—that exclamation is heard from Waukegan to Mars and beyond, in Bradbury's fables. Life is its own end—if one has a soul to tell him so.

The moral imagination is the principal possession that man does not share with the beasts. It is man's power to perceive ethical truth, abiding law, in the seeming chaos of many events. Without the moral imagination, man would live merely from day to day, or rather moment to moment, as dogs do. It is the strange faculty—inexplicable if men are assumed to have an animal nature only—of discerning greatness, justice, and order, beyond the bars of appetite and self-interest. And the moral imagination, which shows us what we ought to be, primarily is what distinguishes Bradbury's tales from the futurism of Wells' fancy. For Bradbury, the meaning of life is here and now, in our every action; we live amidst immortality; it is here, not in some future domination like that of Wells' *The Sleeper Awakens*, that we must find our happiness.

So it will not do to treat of Ray Bradbury, despite his abhorrence of much in the modern world and despite his distrust of man armed for the conquest of space, as if he were a prophet of the coming doom. For no recent writer is more buoyed up by the ebullient spirit of youth, and none more popular with intelligent young readers. Probably no one ever has written so understandingly of twelve- and thirteen-year-old boys as Bradbury does repeatedly, particularly in *Dandelion Wine,* with its prosaic-romantic setting of Waukegan, Illinois (Bradbury's birthplace) and a thousand other American towns about 1928. Perpetual youth, and therefore perpetual hope, defy in Bradbury's pages the fatigue of this century and the ambitions of exploiting scientism.

If spirits in prison, still we are spirits; if able to besmirch ourselves, still only we men are capable of moral choices. Life and technology are what we make of them, and the failure of man to live in harmony with nature is the failure of moral imagination. That failure is not inevitable. To understand Bradbury's disquietude and his high hopes, we may look at his book about the tragic human conquest of Mars, *The Martian Chronicles;* and at his book about the wonder and terror behind the facade of any little town, *Something Wicked This Way Comes.*

Depravity and Courage in Modern Fable

The love of life burns brighter in Ray Bradbury than in any other man of letters I have known—except, possibly, Roy Campbell. "The thing that drives me most often," Bradbury wrote to me not long ago, "is an immense gratitude that I was given this one chance to live, to be alive the one time round in a miraculous experience that never ceases to be glorious and dismaying. I accept the whole damn thing. It is neither all beautiful nor all terrible, but a wash of multitudinous despairs and exhilarations about which we know nothing. Our history is so small, our experience so limited, our science so inadequate, our theologies so crammed in mere matchboxes, that we know we stand on the outer edge of a beginning and our greatest history lies before us, frightening and lovely, much darkness and much light."

The Martian Chronicles are chiefly a record of darkness—with light breaking through at the very end. They cover the years 1999 to 2026. In little more than a quarter of a century, man invades Mars, extirpates its inhabitants, effaces its culture, ravages its beauty, transplants all the afflictions of his homeland, destroys civilization upon Earth—and then sets out to restore, upon Mars, the ancient loveliness.

All this becomes quite believable—even, or perhaps especially, the pathetic Martian ghosts that simulate human beings and try to insinuate themselves into human families, seeking to be loved. But it is not Bradbury's imaginary Martians who matter. What gives these stories their cunning is their realism set in the fantastic: that is, their portrayal of human nature, in all its baseness and all its promise, against an exquisite stage-set. We are shown normality, the permanent things in human nature, by the light of another world; and what we forget about ourselves in the ordinariness of our routine of existence suddenly bursts upon us as fresh revelation.

Wells would have had man usurp the throne of God. Bradbury's hope is that man will let God work through him; for it is not the dead universe which is divine, but "God fleshing himself in sentience"—the living God making Himself felt through human energies. "I speak of no errant usurpation from the Deity. I speak of no paranoiac illusion of mythology which would supremacize man to the detriment of the Supreme Being. I seek only to weld the two. I seek to fuse them in religious fervor until they cleave, entwine, are bound so feverish tight no light can be seen between them: they *are* the light." If man flings himself from Earth to other planets, it will be the act of God, who "does not intend to risk His sentience, His awareness, His chance for eternity, by allowing Himself to remain upon one lonely planet earth."

When called a moralist, Ray Bradbury accepts the impeachment willingly. The desiccated intellectuality of Logicalism is a dying or dead thing; and therefore it is evil, for life is good, and its own object. One of his early explorers of Mars discovers that the extinct Martians had lived by a truth which modern man has lost:

"They knew how to live with nature and get along with nature. They didn't try too hard to be all men and no animal. That's the mistake we made when Darwin showed up. We embraced him and Huxley and Freud, all smiles. And then we discovered that Darwin and our religions didn't mix. Or at least we didn't think they did. We were fools. We tried to budge Darwin and Huxley and Freud. They wouldn't move very well. So, like idiots, we tried knocking down religion.

"We succeeded pretty well. We lost our faith and went around wondering what life was for. If art was no more than a frustrated outflinging of desire, if religion was no more than self-delusion, what good was life? Faith had always given us answers to all things. But it all went down the drain with Freud and Darwin. We were and still are a lost people."

Yet the Martians, become aware of this apparent conflict between science and faith, had refused to destroy themselves by a corrosive materialism. "They quit trying too hard to destroy everything, to humble everything." With the Martians, science and religion enriched one another. "The men of Mars realized that in order to survive they would have to forgo asking that one question any longer: *Why live?* Life was its own answer. Life was the propagation of more life and the living of as good a life as possible." They knew that "science is no more than an investigation of a miracle we can never explain, and art is an interpretation of that miracle."

Among Martian ruins, at the beginning of the twenty-first century, these insights burst upon us; but not there only. For Ray Bradbury discovers the same ancient truths beneath the surface of existence in Waukegan, Illinois, say, about 1928. The outer life of good and evil in an American town is described in *Dandelion Wine;* the subterranean, inner reality, in *Something Wicked This Way Comes.*

A carnival comes to a small town; and two boys, thirteen years old, Jim and Will, are fascinated by it. But this particular carnival is not merry. Its master is the Illustrated Man, Mr. Dark, seeking whom he may devour. His captive freaks are sinners whose monstrous bodies are the personifications of their sins. His carousel, running forward or backward at great speed, will give human beings their desire of youth regained or age attained—and send the iron into their souls. His Mirror Maze will entrap the folk who seek what is not in nature, and will convert them into caricatures of themselves. Mademoiselle Tarot, the Dust Witch, can murder with a whisper. For centuries, preying upon frailty and folly, this carnival has wandered the world, its proprietors setting their snares for the unwise and the unwary, and often with success.

Only one man in town—Will's father, the library janitor, growing old—recognizes the carnival for what it is. The carnival is not Death. "But I think it uses Death as a threat," says Charles Halloway, the janitor, to the terrified boys. "Death doesn't exist. It never did, it never will. But we've drawn so many pictures of it, so many years, trying to pin it down, comprehend it, we've got to thinking of it as an entity, strangely alive and greedy. All it is, however, is a stopped watch, a loss, an end, a darkness. Nothing. And the carnival wisely knows we're more afraid of Nothing than we are of Something."

This carnival is the evil that men do to one another, and to themselves; it is fed by pain and fear. What Cooger and Dark's Carnival desires is not worthless dead souls, but ulcerated egos, given up to will and appetite. "A dead soul is no kindling. But a live and raving soul, crisped with self-damnation, oh that's a pretty snoutful for such as them." Enslaved to the freak-masters, such souls in agony supply the fuel for the carnival's perpetuity. For every need, want, and desire the carnival proprietors promise a satisfaction beyond the bounds of nature. But their victims fall, instead, into madness and ghastly distortion. There is no need for devils to buy souls, for "most men jump at the chance to give up everything for nothing." This carnival has "traveled a long way on an easy map, with people handy by every crossroad to lend it lustful pints of agony to power it on. So maybe the carnival survives, living off the poison of the sins we do each other, and the ferment of our most terrible regrets."

This carnival's power is mighty, and it converts the lightning-rod salesman into a hideous crumpled dwarf, old Miss Foley into a lost child. Jim, who would grow up too soon, stands on the brink of being whirled by the carousel into monstrosity. By lusting after the abnormal, by flouting the nature of things, old and young betray themselves into the freak-masters' clutch.

Yet one power is stronger than the temptations and threats of the carnival; and that power is laughter. We laugh at the incongruous, at the absurdity of the unnatural. Rediscovering the weapon of humor, Halloway first baffles the Dust Witch, and then shoots her dead with a bullet on which he has imprinted a smile. Evil, after all, is ludicrous; and though God is not mocked, those creatures who batten upon tormented souls are aghast at healthy mockery.

Just when all had semed lost, Halloway and the boys destroy the carnival by mirth. But other creatures who prey upon warped souls will come to town presently, in some other disguise, and the fools who want everything will become their freaks.

Evil, in essence, is the appetite to undo the natural order of things. It is the glorification of abnormality. And the price one pays for clutching at the unnatural is metamorphosis into a freak, or into a freak-master.

In Bradbury's fables of Mars and of the carnival, fantasy has become what it was in the beginning: the enlightening moral imagination, transcending simple rationality. The everyday world is not the real world, for today's events are merely a film upon the deep well of the past, and they will be swallowed up by the unknowable future. The real world is the world of the permanent things, which often are discerned more clearly in the fictional dead cities of Mars or the fictional carousel of Cooger and Dark than in our own little private slice of evanescent experience. And—what is a wondrous thing in itself—the new generation of Americans are not blind to the truth of the fabulists, for Bradbury is their favorite author.

The trappings of science-fiction may have attracted young people to Bradbury, but he has led them on to something much older and better: mythopoeic literature, normative truth acquired through wonder. Bradbury's stories are not an escape from reality; they are windows looking upon enduring reality. As C. S. Lewis remarks, those who attack the fantasy of moral imagination as trifling or baneful "escape literature" have shut themselves up in Bentham's Panopticon. The ideologue, in particular, denounces "escape"; for he is the prisoner of his own political obsessions, and misery loves company. Lewis writes that he never fully understood this denunciation of "escape," this hatred of mythopoeic literature, "till my friend Professor Tolkien asked me the very simple question, 'What class of men would you expect to be most preoccupied with, and most hostile to, the idea of escape?' and gave the obvious answer: jailers. . . . But there is perhaps this truth behind it: that those who brood much on the remote past or future, or stare long at the night sky, are less likely than others to be ardent or orthodox partisans."

Bradbury, with Lewis and Tolkien and Collier and some few others, is nobody's prisoner and nobody's jailer. For our modern fabulists have made a breach in Giant Despair's castle.

VI. THE FICTION OF POLITICS
AND POVERTY

Examining Politics through the Novel

IN A TIME SO OBSESSED BY POLITICS—OR RATHER, BY IDEOLOGY —as ours, the influence of political convictions upon humane letters often is either repressive or corrupting. Yet it need not be so. As literature is meant to describe the norms for the person, so it may be employed to describe the norms for the republic—and without degrading the good writer.

In this chapter, I shall touch upon the literary possibilities latent in political subjects; upon the "problem" of poverty, which has become a political question in recent years more than ever it was before, and upon the life of the poor as a theme for humane letters; finally, I shall offer some account of George Orwell as a writer who understood much more about poverty, and somewhat more about political limitations, than most men of letters understand.

Even though the best-seller lists exhibit every season some monstrous fat success purporting to be a novel of political questions, most of these books are not worth reading; nay, they are not worth criticizing. They are tracts, and confused tracts at that, with almost no touch of imagination or humane insight. Their characters are stock figures; their style does not deserve the epithet "pedestrian"; they are humorless and pontifical, and they are justly forgotten in a year or two. Also they tell us very little about politics that could not be gathered by reading a newspaper occasionally. And if one requires practical information about our present discontents, or prudential judgments on proposed legislation, it is better not to turn to a romancer.

I confess that some of these political sermons under the guise of fiction do produce consequences—occasionally for good. A shrewd and commonsensical political manipulator once remarked to me that most members of Congress never had scrutinized the efficacy of the foreign-aid program until their wives read *The Ugly American* and then asked their husbands awkward questions. Yet is it impossible for the political novel to be anything better than a polemic with a sugar coating of fiction? Actually, the realm of practical politics is intricate, often amusing, and full of genuine characters, from the township board to the White House.

One of our troubles is that those "novelists" with some genuine experience of political life rarely can write much better than the average newspaper reporter, while in recent years the men of letters who have turned to politics for a theme possess no mastery over political reality. Even if they can write, their fictional politicians become preposterous heroes or scoundrels, and they miss nearly all the subtle variety of political contest. Or sometimes these writers are ideologues, expecting utopian results from mere legislation, and railing against the weary procedures of constitutional government, out of melioristic illusions.

An aspirant to improvement in this neglected branch of imaginative literature might re-read Anthony Trollope's Parliamentary novels. With his high talent for creating character, Trollope employed English politics as the backdrop for witty sketches, conversations, and episodes which also contained much good-natured political sagacity. His touches of irony and pathos are not to be encountered in American political fiction nowadays; yet the pattern of our politics is no less diverse than that of Victorian England.

Can it be that to depict the reality of national political maneuvers would seem too fantastic? Senator Goldwater once said to me that were he ever to publish his candid memoirs of many senatorial colleagues and men in the seats of the mighty, his book would make *Advise and Consent* sound like *The Tale of Peter Rabbit*. Taking counsel of Democritus, the novelist might find it necessary to laugh always, lest he cry himself into madness. But endowed with a sense of humor and some compassion, a talented writer could scourge the naked follies of the time—and still be something better than a dull and pharisaical doctrinaire.

Time was, Lionel Trilling says, when the novel depended principally upon the contrasts of social class. But with the decay of class and manners, this source for imaginative writing dries up. Mr. Trilling suggests that the labyrinth of ideology, in which men of this century wander, may provide a new field for important fiction. His *The Middle of the Journey,* incidentally, is written upon this postulate—and is the most impressive of the political, or quasi-political, novels of these years.

Ideology, we must remember, is the science of idiocy, as John Adams declared: political delusion, an attempt to create the Terrestrial Paradise by destruction of old institutions and invention of new. By its nature, ideology is abstract and sterile. What can be done with such matter, Joseph Conrad accomplished in *Under Western Eyes* and *The Secret Agent.* Conrad and Trilling will be worth reading for a great while; but the political fanatic essentially is a dreary type, and though we admire one or two novels of Koestler, we would not live on a diet of such. "Politics," George Gissing wrote, "is the preoccupation of the quarter-educated"; and he had in mind the ideological politics of his own youth.

So I do not share Trilling's hope of a future for the novel in the wasteland of ideology. The proper subject of good fiction is not what Burke called "metaphysical madness"—the abstractions of the closet-politician—but rather human character in its proliferating variety. When I commend the political realm to men of literary talent, I do not mean either the Marxist propaganda-novel or a long series of stories about poor wretches caught in the toils of party discipline and stupidity. Ideological pressures flatten a man; there would be a dismal sameness and thinness about characters in such books.

Neither political didacticism, then, nor a fatigued plodding through the desert of political abstraction, can reward the writer and the reader. When I perceive some promise for political fiction, I mean instead a concern with *organic* politics—with political contest and political talk as moulders and mirrors of character, from courthouse to Capitol Hill.

The real John Randolph of Roanoke, who—to his regret—spent

almost thirty seasons in Washington, was more brilliant and more fantastic than any character political novelists dare to draw nowadays. Nor is the breed extinct: take Representative Clare Hoffman, recently retired from Congress, who had all his suits made without pockets, and who cried defiance to every popular pressure.

Novelists will bring into being no "Great Society" by converting themselves into political pedants. It remains true, nevertheless, that nature does imitate art. The whole tone of American political conduct might be elevated somewhat by the skillful and yet charitable satirist, or the writer with some vestigial apprehension of tragedy. From the high old Roman virtue of Robert Taft to the farces of Bobby Baker, American politics still contains the substance of creative literature—and I fancy that the public remains capable of appreciating something in this province more ambitious than a political puppet-show, with touches of "righteousness" and sex.

Literary Riches of the Poor

Poverty is not a "problem," but a condition. On the highest authority, "The poor we have always with us." It is grimly amusing that politicians have begun to talk in utopian fashion of abolishing poverty through positive law in a time when, throughout most of the world, poverty—even destitution—increases with dreadful speed.

In the United States, the complex of social difficulties ordinarily, and shallowly, described as "the problem of poverty" actually has little connection with the low-wage-rate poverty of the Bleak Age. The American slum-dwellers may receive very good wages—when they work. Their trouble is that they are the uprooted, socially and morally. They have lost community, and many of them have lost any sort of moral coherence. Their failure, perhaps in the majority of cases, is a failure of will, complicated and in part produced by the destruction of family and the landmarks of community. Often they are the victims of certain public measures allegedly humanitarian in intent—"urban renewal," for instance, which destroys their neighborhoods without creating genuine new communities; and allowances for dependent children which, in application, make the rearing of bastards profitable and create a generation literally fatherless.

Our politicians, nearly all of them, have failed to apply political imagination to the alleviating of broken community and personal anarchy in our cities. It seems to be time for men of letters to apply their talents to these grim concerns.

Although Americans have rediscovered poverty, and tracts about the needy have been a principal cause of programs for political action during the past five years, our imaginative literature is curiously unconcerned, in any deeper sense, with the American poor. We have novels by the score about racial antagonism, of course, and others about Southern rural decadence; but though these books sometimes touch incidentally upon poverty, generally their authors assume that poverty is the cause, rather than the consequence, of the ills they lament. And despite a show of naturalism, their attitude toward the poor remains quasi-romantic, and thoroughly sentimental.

Until our century, humane letters in this country rarely touched upon the poor at all. The "social" novels, stories, and plays of our age have been calculated to shock, rather than to inform or to develop understanding. From Jack London through Upton Sinclair to John Steinbeck and Erskine Caldwell, our writers have treated poverty as a scandalous phenomenon that is Somebody's Crime—but their work has been somehow unconvincing, even when the writers actually knew a good deal about the material circumstances they described. With them, the poor, for the most part, were stock victims of circumstance, and their interior life went unexamined.

The proletarian novel of thirty, forty, or fifty years ago is unread today—because it is not literature. Only now and then, over the decades, has an author of talent penetrated to the reality of slum-life or has related without ideological obsession "the short and simple annals of the poor." Stephen Crane's *Maggie,* Ernest Poole's *The Harbor,* and portions of John Dos Passos' novels ring true; but little else does.

Nor has the Negro revolt produced an admirable literature of the poor. Some of the books by colored authors are ferocious to the point of madness; most are distorted by ideological passion; next to none will endure. The reviewers for the mass media, of course, praise to the skies certain pieces of fiction and polemic which, were they written by white men, they would not condescend to review. (I think of a review in the *Times Literary Supplement* of one of the multitudinous "historical" cloak-dagger-and-bosom romances of a successful literary hack who happens to be colored. The reviewer referred to a "genuine moral nobility" in this piece of trash. Nothing of the sort was present there, actually, for the author's only ambition was to enrich himself; but to the disintegrated-liberal critic, pigmentation of the skin has become in itself an evidence of moral nobility.)

My chief exception to this harsh judgment is that powerful novel blending symbolism and realism by Ralph Ellison, *The Invisible Man.* Mr. Ellison has vision, and he can write, and very early he fought free of ideology. He knows the Negro, and he knows the poor. He does not fall into the delusion, even in its inverted sense of "belligerent negritude," that there is something *wrong* about being colored or about being poor. He understands that the *circumstances* of poverty, and the way in which a man bears his poverty or his color, are what matter. He is aware of what nearly everyone else has forgotten, that the poor, suffer though they may, are especially blessed of the Lord; and that some of them show it. He does not mean to whitewash the colored man, or to convert all the poor into dully affluent suburbanites. He is endowed with the tragic sense of life.

Despite this general misunderstanding of the life of the poor— which, in America, generally has been the life of the socially uprooted, in the Five Points or in Harlem—for the novelist and the poet and the dramatist the conditions of modern poverty ought to be more interesting than the life of suburbia or of urban material success. The culture of poverty still is turbulent, comic, pathetic, tragic, and intricate. One might expect the emergence of writers as convincing and gripping as were George Gissing and Arthur Morrison, when they wrote about the London poor nearly three-quarters of a century ago. Where, however—with such few exceptions as *The Invisible Man*—are our counterparts of *The Nether World* or *A Child of the Jago?*

The genuinely and permanently poor almost never write about themselves, because they do not write at all. Crabbe in the eighteenth century, Hogg in the nineteenth, are partial exceptions—but they spoke for the rural poor, not for the characteristic poverty of the industrial age. It is the educated man temporarily impoverished, or the detached connoisseur of slums, who sees the poor as they cannot describe themselves. Just now we have a crowd of socially conscious and self-conscious young people who endeavor to make the cause of the poor their own, and talk about "organizing" the poor, much in the vein of Jack London. (Thus far, their organizing has been disastrous to the poor people upon whom they fix their ideological fantasies.) Also we have the beatniks and the hippies, who embrace the outer and inner anarchy of urban and private disintegration. These are deficient, nevertheless, in the moral imagination and in the wry humor essential to any illuminating and readable treatment of the poor in literature.

Few of the American poor are merely middle-class folk somehow deprived of good incomes. Actually, they think and behave quite differently from the humanitarians and latter-day bohemians who try to acclimatize themselves in the city jungle. For the most part, our poor are displaced persons: southern Negroes or mountain whites transported to northern city cores, forlorn "old soldiers" of Skid Row, dirt farmers propelled by necessity to industrial existence, Puerto Ricans or Mexicans or Indians drifted into an alien civilization, the second or third generation of the welfare rolls, the emotionally disoriented victims of the decay of family, old people cut from their moorings and afflicted by the rising cost of living. Geographically and culturally, they are uprooted.

These impoverished do not form as yet a mass proletariat, though America begins to know that ugly phenomenon. The congregations of the "store front" churches, the patrons of the hillbilly taverns up North, the Spanish-speaking "ethnic minorities," the Negro ghetto-denizens, still retain some convictions, memories, and aspirations from different modes of existence—or the older individuals do, at least. Therefore they often are interesting people, worth talking to and writing about precisely because they are not yet assimilated to standardized comfort and mass conformity.

Real proletarians, by contrast, are uninteresting, as well as miserable; that is why the truly "proletarian" novel is either boring or unreal. In the root meaning of the term, a proletarian is a person who gives nothing to the commonwealth but his body and his off-spring. Impoverished spiritually and intellectually, not only materi-ally, a proletarian class like the *lazzaroni* of Naples displays only monotony of character and destitution of mind; however fascinat-ing to the sociologist, such people cannot rouse the writer's imagi-nation. A proletarian is not necessarily in physical want; one may conceive of a vast well-fed proletariat of the future; so writing about the poor is not identical with sermonizing about the proletariat.

Indiscriminate pity or ideological abstraction unfit the writer for the themes of poverty. Gissing, Morrison, and Orwell knew the poor as individuals, not as a mass phenomenon: they knew their oddities, their virtues, their vices, their comic aspects. So the poor *live* in their books, while the communist novel is the dead and face-less realm of the "terrible simplifiers."

Since very few of the American poor think of themselves as proletarians, or even as a "working class," the writer who so re-gards them must fail to understand them. But if the writer accepts the poor as a miscellaneous collection of people—often of lively character—from diverse origins, uprooted though not yet alto-gether depersonalized and deprived of culture, then he may make more of them than social statistics. I suspect that poor men appre-ciate the comic better than do affluent men. Sitting once in a shabby little park, with shabby and talkative "old soldiers" on the next bench, a friend of mine watched the shuffling approach of a ragged boon companion. "Here comes the Ambassador from Poland!" said a wag with a broad-brimmed old hat shading his eyes. The Ambas-sador gave as good raillery as he received.

Or the writer may learn fortitude from them. On one occasion I walked through the remains of Corktown, mostly demolished by the Federal bulldozer, in Detroit, in company with a young man of Maltese family. My companion was then under indictment for mur-der; he had been graduated from high school a few months earlier. He was trapped in the slums, but he showed no trace of self-pity, talked amusingly of characters and conditions, and clearly was no proletarian. He was not tired of life; and since then, he has amended his own.

In the German folk-tale, Iron Hans tells the youth who has been his feckless servant, "Now you must go forth into the world and learn the meaning of poverty." The injunction of Iron Hans would benefit many an aspiring American writer. At a night club, recently, a very well-known man of letters, who made his early reputation by chronicling the seamy side of life, affluently told his affluent companions, "Hell, you can't live on less than thirty thousand dollars a year!" Well, really you can live on less than that sum—I always have. And people whose family income is a mere tenth of that amount may give you more to write about than can any number of courses in creative writing.

George Orwell's Despair

In the twentieth century, no novelist has exerted a stronger influence upon political opinion, in Britain and America, than did George Orwell. Also Orwell was the most telling writer about poverty. In a strange and desperate way, Orwell was a lover of the permanent things. Yet because he could discern no source of abiding justice and love in the universe, Orwell found this life of ours not worth living. In his sardonic fashion, nevertheless, he struck some fierce blows at abnormality in politics and literature.

George Orwell was a left-wing professional journalist, with some of the faults which that unhappy conjunction encourages. Occasionally he wrote hastily and carelessly; he was bitter and arrogant; desiring men to be as gods, he despised them because they had the effrontery to be loud and smelly and stupid. But also Orwell was much more than a left-wing professional journalist. He was fearless, kind, honest, consumingly earnest, and very English. He was the latest representative of the English radical tradition which extends through Langland, Bunyan, Cobbett, Dickens, and Chesterton—a paradoxical radicalism rooted in the experiences and the prejudices of a strong people. In a number of ways—his origins, his poverty, his pessimism, his mingled hatred and pity for the poor, in the subjects of his books—he resembled George Gissing, who died at a similar age of similar causes after a similar life. Orwell's was that radicalism which is angry with society because society has failed to provide men with the ancient norms of simple life—family, decency, and continuity; the sort of radicalism which does not mean to disintegrate the world, but to restore it. Take him all in all, Orwell was a man, and there is none left in England like him.

English colonials are more conspicuously English then are true-born Englishmen; and Orwell was a colonial born in India in 1908. Also he was an old Etonian. In Burma he was a good policeman for five years, though he hated the work; he became a beggar and a slavey in Paris and London; he taught in England. Then he went to Spain, where he fought as a member of the anarchist P.O.U.M. —for Orwell, despite the flavor of Marxism in his books, detested Communists and Communism. Afterward he wrote much for the leftish press, but was suspect as a deviationist in that quarter. He had no great reputation until *Animal Farm* was published, in 1945; and he died shortly after the publication of *1984*. His was a short life, and not a merry one.

In *The Road to Wigan Pier* (1937) occurs this passage that reveals much about Orwell:

"Once when I was thirteen, I was in a train coming from a market town, and the third-class carriage was packed full of shep-herds and pig-men who had been selling their beasts. Someone had produced a quart bottle of beer and passed it round; it travelled from mouth to mouth, everyone taking a swig. I cannot describe the horror I felt as that bottle worked its way towards me. If I drank from it after those lower-class mouths I felt certain I should vomit; on the other hand, if they offered it to me I dared not refuse for fear of offending them—you see here how the middle-class squeamishness works both ways."

This reminds one of Swift's disgust with the coarse physical gar-ment of man, and of the same characteristics in Aldous Huxley. We find this loathing repeatedly in Orwell's descriptions of the hideous-ness of life in 1984. Influenced by Marxist theory, Orwell attributed this revulsion to his class-consciousness; but I suspect that it goes deeper. Like all true satirists, Orwell was allergic to *people*. He adored the Platonic idea of a man; he could not abide the vulgarity of the flesh. What he really hated about modern society was its ugliness, its monotony, its cheapness, its commonness. These are like the opinions of Ruskin, but they are not the impulses of a typical collectivistic revolutionary.

If Hume was a Tory by accident, Orwell was a Leftist by acci-dent. His instincts were more aristocratic then egalitarian; and, like the genuine aristocrat, he held a thoroughgoing contempt for commercialism and crassness. In words like those of George Gissing, he wrote in *Down and Out in Paris and London* (1933).

"In all the modern talk about energy, efficiency, social service, and the rest of it, what meaning is there except 'Get money, get it legally, and get a lot of it?' Money has become the grand test of virtue. By this test beggars fail, and for this they are despised."

And so Orwell's socialism was that skimpy and contradictory socialism which so often pops up upon the Labour back benches, astounded at the bill for nationalizing steel or enraged at petty interferences with Her Majesty's subjects. Orwell frankly disliked and feared "scientific" Marxists; he sympathized with the confessedly muddled socialism of the ordinary British workingman, who thought of socialism simply as shorter hours, better wages, and less bossing about. Of such a workingman he wrote in *Wigan Pier:* "Often, in my opinion, he is a truer Socialist than the orthodox Marxist, because he does remember, what the other so often forgets, that Socialism means justice and common decency."

This is the sort of socialism which literary men like William Morris and Cunninghame Graham stood for—a socialism perfectly impractical, hopelessly sentimental, but generous, intensely human, and not unlike Tory radicalism. When a man like Orwell begins to see what State Socialism really must become in the age that is dawning, he writes *1984,* grits his teeth, and dies.

He loathed the utopianism of H. G. Wells much as William Morris was infuriated at the utopianism of Edward Bellamy. Orwell despised, indeed, nearly all his fellow-socialists. "The typical Socialist is not," he wrote in *Wigan Pier,* "as tremulous old ladies imagine, a ferocious-looking working man with greasy overalls and a raucous voice. He is either a youthful snob-Bolshevik who in five years' time will quite probably have made a wealthy marriage and been converted to Roman Catholicism; or, still more typically, a prim little man with a white-collar job, usually a secret teetotaller and often with vegetarian leanings, with a history of Nonconformity behind him, and, above all, with a social position which he has no intention of forfeiting."

Orwell's socialism, then, scarcely can be called a position at all, but only an agonized leap in the dark, away from the pain of consolidated, uniform, industrialized modern existence. Orwell was acutely and miserably class-conscious, as perhaps only a poor and puzzled Englishman can be, to a degree most Americans find difficult to understand; he thought of himself always as distinctly middle-class, and he wished he were nothing of the sort. So the best solution which occurred to his mind was the merging of all orders of society into a vast inchoate proletarian body. He predicted in *Wigan Pier,* half in despair, half in hope, that the hard-pressed British bourgeoisie would be reduced to the condition of the working-people:

"And then perhaps this misery of class-prejudice will fade away, and we of the sinking middle class—the private schoolmaster, the half-starved free-lance journalist, the colonel's spinster daughter with £75 a year, the jobless Cambridge graduate, the ship's officer without a ship, the clerks, the civil servants, the commercial travellers and the thrice-bankrupt drapers in the country towns—may sink without further struggles into the working class where we belong, and probably when we get there it will not be so dreadful as we feared, for, after all, we have nothing to lose but our aitches."

Yet Orwell was not candid here. Actually, he was appalled at the idea of being assimilated by the amorphous mess of sweating, cursing, humdrum, unthinking humanity. What he really thought of working-people, in the flesh, is suggested by various descriptions of the "proles" in *1984.* They are not the paragraphs of a man who loves common people with a vast gregarious joviality. Orwell would no more have called Walt Whitman camerado than he would have adored Big Brother.

At heart, Orwell hated all innovation. The most ingenious feature of his last book, over which he must have labored with a mordant pleasure, is his burlesque of recent endeavors to revise out of recognition the English language. I refer, of course, to the appendix on "The Principles of Newspeak." To dehumanize man altogether, Ingsoc has stripped and mutilated the language, converting it into a propagandist's pidgin-English.

What Orwell yearned after was not the gray egalitarian future, but old England, ante-bellum England, England before the automobile and the council-house and the troubles of our times. His praises of English tradition are almost in the tone of Burke. In *Coming up for Air,* Orwell expresses himself through George Bowling, a lower-middle-class, middle-aged man who tries to revisit the scenes of his youth and finds that the country he knew as a boy has been obliterated by suburbia, and then smashed by bombs:

"There's a kind of peacefulness even in the names of English coarse fish. Roach, rudd, dace, bleak, barbel, bream, gudgeon, pike, chub, carp, tench. They're a solid kind of names. The people who made them up hadn't heard of machine guns, they didn't live in terror of the sack or spend their time eating aspirins, going to the pictures and wondering how to keep out of the concentration camp."

Bowling praises continuity, and the placidity that comes with acceptance of immemorial ways: "What was it that people had in those days? A feeling of security even when they weren't secure. More exactly it was a feeling of continuity. All of them knew they'd got to die, and I suppose a few of them knew they were going to go bankrupt, but what they didn't know was that the order of things could change. Whatever might happen to themselves, things would go on as they'd known them." And now the world is falling into the hands of "the stream-lined men who think in slogans and talk in bullets."

The Past, Orwell thought, was gone irretrievably; and yet the decent people in his books are reactionaries, men who try to turn back to the old ways. Little of the Past survives for them to recapture—hardly more than rags and tatters of nursery-rhymes, as in *1984*.

As for the Present, Orwell found it intolerable. He thought of it as the Great Depression of his early years in England: the dole and massive unemployment. He became a Socialist because he believed (knowing very little about economics) that under "capitalism" there must be perpetual unemployment on a vast scale. Worse than the material privations of life on the dole was the damage done to character: he had known many decent workingmen, he said, who had disintegrated morally after a few weeks or months on the dole: denied work, they felt useless, rejected by society, and fell to pieces. They would not be worth hiring again.

The migrant farm-laborer and the London beggar were the subjects of his second novel, *A Clergyman's Daughter* (1935). There has been no truer or more dreadful writing about the lot of the destitute and the outcast. The scene of the derelicts—men and women—in Trafalgar Square at night has the wild power of *Lear.* Yet it is possible to conceive of a degradation worse than this.

For if the present is Purgatory, the probable future will be Hell. Orwell foresaw the approach of a totalist society from which faith, custom, common sense, justice, order, freedom, brotherhood, art, literature, and even sexual love would be eradicated. The new "socialist" oligarchy would live for the intoxication of brutal power; the administrative and technical people, party members, would live in terror and stupor; the proletarian masses would exist on the level of beasts. This new society never will end, says O'Brien, the *agent provocateur* in *1984:* it will writhe eternally, its energizing spirit the lust for power. Religion will be dead, but materialism will have failed; freedom will have been exchanged for security, and then security will be chucked through a "memory hole" into the central incinerator. O'Brien is candid with his victim Winston:

"Do you begin to see, then, what kind of world we are creating? It is the exact opposite of the stupid hedonistic Utopias that the old reformers imagined. A world of fear and treachery and torment, a world of trampling and being trampled upon, a world which will grow not less but *more* merciless as it refines itself. Progress in our world will be progress toward more pain. The old civilizations claimed that they were founded on love and justice. Ours is founded upon hatred. In our world there will be no emotions except fear, rage, triumph, and self-abasement. Everything else we shall destroy—everything. Already we are breaking down the habits of thought which have survived from before the Revolution. We have cut the links between child and parent, and between man and man, and between man and woman. No one dares trust a wife or a child or a friend any longer. But in the future there will be no wives and no friends. Children will be taken from their mothers at birth, as one takes eggs from a hen. The sex instinct will be eradicated. Procreation will be an annual formality like the renewal of a ration card. We shall abolish the orgasm. Our neurologists are at work upon it now. There will be no loyalty, except loyalty toward the Party. There will be no love, except the love of Big Brother. There will be no laughter, except the laugh of triumph over a defeated enemy. There will be no art, no literature, no science. When we are omnipotent we shall have no more need of science. There will be no curiosity, no employment of the process of life. All competing pleasures will be destroyed. But always—do not forget this, Winston—always there will be the intoxication of power, constantly increasing and constantly growing subtler. Always, at every moment, there will be the thrill of victory, the sensation of trampling forever on an enemy who is helpless. If you want a picture of the future, imagine a boot stamping on a human face—forever."

This terrifying passage raises a question; and Orwell did not answer that question. Such a triumph of *pleonexia* is more than conceivable: we see it dominating China's "Cultural Revolution," in which the whole heritage of civilization is denounced and destroyed, and in which the only gratification remaining even to the masters of society is stamping upon a human face. But here is the question: what force or appetite, immensely stronger than human wishes, inspires the ambition to trample forever upon an enemy who is helpless?

Just such a culmination of sin is described in Christian orthodoxy. It is called the reign of the Anti-Christ. And it is produced by the intervention of a supernatural hatred, working upon human depravity. It is the overthrow of the normal by the abnormal. It is the apotheosis of Satan.

Orwell saw the Church in disrepute and disorder, intellectually and morally impoverished; and he had no faith. He could not say how the total corruption of man and society would be produced; he could not even refer to the intrusion of the diabolical; but he could describe a coming reign of misrule wonderfully like the visions of St. John the Divine. He saw beyond ideology to the approaching inversion of humanitarian dogmas. All the norms for mankind would be defied and defiled. Yet because he could not bring himself to believe in enduring principles of order, or in an Authority transcending private rationality, he was left desperate at the end. A "desperado," literally, is a man who has despaired of grace.

The politics and the poverty of the future would be indescribably worse than the shabby politics and the grimy poverty of the present age. A few years after Orwell's death, the leader of the vestigial Liberal party announced that he and his colleagues were drawing up a program founded upon "the forward-looking ideas of George

Orwell." This was said without a smile or a grimace. It would not be easy to find a more interesting example of the impoverishment of political imagination.

"There is no such thing as genuinely non-political literature," Orwell wrote in his essay on "The Prevention of Literature" (1945), "and least of all in an age like our own, when fears, hatreds, and loyalties of a directly political kind are near to the surface of everyone's consciousness. . . . It follows that the atmosphere of totalitarianism is deadly to any kind of prose writer, though a poet, at any rate a lyric poet, might possibly find it breathable. And in any totalitarian society that survives for more than a couple of generations, it is probable that prose literature, of the kind that has existed during the past four hundred years, must actually *come to an end*." Soviet Russia supplies the proof: "It is true that literary prostitutes like Ilya Ehrenberg or Alexei Tolstoy are paid huge sums of money, but the only thing which is of any value to the writer as such—his freedom of expression—is taken away from him."

Thus, before entering upon political normality—and, as Orwell wrote, no impenetrable wall of separation can be erected between literature and politics—we come to the concluding topic of these reflections on the norms of humane letters: can literature survive the modern temper?

VII. WILL LITERATURE ENDURE?

The Valley of the Shadow of Books

IT IS NOT UNDER TOTALIST DOMINATIONS ONLY THAT TRUE literature is in danger today. Unscrupulous authors, avaricious publishers, stupid librarians, incompetent teachers, and a reading-public whose taste has been corrupted may do as much injury to humane letters as could any body of official censors. Despite the flood of paperbacks in America, Britain, and some other countries, the old earnest reading-public diminishes, or at least does not grow in proportion to the increase of population. The typical college graduate reads little or nothing except ephemera and the selections of one of the gigantic book clubs. Popular fiction reeks of the brothel or of *Psychopathia Sexualis;* some publishers' editors seem bent on pandering to that poor wretch the literary *voyeur.* Vicarious violence for the sake of violence becomes the literary ration of children. Will the normative function of literature survive at all?

In *1984*, Winston can find only rubbish on what few shelves of second-hand books he encounters in obscure shops; nearly everything published before the Revolution has been burned or pulped. The "democratic despotism" dreaded by Tocqueville might accomplish, without formal political repression, the same result. The content of "basic readers" in American public schools, for instance, has become thinner and thinner during recent decades: the great authors are supplanted by trivia. Or pompous and unread librarian-bureaucrats may eliminate many good books without resorting to the techniques of Bradbury's *Fahrenheit 451*. When, last year, I donated several hundred books to a public library, I discovered soon that nearly half of them had been burnt by order of a district librarian-functionary. This censorship by fire had nothing to do with pornography, and only incidentally was concerned with politics; the librarian in question merely felt that most books written before he was born, or books dealing with nearly anything serious, ought not to clutter library shelves. "We find that the public is not interested in such books." This guardian of our literary patrimony burned, among many other volumes, a set of Macaulay's *History of England* and a set of O. Henry's short stories.

The dwindling of second-hand bookshops is at once symptom and consequence of this decline in true literacy. Once upon a time I was a second-hand-book dealer myself, and I could cite perhaps a hundred instances of the extinction, over fifteen years, of long-established old-book shops that had endured for decades or generations—unto our era of swaggering prosperity and urban disintegration. One pities the rising generation, which may know only the ordered rows of paperbacks, deprived of all the Gothic enchantments and infinite variety that emanated from the dust of the chaotic book-and-curio emporium.

What blight has fallen upon this hoary trade? Why, first, the old-book dealer suffers, like the proprietor of the new-book shop, from the taste of a generation that prefers television and speed to serious reading. But while the new-book store can resort to the public's appetite for "awareness," to the birthday-book market, and to its card and record departments, the dealer in dead authors cannot adjust to modern appetites—except, perhaps, by stocking a little surreptitious pornography.

Also, with few exceptions, the used-book trade generally has been a profitless venture: the average bookseller thought himself lucky to win the wage of management, let alone lay up treasure. Thus the steady inflation of prices and wages hits this occupation brutally. It becomes difficult to find competent help—or perhaps any help—at the rate the bookseller can pay. Pressure salesmanship is impossible in this business, and even the most modest advertising is too costly.

But the worst ravager of the valley of the shadow of books is the wrecker's bulldozer. "Urban renewal," "slum clearance," and the general passion for demolishing and rebuilding in every city write *finis* across the grimy plate glass of that marginal enterprise the book grotto. Most little dealers cannot possibly afford the rent of comparable cubic space in a new building. Besides, how can one shift many thousands of books (the hardest and heaviest articles to move) to a new location, and get them on the shelves once more, when their average value is only a few cents? Some of them have mouldered up near the ceiling for decades, pitifully awaiting a purchaser; and some of those books ought to perish; but in this exigency, off all must go to the wastepaper dealer, or perhaps to the bonfire. Like certain sensitive plants, the old-book shop rarely takes root in new soil.

Some fusty caverns stuffed with quartos and duodecimos always will defy the lust for innovation, one trusts. In old Bristol, the bookshops along Christmas Steps may be invulnerable to the urban redesigner (a real Philistine, in unfortunate Bristol), because they twist up a hillside. Probably the Third Avenue dealers will contrive to live through the monstrous alteration of Manhattan. Godfrey's Bookshop, sprawling through the rooms of an ancient half-timbered house in the oldest quarter of old York, probably will not be demolished to make way for a new and nasty commercial building—not for a few years, anyway. Part of Bloomsbury, with its well-stocked bookshops, will vanish, but not all. Boston and Philadelphia will spare a few forlorn dealers of the old breed.

Yet I wonder how much longer I will be able to descend into the bowels of that immemorial Edinburgh bookshop which extends downward from an eighteenth-century bridge to the squalor of the Canongate, five floors crammed with hard-to-find works, mostly religious—where I used to pick up volumes of W. H. Mallock or John Henry Newman for sixpence?* How much longer, indeed, will one encounter the book-carts of Rome or Glasgow, one of the most minute forms of private enterprise still existing in the Western world? As for the dim, unprosperous, higgledy-piggledy, dirt-cheap bookshops that formerly scrabbled for life on the verge of the Skid

---

* Since I wrote these sentences, indeed the Edinburgh bookshop to which I referred, with its civil clerks, has disappeared. For that matter, the sixpence, too, is to be abolished soon—as Orwell said it would be.

Rows of Detroit, Chicago, or Cleveland—why, we shall not look upon their like again.

Reading a book borrowed from a college or public library is a sorry substitute for grubbing out your very own infinitely precious, infinitely cheap copy from the ragged regiment on the book-cavern's shelves or the heaps upon the floor. George Gissing (or Henry Ryecroft) took a deep and laborious joy in lugging the length of Tottenham Court Road, trip after trip, the quartos of the splendid set of Gibbon's *Decline and Fall* he had acquired for a few shillings. One *reads* a great work so acquired; while one merely puts the paperback edition on one's shelves, for a rainy day that never comes. (I suppose here that one possesses bookshelves; some model houses are proudly exhibited that provide no space whatso-ever for books.) Once I discovered half a set of Conrad in Lansing, and spent my month's expense-money in making it mine. Years later, in Salt Lake City, I came upon the missing half of that very broken set, and acquired it out of my private's pay. The regimented crowds of young people on our mass campuses, occasionally spend-ing an hour in the assigned-reading room so as to qualify for a diploma (or sociability-certificate), never will know that shadowy kingdom of the old-book shop, in which was all manner of delight.

It seems improbable that any abrupt alteration of the modern taste, temper, and economy may rescue the old-fangled bookseller from the fate of the dodo. Yet as the wrecker's ball makes dust and ashes of our cities' cores, we might remind one another that old books, like the poor and like the denizens of Skid Row, have to go somewhere—unless we mean to extirpate them. Much of our "urban renewal" really is urban devastation. Rehabilitation, and judicious sparing of mean but living streets, is far preferable. All the odd little shops and corners that make towns worth wandering through—as Jane Jacobs suggests in her *Death and Life of Great American Cities*—are more humane than are arid vistas of glass and steel. So it is with the perishing bookshop.

Good second-hand bookshops rarely will be sleek and profit-making. We still can afford, I hope, some untidiness in modern existence. A people can come to know the price of everything and the value of nothing. Of this bent are folk who think they can leave no spot in town for anything which, like the book trade, does not adhere to the nexus of cash payment; who would prune from the civil social order all diversity and privacy and dustiness—and old-book browsing. For every pulped or burned book, they must pay a nasty price in boredom and blighted imagination.

Normality Reaffirmed

In concluding this section of the present book, I venture to state again the definition of normality, and to reaffirm the importance of literature as a transmitter of standards.

Normality is the character or state of being normal—of according with a rule or standard. The term implies the existence of "norms," or authoritative principles and models. Derived from the Latin *norma,* a carpenter's square, "norm" signifies a measure generally accepted and virtually immutable.

In recent decades, numerous professors of education, sociologists, and other writers have used the words "norm," "normal," and "normality" to describe a measure of average performance, a mathematical median or mean, or characteristic popular behavior of the hour. Such usages, however, are corruptions of the original significations. As a term of morals, politics, and natural science, "normality" (strictly employed) generally refers to some enduring standard or measurement, transcending local or temporary deviations from the norm; it is *not* synonymous with "average" or "typical."

Thus ethical normality is determined not by mass behavior at any particular moment, but rather by the custom and consensus of many civilized generations, and by reference to ethical standards long accepted by moralists, jurists, and religious teachers. Similarly, political normality depends upon conformity to long-observed phenomena and rules of the civil social order, not merely upon the conduct of a particular majority in a particular political community in a particular year or decade.

Norms, and a consequent condition of normality, may be derived from "revealed" truth; from the long experience of human beings living in community; from intellectual and spiritual "leaps in being" —that is, from the perceptions of men of genius; from accurate scientific measurement of behavior over a lengthy period of time and in many circumstances. Sometimes—as Hume said of moral ideas—the sources of normative concepts may be unknowable.

Whatever the origins of normative understanding, "normality" and its associated words imply permanence and reference to a standard superior to average behavior at any given time. Set against "abnormality," the term normality is founded upon a conviction that judgments may be formed, and actions undertaken, upon patterns or rules which recognize the enduring nature of certain moral and social qualities.

Great literature possesses its own general norms; but, still more important, literature is a chief means for passing on to posterity the normative knowledge of a culture—and a means for censuring the abnormity of every age. Through the body of humane letters, we are provided with models for emulation and precepts for guidance. We learn from literature, far more than from personal experience, the character of the saint, the hero, and the philosopher. We learn from literature those insights into the human condition which make life worth living.

So if true literature does not survive—and does not influence in some degree the mass of men—neither will civilization long survive. Only the most primitive economic activities, for instance, would outlast the collapse of literary culture; for men deprived of inherited wisdom soon would find themselves unable to band together for any productive purpose.

The oldest civilized continuity, indeed—China's—was maintained almost wholly by literature and custom, without the light of revelation in the stricter sense, and without aristocracy in the Western sense. Therefore the ferocious attempt of Mao Tse-tung to obliterate the remnants of Chinese literary and artistic culture is an attempt to destroy wisdom: it is literally madness. For if man rejects the wisdom of his ancestors, communicated to him by humane letters, he must fall into the abyss. This hard truth was perceived by Chinese philosophers some twenty-three centuries ago.

Consider Hsun Tsu, who was born about three hundred and twelve years before Jesus of Nazareth. Some people who ought to know better think that the doctrine of human depravity is purely Christian in origin. But really that doctrine is part of the religion which has existed since the beginning of the world, even if St. Augustine gave it the form which we know. Here are some passages (in Burton Watson's translation) from the treatise of Hsun Tsu on evil.

"Man's nature is evil; goodness is the result of conscious activity. The nature of man is such that he is born with a fondness for profit. If he indulges this fondness, it will lead him into wrangling and strife, and all sense of courtesy and humility will disappear.

"He is born with feelings of envy and hate, and if he indulges these, they will lead him into violence and crime, and all sense of loyalty and good faith will disappear.

"Man is born with the desires of the eyes and ears, with a fondness for beautiful sights and sounds. If he indulges these, they will lead him into license and wantonness, and all ritual principles and correct forms will be lost.

"Hence, any man who follows his nature and indulges his emotions will inevitably become involved in wrangling and strife, will violate the forms and rules of society, and will end as a criminal. Therefore, man must first be transformed by the instructions of a teacher and guided by ritual principles, and only then will he be able to observe the dictates of courtesty and humility, obey the forms and rules of society, and achieve order. It is obvious from this, then, that man's nature is evil, and that his goodness is the result of conscious activity."

By denouncing all traditional teachers and all ritual principles, the fanatics of the "Cultural Revolution" not only cast away all Chinese philosophy: in an immediately practical sense, they set loose the evil in man's nature that was restrained by precept and custom. That is why "Maoism" cannot create, atomic bomb or no atomic bomb; it can only destroy.

"A warped piece of wood must wait until it has been laid against the straightening board, steamed, and forced into shape before it can become straight," Hsun Tsu continued; "a piece of blunt metal must wait until it has been whetted on a grindstone before it can become sharp. Similarly, since man's nature is evil, it must wait for the instructions of a teacher before it can become upright, and for the guidance of ritual principles before it can become orderly."

The West, too, experiences its cultural revolution: in general not through violence, but through error, indifference, materialism, scientism, and appetite for novelty. People like C. P. Snow, pretending to desire the reunion of science and humane learning, actually hope to submerge the old literary culture altogether. (Snow is an ardent admirer of Mao Tse-tung's achievements.) And in the West, as in China, the cultural revolution, if triumphant, would bring down in ruin the material achievements it praises, by destroying the moral basis of society—the cement of which is humane literature.

Literary culture will survive if enough men and women become aware that the purpose of literature is not simple amusement, but rather the guarding and advancement of the permanent things. If literature has no end, it does not deserve to survive. A large number of writers and publishers and reviewers clearly are of the opinion that literature exists only to fill their pockets and tickle their vanity. Any honest physical labor is more edifying than that. But perhaps we see the commencement of a reaction against such decadence in letters, if only from mankind's primal instinct for the perpetuation of the species.

People like Lord Snow may be merely silly; Mao Tse-tung, though not silly, may be mad. Yet it is through silliness and madness that the diabolical commonly enters into mundane affairs. "All sin is childish," an old man of the clergy (who was also a classical scholar) told me once. I have found that to be true. The rejection of humane letters is an act of childish impatience and arrogance. The consequences of that rejection, nevertheless, are not restricted to juvenile years, but may be perpetual. When the great books are forgotten or burnt—why, "here comes a chopper to chop off your head." So I conclude my vaticinations with some comments on a silly little non-book, therefore, believing that silliness can be most sinister.

The Iceman Cometh

The hater of mankind's past usually is also a hater of Shakespeare—and by no accident. For Shakespeare, amid the splendor of his language, was concerned always with the constant in human existence. And the futurist, furiously denying that human nature is constant, rightly discerns in Shakespeare a formidable knight-errant of the permanent things.

Some few years past, an educationist demanded that Shakespeare no longer be taught in American public schools, because Shakespeare "wrote in an anti-democratic era." This is the voice of the egalitarian futurist; but there are other varieties of the attitude. With sound insight, Aldous Huxley, in *Brave New World*, sets against the future society of gratified gross appetites that understanding of the human condition which was Shakespeare's.

These reflections are provoked by a recent oddity of American scientism, a book called *The Prospect of Immortality*, by Robert C. W. Ettinger, a teacher of physics in a junior college. Ettinger, you may recall, is the gentleman who wishes to freeze us all, that we may live forever. (Enthusiasts for his scheme now call such projected treatment of corpses "cryogenic interment.")

Some reviewers and readers suspected that Ettinger's book about the coming "Freezer-Centered Society" was an elaborate spoof, worthy almost of Swift, reducing to absurdity our American credulousness before pseudo-science, and our dread of death. But through correspondence with Mr. Ettinger, I have discovered him to be a sincere person, eager to proselytize, in dead earnest about freezing us like beefsteaks—and about making freezing of corpses compulsory, on pain of trial for negligent homicide. A little cult already has sprung up round Ettinger's book: odd societies dedicated to perpetual survival of the individual on earth, and such votaries as a professor of classics, a female journalist, even a clergyman or two.

The Prospect of Immortality being neither a scientific nor a philosophical treatise, it interests me chiefly as an illustration of the mentality of the Shakespeare-hater. In a section entitled "Beyond Beowulf," Ettinger makes himself clear:

"I am convinced that in a few hundred years the words of Shakespeare, for example, will interest us no more than the grunting of swine in a wallow. (Shakespeare scholars, along with censors, snuff grinders, and wig makers, will have to find new, perhaps unimaginable occupations.) Not only will his work be far too weak in intellect, and written in too vague and puny a language, but the problems which concerned him will be, in the main, no more than historical curiosities. Neither greed, nor lust, nor ambition will in that society have any recognizable similarity to the qualities we know. With the virtually unlimited resources of that era, all ordinary wants will be readily satisfied, either by supplying them or removing them in the mind of the individual. . . . Competitive drives, in the inter-personal sense, may or may not persist; but if they do, it will be in radically modified form."

What a charming prospect! Ettinger informs us that, thawed out after some years or centuries of cryogenic interment, we all shall be as gods—the original promise of the Tempter, never fulfilled. For Science will have remedied all ills, physical or moral, to which flesh is heir. By 2258, the median individual income will be eight million dollars annually; we shall have occupied the planets and the stars; self-reproducing thinking-machines will perform all the work, and the citizen "will be allowed a basic income just for breathing"; motherhood will have been abolished—good riddance to bad rubbish—by ectogenesis; the sexes will be virtually indistinguishable. And how very happy and very different we defrosted survivors from quasi-Shakespearean savagery will be! Not only will the scientists of the future repair our archaic frozen bodies, but they will alter our minds radically—through "brute force," if need be, Ettinger says. Here is the prospect for the thawed-out citizen:

"After awakening, he may already be again young and virile, having been rejuvenated while unconscious; or he may be gradually renovated through treatment after awakening. In any case, he will have the physique of a Charles Atlas if he wants it, and his weary and faded wife, if she chooses, may rival Miss Universe. Much more important, they will be gradually improved in mentality and personality. They will not find themselves idiot strangers in a lonely and baffling world, but will be made fully educable and integrable."

Ettinger confesses that severe brain-damage may result from the process of freezing—or that the individual's mind may not have been worth much to begin with. But why worry? By 2258 A.D., and presumably much earlier, computing machines will have been so perfected that ingenious computers may be substituted for part or all of the subject's brain-tissue. O happy robots, clad in ancient flesh!

We encounter in this bathos what has been called "the spectre of predictable man," once more. In the totalist order of scientism, the tragic sense of life would be eliminated, together with tragedy, comedy, history, Shakespeare—and hope. Every man would be Charles Atlas—unnumbered millions of Charles Atlases, like peas in a universal pod—and every woman would be Miss Universe, vacuous simper and all. This is H. G. Wells' *Men like Gods* taken seriously. And, as in *Men like Gods*, life would be too unutterably boring to be worth living; but, death from "natural causes" having been abolished by compulsory cryogenic interment, the final escape-hatch would be sealed. Christian doctrine has a word for that condition: Hell.

Cheerfully and zealously, then, Ettinger advocates what C. S. Lewis called "the abolition of man." (Some of Ettinger's predictions and recommendations interestingly resemble those of the scientist-reformers in *That Hideous Strength*.) Intent upon the conquest of death, the "Freezer-Centered Society" ideologues (not much madder than other ideologues) are quite willing—nay, eager —to sacrifice normal humanity for the sake of an intolerable earthly "immortality." One remembers that the only thorough experiments in freezing human beings, so far, were conducted in Nazi concentration camps.

To accomplish the abolition of man, great literature, with its ethical end and its rousing of the spirit, must be struck down by the futurists; memories of love and death and hope and proliferating variety must be effaced altogether. Though even such a literary prostitute as Ehrenburg would have spared Shakespeare (reviving him, indeed, through a different sort of thaw), the more thoroughgoing scientistic totalists, as represented by the Merciful Frost set, know Shakespeare's phrases for "the grunting of swine." Hate Shakespeare, for he is human, all too human, and declines to be quick-frozen! Until Shakespeare is forgotten, who but a faithful few will swear by Ettinger and the frosty coffin?

The march of Progress, says the futurist, will rid us of Shakespeare and all the rest of that cultural baggage with which we are encumbered in this Purgatory of ours; only ensure that your senescent tissues are frozen in every particle, and you will wake in the Golden Age. Such metaphysical madness is but the fulfillment of the progressivism which Jakob Burckhardt described a century ago:

"Our assumption that we live in the age of moral progress is supremely ridiculous when we look back on those perilous times out of which the free strength of ideal desire rises to heaven in the lofty spires of a hundred cathedrals. The matter is made worse by our vulgar hatred of everything that is different, of the many-sidedness of life, of symbolic rites and privileges half or quite in abeyance, by our identification of the moral with the precise and our incapacity to understand the multifarious, the fortuitous."

Understanding Burckhardt's "many-sidedness of life," expressing the multifarious, the fortuitous, Shakespeare necessarily is detested by the metaphysically mad futurist. How very tidy would be the future world of cryogenic interment and resurrection! How dreadfully untidy, how nastily human, Shakespeare is! Blow, O blow, ye winter winds; Frost's not half so unkind as man's obstinacy.

And there's this, too, against Shakespeare: he puts wisdom into the mouths of fools; he seems so vexatiously sane even in raving fits. If only he had been frozen in 1616, we might operate, willy-nilly, on his brain cells, when the Golden Age arrives, and make him nearly as intelligent as a thinking-machine, or as Robert C. W. Ettinger. Aye, there's the rub: confounded old-fangled sanity. If we could be rid of that, as expressed in Shakespeare, soon we might convert the earth into one enormous ice-box.

Yet, as readers may have gathered, I am of another mind. I give you the counsel of Edgar, in *King Lear:* "Take heed o' the foul fiend: obey thy parents; keep thy word justly; swear not; commit not with man's sworn spouse; set not thy sweet heart on proud array. . . . Keep thy foot out of brothels, thy hand out of plackets, thy pen from lenders' books, and defy the foul fiend."

Part Three

THE NORMS OF POLITICS

❋❋❋❋❋❋❋❋❋❋❋❋❋❋❋❋❋❋❋❋❋❋❋

I. THE DRUG OF IDEOLOGY

The Meaning of Ideology

IN OUR AGE, MOST OF THE WORLD HAS FALLEN INTO PROFOUND political disorder; and while the United States may seem an island of tranquillity, comparatively speaking, in a sea of troubles, nevertheless we are not secure. In politics, as in letters, abnormity gains ground. The following chapters are intended to describe the decay of political normality, and to suggest that it is possible to recover the norms of the civil social order.

One may discern the principal causes of social disorder. Some of them are the consequences of swift economic and technological change, and those cannot be examined at any length here. But also a social order begins to disintegrate—or is supplanted by a very different domination—when political custom and political theory are overwhelmed by ideology; and when established political institutions are abandoned or permitted to decline, out of popular indifference and ignorance. In these chapters, I am concerned with the desertion from political theory and tradition, and what may be done about it; with the neglect of institutions that maintain order and justice and freedom, and with the results of such dereliction. The permanent things of the commonwealth stand in peril, throughout the world. Our first necessity is to understand the nature of ideology.

"Ideology" does not mean political theory or principle, even though many journalists and some professors commonly employ the term in that sense. Ideology really means political fanaticism—and, more precisely, the belief that this world of ours may be converted into the Terrestrial Paradise through the operation of positive law and positive planning. The ideologue—Communist or Nazi or of whatever affiliation—maintains that human nature and society may be perfected by mundane, secular means, though these means ordinarily involve violent social revolution. The ideologue immanentizes religious symbols and inverts religious doctrines.

What religion promises to the believer in a realm beyond time and space, ideology promises to everyone—except those who have been "liquidated" in the process—in society. Salvation becomes collective and political. "When the intellectual feels no longer attached either to the community or the religion of his forbears," Raymond Aron writes in *The Opium of the Intellectuals,* "he looks to progressive ideology to fill the vacuum. The main difference between the progressivism of the disciple of Harold Laski or Bertrand Russell and the Communism of the disciple of Lenin concerns not so much the *content* as the *style* of the ideologies and the allegiance they demand."

As a term of modern politics and sociology, "ideology" may be defined tentatively. It is an alleged science of politics, dogmatic and often utopian, closely allied with the interests of a particular social class or political sect. Several powerful ideologies or quasi-ideologies have been at work in the nineteenth and twentieth centuries. This word has passed through complicated changes of meaning, however, and often is misapplied.

In France, at the close of the eighteenth century, the term was employed by the disciples of Condillac, particularly Destutt de Tracy, whose *Les éléments d'idéologie* appeared in five volumes between 1801 and 1815. The original "ideologists" or "ideologues" believed that all knowledge is derived from sensation, and that a science of ideas could be developed upon this basis, describing the history and evolution of thought, and applicable to politics, ethics, and pedagogy. Thus originally "ideology" was a kind of climax of the rationalism of the Enlightenment, an attempt to systematize and apply knowledge obtained from sensory perception. The intellectual origins of ideology are described by a number of writers, perhaps most recently in two books by Thomas Molnar, *The Decline of the Intellectual* and *Utopia, the Perennial Heresy*.

Napoleon, in 1812, looking with disfavor upon the ideological school, ridiculed Destutt de Tracy and his associates as "ideologists," men of hopelessly abstract and fanciful views, unacquainted with the realities of the civil social order. From an early date, accordingly, "ideology" and "ideologist" or "ideologue" became terms of derogation, implying misguided intellectuality as banefully applied to social concerns. Thus John Adams, in 1813, wrote of ideology: "Our English words, Idiocy or Idiotism, express not the force or meaning of it. It is presumed its proper definition is the science of Idiocy. And a very profound, abstruse, and mysterious science it is. You must descend deeper than the divers in the Dunciad to make any discoveries, and after all you will find no bottom. It is the bathos, the theory, the art, the skill of diving and sinking in government. It was taught in the school of folly; but alas! Franklin, Turgot, Rochefoucauld, and Condorcet, under Tom Paine, were the great masters of that academy!"

The chief political thinkers of the English speaking world, at least, have abjured ideology. In his *Logic*, John Stuart Mill declares, "I would willingly have . . . persevered to the end in the same abstinence which I have hitherto observed from ideological discussions." In America and Britain, long hostile toward what Burke called "the abstract metaphysician" in politics, the concept of ideology always has been unpopular—at least until quite recently.

About the middle of the nineteenth century, Karl Marx and his disciples considerably altered the meaning of "ideology." According to Marx—particularly in his *Poverty of Philosophy*—ideology is a cloak for class interests, an outwardly rational instrument of propaganda, a veil of argument produced to disguise and defend an established social order. In Marx's phrases, "The same men who establish social relations conformably with their material productivity, produce also the principles, the ideas, the categories, conformable with their social relations." Thus Marx attacked the social theories of his own time and of earlier ages as ideologies meant to maintain capitalism, feudalism, imperialism, and other systems.

Marxism itself, however, rapidly developed into an ideology, or dogmatic system of politics professing to found its structure upon a "reality" ascertained by sensory perception alone.

In the present century, Karl Mannheim distinguished between the "particular" and the "total" meanings of ideology. "The former," Mannheim wrote, "assumes that this or that interest is the cause of a given lie or deception. The latter presupposes that there is a correspondence between a given social situation and a given perspective, point of view, or apperception mass." In general, Mannheim takes the view that ideology is irrational, and in modern times merges with utopianism.

Since the Second World War, in serious discussions, "ideology" usually has meant a dogmatic political theory which endeavors to substitute secular doctrines and goals for religious doctrines and goals—what J. L. Talmon calls "political messianism." The ideologue promises social, rather than personal, salvation; and this salvation, occurring in time, is to be achieved through a radical transformation of social institutions, involving the destruction of existing law and institutions, and probably requiring violence against the present possessors of power. On principles allegedly rational and scientific, ideology is meant to reconstruct and perfect society and human nature.

It follows that the various ideologies which have arisen since the concluding years of the eighteenth century—Jacobinism, socialism, communism, anarchism, syndicalism, fascism, Naziism, and others —all are opposed by conservatism, which is founded upon the concept that politics is the art of the possible, and the concept that the old and tried is preferable to the new and untried. In the aphorism of H. Stuart Hughes, "Conservatism is the negation of ideology."

Yet, as I remarked earlier, today "ideology" frequently is used as if the term were synonymous with "political philosophy" or "political theory." Tacitly, this assumption suggests that any theoretical foundation for politics or sociology must be involved either with social utopianism (often fanatical) or with veiled class interests, or with both. This corruption of the term, produced in part by a vulgarizing of the concepts of Marx and Mannheim, makes sober examination of social first principles more difficult, particularly in a time when ideological passions and prejudices retain power throughout most of the world.

Real thinking is a painful process; and the ideologue resorts to the anaesthetic of social utopianism, escaping the tragedy and grandeur of true human existence by giving his adherence to a perfect dream-world of the future. Reality he stretches or chops away to conform to his dream-pattern of human nature and society. For the concepts of salvation and damnation, he substitutes abstractly virtuous "progressives" and abstractly vicious "reactionaries."

The twentieth-century ideologue, after the manner of Robespierre, thinks that his secular dogmas are sustained by the Goddess Reason; he prides himself inordinately upon being "scientific" and "rational"; and he is convinced that all opposition to his particular wave of the future is selfish obscurantism, when it is not direct vested interest. One may add that ever since the modern scholar began to call himself an "intellectual," he has tended to fall addict to the opiate of ideology; for the word "intellectual" itself, used as a noun of persons, implies an overweening confidence in Reason with a capital R, to the exclusion of faith, custom, consensus, humility, and sacred mystery.

The ideologue, in brief, is one of Orwell's new-style men "who think in slogans and talk in bullets." For the ideologue, humankind may be divided into two classes: the comrades of Progress, and the foes attached to reactionary interests. All human actions may be judged in terms of ideological motive, the ideologue is convinced. An African leader who wishes to settle for the practicable and to maintain amicable relationships with Europeans, for instance, must be a tool of "colonialists" or in the pay of a sinister capitalistic cartel; it is inconceivable that such a leader should be sincere in his course of action. On the other hand, a revolutionary, in Africa or elsewhere, always is right: just conceivably he may be over-zealous on occasion, but the purity of his motives is beyond question. The ideologues are Burckhardt's "terrible simplifiers." They reduce politics to catch-phrases; and because they will tolerate no stopping-place short of heaven upon earth, they deliver us up to men possessed by devils.

Ideology, Objectivity, and Scientism

"Ideology is existence in rebellion against God and man," Eric Voegelin writes. "It is the violation of the First and Tenth Commandments, if we want to use the language of Israelite order; it is the *nosos*, the disease of the spirit, if we want to use the language of Aeschylus and Plato. Philosophy is the love of being through love of divine Being as the source of its order." For a great while, Voegelin continues, ideology has held a mortgage upon science— that is, upon systematic thought.

But the ideologue does not think of himself as a simplifier or a sloganizer. He believes that he is objective and scientific, even dispassionate. An anti-collectivist ideologue (rather a rare breed, in this century), Miss Ayn Rand, even concocts a rigorous ideology called "Objectivism." All faithful followers of systematized ideologies believe themselves to be objective; their adversaries, to a man, are subjective.

So permit me to digress here concerning "objectivity," a word as much abused as "ideology." The modern devotee of objectivity prides himself upon being a realist, a man who perceives the world as it truly is, without being deluded by visions, personal interests, or irrational emotions. But no man is more unphilosophical than one who fancies that he is totally objective.

Objectivity means the property or state of being objective. The word now implies absorption in, or concern with, external objects, as opposed to "subjectivity," or concern with self and the interior life.

Yet historically considered, the terms "objectivity" and "objective" meant to medieval and Renaissance scholars quite the contrary of their twentieth-century connotations. From about 1300, when Duns Scotus defined the term, until late in the eighteenth century, "objectivity" and "objective" were generally understood to refer to things perceived or thought, intentional, or representative; while "subjective," during those centuries, meant things in their own form. This earlier usage is suggested by Bishop Berkeley

(1709): "Natural phenomena are only natural appearances. They are, therefore, such as we see and perceive them. Their real and objective nature are therefore the same."

For the past two centuries, however, "objectivity" has connoted "real" objects, as opposed to "subjectivity," or concern with the subject of cognition, the mind. In addition, "objectivity" has come to imply concentration upon external objects of thought—things or other persons—as against attention to one's self, one's own ways, one's own sensations. In this sense, the "objective" man is one who concerns himself with external facts or what he believes to be "objective" reality, rather than with his own emotions, personality, and thoughts. The rationalistic, nineteenth-century usage is exemplified by a remark of John Fiske: "The only healthful activity of the mind is an objective activity, in which there is as little brooding over self as is possible." Fiske is echoed by another enthusiast for this sort of objectivity, John Dewey, in *Democracy and Education:* "The idea of perfecting an 'inner' personality is a sure sign of social division. What is called 'inner' is simply that which does not connect with others—which is not capable of free and full communication. What is termed spiritual culture has usually been futile, with something rotten about it, just because it has been conceived as a thing which a man might have internally—and therefore exclusively."

In the "objective" paradise of Dewey and his disciples, as in Huxley's *Brave New World,* everybody belongs to everybody else— and not one's body merely, but one's mind, becomes public domain. Dewey was bent, though perhaps only half-consciously, on creating an impersonal society: that is, a society in which strong personalities would be eliminated. For there is no personality, really, except inner personality, subjective personality; if, then, its perfection is denounced as rotten, human beings are expected to efface personality altogether. They become "other-directed men." Lacking belief, loyalty, and self-reliance, dependent upon an unattainable perfect objectivity, they are moved only by fad and foible, and are blown about by every wind of doctrine. Objectivity of this sort terminates in pusillanimity.

Many twentieth-century writers and scholars praise "objectivity" as impartial and accurate; and they disparage "subjectivity" as sliding toward illusion, partisanship, and emotional disturbance. Thus most sociologists, say, profess devotion to objectivity; while poets, concerned with personal experience, are allegedly immersed in subjectivity. It remains most doubtful, nevertheless, whether any man may so wholly divest himself of prejudice, early opinions, and private experience as to manifest a thoroughgoing objectivity.

In the social studies, for instance, not a few doctors of philosophy call "objectivity" what really is their own ideology. Thus they praise to the skies a book that advocates a positivistic view of man and society; if that book espouses the cause of centralized planning, the omnicompetent state, and the progressive standardizing of all aspects of life, it is "objective"—that is, the book conforms to reality, or to what should be reality. If a book takes another tack, holding by religious conceptions of man and prescriptive opinions of the free and just society—why, the authors of so disagreeable a work must be nasty subjectivists.

For in an age of strong ideological tendencies, many people who profess devotion to "objectivity" may be self-deluding victims of a curiously inverted "subjectivity," indulging an intolerant zeal for "tolerance," a passionate attack on passion, a bigoted denunciation of bigotry. In such circumstances, "objectivity" is confounded with ideological preference, and the "objective" ideologue demands conformity to his notion of reality—or of what ought to be the state of society.

In actuality, "objective" and "subjective" approaches to true perception are not inimical, but rather co-ordinate, and even symbiotic. Accurate understanding of external objects, distinct from consideration of self, is the essential method of modern science; but the knowledge gained from personal experience and meditation is necessary for the classification and ordering of phenomena. Thus poetic insight, if "subjective," nevertheless broadens and deepens the vision; while scientific examination, if "objective," confirms or corrects the private judgment.

To resume, nevertheless the typical ideologue thinks of himself as perfectly objective. The core of his belief is that human nature and human society may be improved infinitely—nay, perfected—by the application of the techniques of the physical and biological sciences to the governance of men. Nearly all nineteenth- and twentieth-century radical movements drew their inspiration in considerable part from this positivistic assumption; Marxism is only one of the more systematic products of this view of life and thought.

For the convinced positivist-ideologue, traditional religion has been a nuisance and a curse, because it impedes the designs of the ideological planner. Science, with a Roman S, should supplant God. The religious teacher would give way to the "scientific" manager of the new society.

This rather vague claim that society ought to be regulated on "scientific" principles has held an appeal for some physical and biological scientists; and the less such scientists have known of humane letters, history, and political theory, the more enthusiastic they have tended to be for a new order which would sweep away all the errors and follies of mankind by a rational application of scientific theory and method. The high achievements of physical and biological science in the nineteenth century gave powerful reinforcement to the advocates of "scientism" in sociology and politics. Religion, moral tradition, and the complex of established political institutions were irrational and unscientific and subjective, it seemed; surely the scientists must show the preachers and politicians the way to a better world. H. G. Wells was the ablest vulgarizer of scientistic ideology.

But since the middle of the twentieth century, a good many intelligent people have been taking a second look at the claims of pure science, of the "science of society," and of religion. Fresh scientific speculation has called into question the soundness of many of the assumptions of the mechanistic physics and the Darwinian biology of the nineteenth century; while a revival of serious theology and a renewed interest in political theory have strengthened the positions of people who think that they were not born yesterday. The catastrophic social events of our century, moreover, have caused some of us to inquire whether there is not something fundamentally wrong with philosophical and scientific and sociological postulates which promise us the terrestrial paradise but promptly deliver us at the gates of a terrestrial hell. Fascism, Naziism, and communism all have claimed to be scientific.

A good representative of reformed scientific opinion is Dr. Edmund W. Sinnott, dean of the graduate school of Yale University, writing in *The Bulletin of the Atomic Scientists* (December, 1956). After presenting very fairly and even evangelically the case for scientific positivism and objectivity, he proceeds to demolish it. With Aristotle, Sinnott recognizes final causes: he is a teleologist.

What animates every organism, what constitutes its nature, is *purpose:* "If it be accepted, the idea of purpose, of intention, of the motive power of a goal or ideal rather than of an organic 'drive,' changes the orientation of our psychical lives." Man, he argues, is drawn toward a goal; and that goal often cannot be perceived or apprehended through the methods of exact science. "The closest contact with reality for many people is through this unexplained, mysterious urgency in life experienced in flashes of insight, for these carry with them a great weight of authority." So here an eminent professor of science has stood up for subjectivity, for the man of vision, for Carlyle in Leith Walk or Pascal murmuring "Fire, fire, fire!"

"The days of the evolutionary optimists are gone," Sinnott continues, "who believed that progress is inherent in the nature of things and that man is bound to grow better almost automatically. If we are to find a way out of our troubles, we must appeal not only to the rational attitudes and methods of the scientist but also to man's inner spiritual motivation. Love may turn out to be a more valuable resource than logic."

For Sinnott, science cannot supplant religion; both science and religion "have indispensable contributions to make to the great task of building a society in which men will not only be safe and wise and happy and loving but will gain the serene confidence that their lives are in harmony with the universe itself."

So scientism—the facile application of the teachings of natural science to the affairs of mankind—is on boggy ground today: social "objectivity," like social Darwinism, is parting company with much present scientific theory. The representative ideologue is unaware how very old-fangled he is becoming in his notion of what pure science teaches.

Yet it would be foolish optimism to mistake the speculations of some leading philosophers of science for the convictions of the whole body of teachers of science, researchers, and scientific technicians. A professed man of science still may remain as much an ideologue as any agent of the Chinese "Cultural Revolution."

At the convention in 1956 of the American Association for the Advancement of Science, for instance—meeting only a short time after Professor Sinnott wrote—there still were exhibited (together with more encouraging opinions) certain depressing examples of the influence which scientistic ideology still exerts upon American society. Consider a research-project in "intellectual potential" described to the Association by its authors, an associate professor of psychiatry and an associate professor of pediatrics at Ohio State University.

The purpose of this research-project was to discover whether heredity determines individual intelligence to any marked degree. These two professors studied the behavior of a thousand infants in Baltimore, all about forty weeks old, excluding babies with damaged brains from consideration in their general conclusions. Upon the "developmental score" employed in this study, ninety per cent of the infants scored between 90 and 120, with 100 as the norm. Race, economic status, and education of parents seemed to have no discernible effect upon the scores of particular babies. Therefore, the professors announced, one baby seems to be as intelligent as another; and undeniable variation of children at a later age must be "wholly a result of education and environment."

"Intelligence," an educationist said once, "is simply what our tests test." This particular research-project appears to me a tolerable example of an ideological mortgage upon the work of science. Leaving aside certain logical and statistical fallacies involved in this project, still the range between 90 and 120 indicates a very considerable difference in infant minds. But the principal foolishness of such a survey is its claim to measure human intelligence at a stage when the human creatures concerned could not yet be called rational human beings. One might as well try to determine the swiftness of a fawn by examining the creature in embryo, as to try to determine the power of the human intellect by observing the behavior of a baby a few months old. Man's rationality is made possible by his mastery of words and his employment of his hands. A little baby knows no words, and therefore no general concepts; he can use his hands to little purpose, and therefore is not yet even a tool-using animal. Of course all small babies seem much the same in intelligence; for none of them has, at that stage, much intelligence distinctively human; they are almost identical in their poverty. If a thousand forty-weeks-old baboons or chimpanzees had been observed and tested alongside the human infants, doubtless the apes would have come out much better on the development-score, for their nature matures much more rapidly than does the human.

Therefore, one supposes, we ought to conclude that the differences between baboon baby and human baby are matters of education and environment, and baboons should be entitled to the privileges and immunities of the United Nations' Universal Declaration of Human Rights.

This latter-day *tabula rasa* doctrine of the psychiatrist and the teacher of pediatrics, I suspect—though I do not know the professors in question—is ideologically inspired. It is "democratic," in the Jacobin meaning of that word. All people *ought* to be equal, the egalitarian ideologue commences; but if persons are unequal in intelligence from a very early age, then it may be difficult to establish among them equality of condition; so the "scientific" dogma must be made to fit the ideological dogma, and Jonathan Edwards and Sam Jukes will be demonstrated, by "development-scores," to be naturally as much alike as two peas in a pod. Intelligence is what our tests test; and if tests reveal disconcerting individual differences —why, back to your development-scores, men. Having arrived at a tentative conclusion about certain infants by scientifically dubious means, then the ideologue hastily tacks on to his structure grand generalizations, quite unsupported even by his own evidence, concerning the native intelligence of adults. This is scientism in its worst sense: science enslaved by ideological prejudice.

In genetics, as in other sciences, the ideologue recoils from his own conclusions only when the results indubitably are ruinous—as in the notorious affair, in Soviet Russia, of Lysenko's theories about corn, faithful to Marxism but false to nature and productive of monstrous crop-failures. The ideologue, I am saying, is not genuinely objective and not genuinely scientific. In essence, ideology is a passionate endeavor to overthrow the spiritual and moral order, as well as the social order; and scientific doctrine is no better than a tool for the ideologue. Raymond Aron makes this point:

"Communism developed from an economic and political doctrine at a time when the spiritual vitality and the authority of the Churches was in decline. Passions which in other times might have expressed themselves in strictly religious beliefs were channelled into political action. Socialism appeared not so much a technique applicable to the management of enterprises or to the functioning of the economy, as a means of curing once and for all the age-old misery of mankind.

"The ideologies of the Right and of the Left, Fascism as well as Communism, are inspired by the modern philosophy of immanence. They are atheist, even when they do not deny the existence of God, to the extent that they conceive the human world without reference to the transcendental."

Ideology is intellectual servitude. And emancipation from ideology can be achieved only by belief in an enduring order of which the sanction, and the end, are more than objective, more than scientistic, more than human, and more than natural.

Ideology and American Society

The American soil is not well prepared for pure ideology. Half a century ago, Santayana wrote that "it will take some hammering to drive a coddling socialism into America." The hammering of ideology has been heard since then, but political religion has not yet triumphed. Though, as Aron knows, the United States has its political illusions, these are not precisely identical with the illusions of the French intellectual of the Left:

"The 'American way of life' is the negation of what the European intellectual means by the word ideology," Aron remarks. "Americanism does not formulate itself as a system of concepts or propositions; it knows nothing of the 'collective savior,' the end of history, the determining cause of historical 'becoming,' or the dogmatic negation of religion; it combines respect for the constitution, homage for individual initiative, a humanitarianism inspired by strong but vague beliefs which are fairly indifferent to the rivalries between the churches (only Catholic 'totalitarianism' is considered disquieting), the worship of science and efficiency. It does not involve any detailed orthodoxy or official doctrine. It is learned at school, and society enforces it. Conformism if you like, but a conformism which is rarely felt to be tyrannical, since it does not forbid free discussion in matters of religion, economics, or politics."

Yet a hankering after ideology has existed since early times in America, though never well satisfied; and at moments, during the past forty or fifty years, it seemed as if ideology were about to capture the American mind. That ideology, if it had come to exercise an hegemony over American thought, would have borne the name of Liberalism. Communism, though it contrived to entrench itself in some high places among American intellectuals, never attracted so great a share of them as went over to Marxism in France or Germany or Italy or even Britain; while Fascism took no root here at all.

Something called Liberalism, nevertheless, became very nearly a secular orthodoxy among American writers and (more especially) American professors. No one was quite sure what Liberalism amounted to—which kept it from becoming a full-grown ideology. To some, Liberalism meant anti-religious opinions; to others, socialism, or a managed economy; to a different set, absolute liberty of private conduct, untrammeled by law or tradition; to a number, perpetual doubt for the sake of doubting; to one lot, old-fangled Benthamism.

This Liberal secular orthodoxy is decaying now, to the alarm of its principal champions, some of whom defend it with the zeal of genuine ideologues, although they are not quite sure just what they are defending. Nowadays these champions, confronted with the revival of conservative ideas, alternate between the argument that conservatism is getting nowhere at all, and the contention that conservatism is so dreadfully powerful as to drive persecuted liberals into holes and corners.

As a matter of fact, the precepts of Liberalism still dominate a great many American writers and professors, who sometimes are intolerant in the name of liberal toleration; but the odds are that this Liberal orthodoxy cannot now harden into a true ideology. The fantastics of the New Left dearly would love to embrace a rigorous ideology; but they fall out so much among themselves, and within themselves, that no body of secular dogmas takes form.

America needs nothing less than it needs ideology. Not abstractions, but prudence, prescription, custom, tradition, and constitution have governed the American people. We have been saved from ideology by political tradition. We still subscribe, however confusedly, to the norms of politics; we still cherish the permanent things.

For nearly two centuries, the outward forms of government in this nation have altered little. Although during the past four decades, and particularly during the past ten years, the actual functioning of our political system has changed rapidly, still the facade of the political edifice looks much as it used to. Within, nevertheless, the house is being transformed—even if few desire a radical transformation. No system of laws and institutions is immutable. Can the American Republic direct such change into actions which will reconcile with our historical experience and our prescriptive institutions that spirit of the age which now shakes the house?

Change, as Burke said, is the means of our preservation: as the human body exhausts old tissues and takes on new, so must any vigorous society. Yet rash and mindless change, striking to the heart of society, may destroy the continuity which invigorates a nation. The character of change in America probably will be determined, for good or ill, within the next few years.

Whatever our civil discontents at present, we stand in little peril of a political revolution which would destroy our national foundations. The American people remain, in some ways, the most conservative in the world—even though their conservatism is not so much the product of reflection as it is of habit, custom, material interests, and attachment to certain documents, most notably the Declaration of Independence and the Constitution of the United States. Our difficulty, indeed, is not just now the clutch of ideology, but rather complacency—the smug general assumption that the civil social order, in essence, always will be for our sons what it was for our fathers.

"With conservative populations," Brooks Adams wrote, "slaughter is nature's remedy." He referred to a complacent democratic conservatism of the crowd. If American order, justice, and freedom are to endure, some of us must look into the first principles of politics and apply the wisdom of our ancestors to the troubles of our time. To preserve all the benefits of American society—which may be lost not through revolution, but perhaps in a fit of absence of mind—we must turn political philosophers, as did our ancestors in the last quarter of the eighteenth century.

Like the English, the Americans usually have been reluctant to embark upon abstract political speculation. Except for the period just before, during, and after the Revolution, and—to a lesser extent —the years before and immediately after the Civil War, we have produced little political philosophy; we have trusted, instead, to constitution, custom, convention, consensus, and the wisdom of the species.

Indeed, the Declaration and the Constitution, though drawn up by men of philosophical knowledge and power, are not in themselves manuals of political philosophy. The Declaration of 1776 is simply a declaration—and a highly successful piece of immediate political propaganda; such philosophical concepts as find expression therein are so mistily expressed as to mean all things to all men, then and now. The Constitution is not a tract at all, but a practical instrument of government, molded in part by necessary practical compromises.

We will not repudiate the Declaration, nor much alter the formal Constitution. Yet no society can be bound by parchment. With vertiginous speed, the character of American society is being altered. Can a people whose modes of living, economy, and diversions differ radically from those of the eighteenth century continue to live in harmony and prosperity under a political system developed in very different circumstances? Can a people of whom the immense majority now dwell in megalopolis, for instance, govern themselves on the old principles of American territorial democracy?

For my part, I do not think that we could construct a brand-new constitution better calculated to reconcile the claims of order and the claims of freedom than does our old Constitution—whatever its anomalies and difficulties today. If that is true, then we will do well to seek means for reinvigorating the Constitution and making sure it deals adequately with the conditions of the twentieth century; otherwise it may be altered out of recognition by an extravagant "judicial reinterpretation," unsupported either by precedent or by public consensus—or, in the long run, it may be discarded altogether by an impatient Executive Force, Congress, and people.

And we must remind ourselves that beneath any formal constitution—even beneath our Constitution, the most enduringly successful of such formal documents—lies an unwritten constitution much more difficult to define, but really more powerful: the body of institutions, customs, manners, conventions, and voluntary associations which may not even be mentioned in the formal constitution, but which nevertheless form the fabric of social reality and sustain the formal constitution.

So the examination of our present discontents cannot be confined to an exercise in formal constitutional law. To discuss the future of American politics, we must confess that, vastly important though they are, the Declaration and the Constitution do not constitute the be-all and end-all of political wisdom; and that, when the file affords no precedent, we must turn from the legal brief to political philosophy.

Recourse to political first principles is attended by risks. Scarcely anything could be more ruinous than to turn the American people into a set of half-schooled coffee-house philosophers, ideologues bent upon gaining Utopia instanter, terrible simplifiers in politics. Yet in the exigencies of our decade, a people cannot govern themselves wholly by the decisions and the rhetoric of 1776 and 1787. The intellectual and political leaders of our age have the duty of guiding public opinion into prudent consideration of the means for harmonizing our prescriptive politics with modern conditions that require some tolerable action. I am saying that there exists real danger of our drifting mindlessly into the mass-age, unaware that order and justice and freedom are fragile; and that today, as much as in 1776 or 1787, we need to discuss questions concerning the vitality of the good civil social order.

Ever since the Civil War, political thought has languished in the United States. For important political theory almost always is developed out of a time of troubles, when thinking men, forced to examine their first principles, seek means to avert the imminent collapse of order, so as to restore some measure of justice and security to a wounded society. The political writings of Plato and Aristotle came out of such an age. So did Cicero's works, and Dante's, and Hobbes's, and Machiavelli's, and Hooker's, and Locke's, and Burke's, and Marx's. The nature of the confusion which provokes the exposition of political theory may be the inadequacy of an old order, morally and administratively, as it was in the society of Calvin and of Rousseau; or the confusion may be the consequence of a new order's search for sanction, as it was in the society of Bodin or of Bentham. Doubt and violence are the parents of social speculation. Prescription, legal precedent, and muddling through suffice for ages or nations that experience no serious threat to things established.

Thus the political ideas of Adams, Hamilton, Madison, and

Jefferson, though rooted in English and colonial experience and mightily influenced by the legacy of English political philosophy, took form as prudent endeavors to restore order and justice to a commonwealth distressed by revolution. Thus the ideas of John Randolph and Calhoun were expressed as a defense of established institutions in the Old South. Once the triumph of the Union, however, had put an end to the debate between North and South, and once the swelling prosperity of the United States after the Civil War combined with the nation's comparative isolation to make any foreign menace trifling, American political speculation sank to a lower level.

No political philosopher of remarkable stature appeared during the closing third of the nineteenth century, and the bulk of what passed for political thought in this country was simply the reflection of various English and German liberal ideas, adapted to the American climate of opinion. There seemed to be no need for reference to first principles; Things were in the saddle, and most men were content to let Things ride mankind. Warning voices like those of Henry and Brooks Adams were rather despairing protests than expressions of political philosophy. As the First World War approached, and as the economic and moral problems of the post-war era became pressing, ideas were granted some small hearing, it is true, so that Irving Babbitt and Paul Elmer More and George Santayana asked the right questions. Yet Things galloped on; the New Deal, fortunately perhaps, was the expression of vague humanitarian aspirations and positive grievances, not of any coherent "liberal" or "radical" system of thought. Nor was America's participation in the Second World War governed by any body of general ideas: caused by the combination of moral indignation with fear of Germany and Japan, American intervention stood bewildered for want of first principle when the problems of the peace had to be confronted.

The genius of American politics, as Daniel Boorstin suggests, consists in an innocence of abstract doctrine and theoretic dogma; and this is quite as true of the genius of English politics. Yet possibly the immunity of these nations from the curse of ideology has resulted not so much from a deliberate contempt for theory, as from two peculiar advantages that today are much diminished: first, a comparative physical isolation from other powers that made possible the postponement of grave decisions; second, an underlying set of moral and political assumptions, common to nearly everyone in these societies, which were the products of a venerable historic experience, and which served the purpose that political dogmas serve in nations less governed by general prejudice, prescription, and custom.

Yet a time may come in the history of nations when the previous security against foreign intervention is destroyed, and when tradition and established usage are so weakened that they cannot stand unbuttressed against the assaults of ideology. Such an era is America's near the close of these 'Sixties. The dissolution of America's old political and military isolation requires no comment; we survived by a single generation the end of Britain's comparative isolation. The breaking of the cake of custom is the subject of many books, though all its intricacies have not yet been explored. It must suffice to say here that with the triumph of modern technology, the ascendancy of general literacy and secularized schooling, the extreme mobility and fluidity of twentieth-century American society, the disappearance of many elements of authority and class, and the diffusion of positivistic ideas—why, tradition and custom in the United States, though by no means effaced, have lost much of their old power. We live, then, in an insecure society, doubtful of its future, an island of comparative but temporary sanctuary in a sea of revolution; and neither the old isolation nor the old received opinions of the mass of men seem calculated to hold out unassisted against the physical force of revolutionary powers and the moral innovations of modern ideologies. This is just such a time as has required and produced, repeatedly in the course of history, a re-examination of first principles and a considered political philosophy.

So the following chapters have to do principally with attempts to form a political philosophy, as opposed to ideology: the renewed search for the norms of politics, of order and justice and freedom, in our rough age. Some of these attempts are doomed to failure; but others may redeem us, as a people, from the Center of Indifference.

❋ ❋

II. LIBERAL FOREBODINGS

Recoiling from Ideology

Three vaguely-delimited bodies of political opinion existed in the
United States when, a few years ago, thinking men began to perceive the necessity for some return to principle, as against mere
muddling through: conservatism, liberalism, and radicalism. All
three of these bodies of opinion were deficient in true political
theory.

American radicalism may be disposed of briefly. This had come
to mean the Marxist ideology, to which real speculative philosophy
is anathema; the other variants of American radicalism, except for
decayed remnants, had withered away or had been merged in
American liberalism. The dread Russian and Chinese examples of
triumphant Marxism, and the nationalist antagonism between the
United States and those powers, have so put down this radicalism in
America—except for the futile and unpopular gestures of the New
Left—that its claims to represent any substantial part of American
opinion need not be considered seriously. We are left with conservatism and liberalism; and neither of these categories of political
belief has admitted of any clear adherence to principles until quite
recently. For that matter, the large majority of American conservatives and liberals still remain ignorant of the history and the probable future of their own body of opinion.

By the end of the 1940's, conservatism in the United States almost had lost the power of language. Often men of conservative prejudices expressed themselves apologetically in the phrases of nineteenth-century liberals; sometimes they even echoed the slogans of old-fangled anarchism. The American conservative interest was composed of various elements, some overlapping: natural conservatives, believing, with Falkland, "when it is not necessary to change, it is necessary not to change"; constitutional conservatives, attached to the inherited forms of American government; economic conservatives, intent upon preserving private property and a free economy; rural conservatives, opposed to the urbanization and consolidation of modern life; "liberal" conservatives, fearing for the survival of personal freedom. Most of these people expressed themselves badly, and few were able to describe any coherent moral or philosophical basis for their beliefs. Though frequently their impulses and prejudices were genuinely conservative in the historic sense of that term, nevertheless they would endeavor to defend themselves by the arguments of their old adversaries—Bentham, for instance, and John Stuart Mill, and Herbert Spencer.

American liberalism failed to crush this conservative rear guard simply because, as a body of belief, liberalism was in no more coherent state. Originally dedicated to emancipation of the individual from all sorts of restraints and obligations, by the 'Forties American liberalism had come to mean, for the most part, an amorphous feeling that society ought to be improved through the agency of centralized government. The liberty which it now sought was "freedom from the consequences of freedom"; and, in Santayana's phrase, the New Liberal desired to relax no bonds except the marriage tie. This liberalism had become a quasi-ideology; from the beginning, indeed, strong ideological tendencies had lurked in its Benthamite foundations—swearing by the god-terms Progress and Equality. It was heavily influenced by the negation of philosophy, pragmatism, and sought futilely to identify itself with the Popular Will. Its sources of support were even more disparate than those of American conservatism—ranging from doctrinaire zealots for emancipation upon the model of Lamartine, to doctrinaire Marxists who hesitated, for all that, to subscribe to Stalinism.

When the truth about Soviet Russia and other collectivistic dominations became undeniable, the liberal camp tended to break up into factions, some moving in a conservative direction, some expressing contrition for their past errors but altering little their practical politics, and some simply repeating, as a ritual, their old slogans, as if by dint of repetition they could give them fresh life. Many spoke vaguely of effecting some compromise between capitalism and socialism, or of reconciling Christianity and pragmatism. It was discouragingly clear that these liberals possessed even less understanding of political principle, of standards, than did the conservatives.

Yet this ignorance of political norms, this disregard of theory among both conservatives and liberals—the forces cf permanence and of change—now seems to be diminishing somewhat. There are signs that, without embracing the fanatic dogmas of ideology, the conservative and liberal bodies of opinion in America are commencing to think things through. I do not mean that they are about to coalesce. Any healthy society requires an enduring contest between its permanence and its progression. We cannot live without continuity, and we cannot live without prudent change. But a conservatism of reflection and a liberalism of reflection, either aware of its own first principles, may serve separately to arrest the decay of our civilization and to make common cause against Giant Ideology, which now threatens to put an end to philosophy and justice throughout the world. The better minds of both bodies of opinion, here in America, are restoring to our consciousness the real meaning of both conservatism and liberalism.

As yet, this return to principle may be discerned only dimly among men of practical partisan politics: the day of the philosopher-statesman has passed, though it may return. The signs of a resurgence of principle are to be found, instead, in the work of certain scholars. And their ideas already are making their influence felt upon the universities, governmental bureaus, the serious journals, and even the popular press.

Already I have mentioned some conservatives of this bent—if by "conservative" we mean a champion of the permanent things; and I shall mention others in later chapters. Just now, however, I hope to describe succinctly the ideas of three liberal writers—if by "liberal" we mean advocates of reasoned change—who are not ideologues: Richard Hofstadter, Louis Hartz, and David Riesman. These scholars may be described as "revisionist" or "prudential" liberals, as opposed to the "ritualistic" liberals trounced by Sidney Hook and the "disintegrated" liberals described by Gordon Chalmers. Professors Hofstadter, Hartz, and Riesman are endeavoring to find new avenues for the liberal impulse, and to emancipate liberalism from the opiate of ideology.

Transcending Liberal Traditions

In most of the world, the voices that speak for tradition are dinned under by more drums than those which beat to drown the last words of Charles I. Yet I think that tradition, like King Charles on the fatal scaffold, will be heard nevertheless, in the age which is dawning. "Nay, but I shall be heard, and that to the end of time."

Still, too much of what is said about tradition in America nowadays is cant or hypocrisy—identification of one's pet ideology or one's private interests with "tradition," or else employment of the word "tradition" to cloak some design for undoing the social order. Therefore it is refreshing to read books that treat of tradition with candor, whatever opinions their authors may have of tradition's worth. Louis Hartz and Richard Hofstadter find that the American tradition is liberal—but that it is insufficient nowadays. They seek something more practical.

I refer to Mr. Hartz's book *The Liberal Tradition in America,* and to Mr. Hofstadter's *The American Political Tradition and the Men Who Made It,* and to his *The Age of Reform.* These writers possess some knowledge of what the political traditions of this country have been, and they believe that those traditions now are obsolete.

Although Professor Hartz retains affection for some elements in those traditions, he tells us that we must transcend them:

"Instead of recapturing our past, we have got to transcend it," Hartz writes. "As for a child who is leaving adolescence, there is no going home again for America. . . . [This challenge] holds out the hope of an inward enrichment of culture and perspective, a 'coming of age,' to use the term of the twenties again, which in its own right is well worth fighting for. What is at stake is nothing less than a new level of consciousness, a transcending of irrational Lockianism, in which an understanding of self and an understanding of others go hand in hand."

If this passage from *The Liberal Tradition in America* seems obscure, I must remark that it is no easier to apprehend in its context; as Dr. Daniel Boorstin says of this book, it is itself an illustration of what ails American liberalism today—abstract, bookish in the bad sense, and insulated against reality. Still, it retains the merit of candor.

Mr. Hofstadter, a better writer and more original thinker, knows more about our political tradition than does Mr. Hartz, and likes it less. The men who made that tradition, according to Hofstadter— the Founding Fathers, Jefferson, Jackson, Calhoun, Lincoln, Phillips, Bryan, Theodore Roosevelt, Wilson, Hoover, F.D.R., and the rest—all were somehow unsatisfactory, captive in some degree to Hartz's "irrational Lockianism."

For Hartz and Hofstadter, tradition is a devil-term: it is something you try to transcend as fast as you can, tugging dull conservatives along behind you. The masters of politics during the past two or three centuries were myopic men, even at their most liberal; from the height of our modern realism we may condescend to smile at their limitations; but we ought to throw off the hand of this dead ancestry and march away in some rational new direction, with our modern pragmatic rationality for guide and governor. An aside of Hofstadter's, in the introduction to his *American Political Tradition,* sufficiently summarizes this view of the past and future of American politics:

"Although it has been said repeatedly that we need a new conception of the world to replace the ideology of self-help, free enterprise, competition, and beneficent cupidity upon which Americans have been nourished since the foundation of the Republic, no new conceptions of comparable strength have taken root and no statesman with a great mass following has arisen to propound them. Bereft of a coherent and plausible body of belief—for the New Deal, if it did little more, went far to undermine old ways of thought—Americans have become more receptive than ever to dynamic personal leadership as a substitute. This is part of the secret of Roosevelt's popularity, and, since his death, of the rudderless and demoralized state of American liberalism."

For Hofstadter, the duty of the statesman is to ride on the crest of the mounting wave of events, furthering "existing tendencies toward organization," though never judging of the moral effects of the "industrial discipline" and "a managerial and bureaucratic outlook" which Mr. Hofstadter notes and smiles upon as the marks of the new America. The future, *somehow,* must be better than the past, if only we apply our rationality toward the hastening of change; in any event, we do not make our world, but merely apologize for it—so Hofstadter thinks. (Here Hofstadter and Hartz fall out, Hartz agreeing with F. S. C. Northrop that history is made by the premises which men hold, but Hofstadter embracing a genteel determinism.)

Hofstadter's and Hartz's version of the history of American politics is that all our leaders labored under a Lockian or "conservative and Manchesterian" orthodoxy, whether they were called conservatives or liberals; we have little now to learn from the achievements of these leaders, though we may profit from a study of their deficiencies.

In justice, I add that both these writers make valuable commen's upon our present difficulties and discontents, reminding us of how old principles, decayed into ideology, can defeat the very end they were intended to attain. Hofstadter and Hartz raise important questions. I am concerned just now, however, with whether these scholars give us an accurate description of American political traditions, and whether they do justice to the role that tradition ought to have in any dramatic rescue of modern society from its difficulties.

Is "Lockianism," or "the ideology of self-help, free enterprise, competition, and beneficent cupidity," the essence of our political tradition? I think not. I agree rather with Daniel Boorstin, who says that the genius of American politics consists in our habit of refraining from abstract doctrine and theoretic dogma; as a people, we have not been doctrinaires, neither bookish adulators of Locke nor speculative Benthamites.

Our principles of self-help, free enterprise, competition, and "beneficent cupidity," though encrusted with a veneer of nineteenth-century dialectic, are of origins much older than the political economy of Manchester or even the Treatises of Locke. Nor are these principles really at the root of the American political tradition. Rather, our political tradition is rooted in two bodies of belief and custom: first, the Christian religion; second, the English and colonial historic experience in politics, with its fruits of representative institutions, local government, private rights, and the supremacy of law.

We have been governed by a genuine tradition—that is, a body of beliefs passed on from generation to generation, as prescriptions, customs—and not by ideology, or rigid and abstract political dogma. As Boorstin writes, the American Revolution was a revolution without dogma; and the whole course of our subsequent political history has taken the Revolution for its model. Clinton Rossiter, in his *Seedtime of the Republic,* puts this clearly: "What is especially amazing about modern American political thought is not that it continues to employ the idiom and exhibit the mood of the Revolution, but that both idiom and mood seem adequate to deal with many present-day problems."

Now this political tradition really is neither Hartz's "irrational Lockianism" nor Hofstadter's Manchesterian ideology. This tradition seems healthy; and its principal ingredients are the Judeo-Christian faith and that legacy of institutions which we all know. It is altogether possible that if we endeavor to "transcend" this tradition, by substituting for our belief and practice some utilitarian or pragmatic system of ethics, and some neat scheme of central administration, then we may not succeed at all in meeting the difficulties of modern society. We may succeed only in breaking that continuity of custom and institution upon which rests any decent social order. Were our political tradition merely the liberal doctrine of yesteryear which Hofstadter and Hartz describe, I would agree with them that it ought to be transcended. But it is more.

"In a corporate and consolidated society demanding international responsibility, cohesion, centralization, and planning," Hofstadter writes, "the traditional ground is shifting under our feet." So it may be; but this does not demonstrate that thoroughgoing centralization and planning are required. Who "demands" such grandiose innovations? I dislike this passive voice. Are we, as the Greeks thought they were, subject utterly to Fate and Fortune? If the traditional ground is shifting under our feet, possibly our real need may be to renew our understanding of our traditions, and to set to work dealing with our present discontents in the light of that knowledge.

Here I have space only to suggest the deficiencies of Hofstadter's and Hartz's analyses of those elements which lie at the heart of our tradition—religious faith and the "giveness" of our political institutions. As for the first, both authors pay merely the briefest respects to our Christian patrimony, which underlies all our political postulates; and much of what they do say is erroneous or misleading.

Hartz, it is true, does remember that the founders of the American Republic "refused to join in the great Enlightenment enterprise of shattering the Christian concept of sin." But he attaches an inordinate importance to the doctrines of Locke, as if he thought that the signers of the Declaration and the framers of the Constitution were *philosophes,* taking their first principles from philosophical treatises. Much of what he calls "Lockian" is infinitely older than Locke: it is bound up with those assumptions concerning human dignity, personality, conscience, charity, and duty which are included in Christian ethics.

Nor would it be difficult to demonstrate that the King James Version and the Book of Common Prayer, rather than Locke's Second Treatise, gave these American minds their cast. If one must turn to philosophers, probably Richard Hooker, directly or indirectly, had more to do with the fundamental opinions of the Founding Fathers than did Locke; certainly Blackstone's direct influence was greater than Locke's. Americans have no difficulty in agreeing with Burke for the reason that they, like Burke, have formed their opinions of human nature and society on the authority of Christian tradition.

Some of Hofstadter's infrequent comments on religion are more misleading than Hartz's. Take this: "The men who drew up the Constitution in Philadelphia during the summer of 1787 had a vivid Calvinistic sense of human evil and believed with Hobbes that men are selfish and contentious." Well! In point of fact, the majority of the framers of the Constitution were not Calvinists, but Anglicans; and almost to a man they were condemners of Hobbes, if they had read him at all. The American statesman with perhaps the most "realistic" view of human nature (Hofstadter's phrase), John Adams, detested the works of Hobbes. As a political theorist, Hobbes is read by modern professors of politics; he never has had much influence on anyone else, except upon some of the nineteenth-century English Philosophical Radicals and Utilitarian writers on jurisprudence. Hofstadter does, indeed, recognize that religious belief exerted influence upon the formation of our political institutions; but a recognition so confused does little to help us understand the American political tradition.

Religious and ethical premises aside, the American political tradition, in essence, has not consisted in "Lockian" abstractions about society, nor in certain Manchesterian secular dogmas. It is embodied, instead, (as Carl Friedrich suggests) in "certain written documents available for inspection and detailed consideration." It takes form in our prescriptive system of government; it is a juridical tradition, sheltered by regular forms of appeal to the courts. It subsists in our township and county political organizations, our state governments, our federal government, our respect for political checks and balances, our division of powers, our principle of a government "of laws, not of men," our protections for minorities, our practice of filtering democracy through a variety of representative bodies. It lives in our political parties and in our jealous regard for private and local rights.

Positive law, or written constitutions, may have given those social forms their guarantee; but the institutions and beliefs I mention have taken on the force of tradition, and now are sustained by popular respect and habit, not by any effectual administrative compulsion, ordinarily. Attacks upon these customs and forms arouse all the dread and indignation which generally are the symptoms of genuine popular attachment to traditions. The "ideology of self-help, free enterprise, competition, and beneficent cupidity" of which Hofstadter writes—so far as that "ideology" is not simply a part of Western civilization—is superficial, compared with the strength of this real tradition of the American Republic.

Hofstadter is one of a number of scholars who are fond of arguing that the character of our traditions is being altered profoundly —or already has been altered—by changes in the racial and cultural character of the American population, together with complex fluctuations in the status of social groups. The immigrants from central and southern Europe, it is argued often, will not be bound by the old American political tradition. Yet the evidence is strong, to the contrary, that most immigrants and their children and grandchildren are even more strongly attached to those political traditions than are Americans of "native" stocks. For they have to ac-

quaint themselves with the traditional documents to which Friedrich refers, in applying for citizenship; or, conscious of their new-
ness in America, members of these ethnic groups often feel a compulsion to understand and support American establishments.

Whether one wishes to preserve a tradition or to transcend it, he
needs first to make sure of what that tradition is, and of what it has
done to nurture a nation's life. Nations do not endure without traditions. Some traditions may grow obsolete; all require respectful
scrutiny, now and then, in the light of the age, lest they ossify.
Traditions do take on new meanings with the growing experience of
a people. And simply to appeal to the wisdom of the species, to
tradition, will not of itself provide solutions to all problems. The
endeavor of the intelligent believer in tradition is so to blend ancient usage with necessary amendment that society never is wholly
old and never wholly new. He believes that tradition is a storehouse
of wisdom; as Dwight Macdonald says, tradition nourishes. Sudden
parting from tradition, however abstractly rational, may sweep
away much that is good together with a little that is bad.

Now I do not think that Hartz and Hofstadter, for all their learning, really apprehend the significance of the American political tradition; nor do they attach sufficient importance to the civilizing
influence of tradition in general. In "transcending" our traditions,
derived from religious faith and from the civil social experience of
British and American history, they soon would come under the
necessity of recognizing or establishing some alternative set of principles. But the alternative to tradition is ideology; and Hartz and
Hofstadter are nearly as uneasy with ideology as they are with
tradition. So they offer us nothing distinct.

The virtues and shortcomings of the approach of these revisionist liberals may be discerned more clearly by an examination of
their remarks on Woodrow Wilson, whom they have determined to
cast out of the liberal pantheon. For that matter, the drift of American liberalism since Wilson's time has considerable relevance to
our larger question of the renewed search for political principle.

Woodrow Wilson and the Antagonist World

Few great names have gone out of favor more rapidly than that of Wilson. The reason is not far to seek. Wilson's fervent admirers, in the 'Twenties and 'Thirties, were progressives and liberals; they it was who enshrined him in that curious pantheon honoring Jefferson, Jackson, Wilson, and Franklin Roosevelt as the deities of American liberalism. But now the liberals have discovered that Wilson never really was one of their number; he had feet of clay; he was a natural conservative. And therefore Wilson has been cast into the outer darkness.

It seems surprising, looking back at Wilson and his era, how the liberals ever blundered into this embarrassing error. For Wilson openly proclaimed himself a disciple of redoubtable American and English conservative thinkers; the aim of his practical politics was to preserve traditional America and, if possible, to restore some things that were passing out of American society. Whenever he did adopt a policy unmistakably liberal, it was more or less against his will, and out of force of circumstance: the income tax, for instance, was thrust upon him—as upon Gladstone—by financial exigencies, but he abhorred it.

Accident has much to do with careers. Wilson the natural conservative became almost by chance the presidential candidate of the liberals, and found himself head of a party which barely knew him. Politicians, even the best of them, to some extent must speak the language of their followers: Wilson did so, but more from the exigencies of the situation than from any voluntary commitment. Interesting parallels have been drawn between Wilson and Gladstone —who, of course, at one time was the leading light of Toryism, but through rivalry with Disraeli found himself at the head of Liberalism.

Yet the superficial conjunction of Wilson with Progressivism deceived liberals in the years following Wilson's death; they took the natural and philosophical conservative for the liberal ideologue, endowing the sober Princeton professor with their own aspirations. Only now are they undeceived, when the real distinctions between conservative and liberal thought have become clearer than at any time since the Civil War. And it should be remarked, in justice to Wilson's liberal admirers and critics, that Wilson's language and action, during the War and the making of the Peace, provided some excuse for this confusion. It is difficult for a public man to escape becoming what his associates insist he is. Moreover, the climate of liberal opinion was powerful then; in office, Wilson experienced the seductions of that liberal climate of opinion—as did John F. Kennedy, much later—and to some extent abandoned his conservative principles for liberal abstractions.

When I was a schoolboy, we were told to write essays on how President Wilson would have made this sad old world into a terrestrial paradise, if only he had not been hampered (transiently, we were to trust) by a few Wicked Men in France and Massachusetts and Idaho. In all innocence, I wrote an essay about Wilson which deviated from this view, and was reproved by the teacher. That attitude of unquestioning admiration has passed now. One cannot read without a smile such sentences as this of Harold B. Howland (in his *Theodore Roosevelt and his Times,* published in 1921) concerning the presidential contest of 1912: "One thing was clear from the beginning: the day of conservatism and reaction was over; the people of the United States had definitely crossed their Rubicon and had committed themselves to spiritual and moral progress." Whatever sort of progress we have experienced since 1912, and no matter how many Rubicons we have crossed, we have not known Wilson's New Freedom, and it is difficult to discern the marks of our predicted spiritual and moral elevation.

Surely Wilson, despite the phrase "The New Freedom," by 1912 had shown few signs of being anything but a prudent conservative reformer, desirous of keeping America what she had been. He put no faith in schemes for altering profoundly the political and economic structure. At a time when there was talk of modelling the federal administration after the British Parliament, with cabinet responsibility and Congress put in the role of a body of critics, Wilson was prompt to declare the imprudence and impossibility of any such importation of parliamentary institutions grown up from roots quite different from those of American federalism. This is but an example; in many other matters, by 1912, Wilson had written and acted as a reflecting conservative.

Nowadays, adulation of Wilson is confined chiefly to circles of old-fangled doctrinaire liberals unlike Wilson himself; their fondness for the political absolute has gone far beyond him. His name is muttered occasionally as an incantation to sanction proposals for a World State quite contrary to his idea of national self-determination, or to endorse egalitarian schemes which would have been anathema to him. I speak here of the bewildered breed called the ritualistic liberal; the attitude of the younger revisionist liberals among us is different. So we return to Richard Hofstadter and Louis Hartz.

"His hard doctrinaire mind," Hartz writes about Wilson, "taken as a whole, was not of the American type." And Hartz continues, in *The Liberal Tradition:* "The policy of Wilson in peace, so striking a contrast to the realpolitik of the Old World and ultimately so abject a victim before it, was shot through and through with the absolute 'Americanism' on the basis of which the war was fought. His central dilemma, what Walter Lippmann called 'the inner contradiction' of his thought, is by now a commonplace: the attempt to apply to a world in crying need of integration and on the brink of capitalist decline the political formulas of nationalism and free trade that the nineteenth century evolved. But to say merely this, to classify Wilson as a decadent disciple of Gladstone, is not only to miss the American contribution to his perspective, but actually to obscure it. Wilson's blindness was not only philosophic, it was empirical as well, the product of a peculiar historic experience . . ."

Hofstadter is harder still upon Wilson, because Wilson really was old-fashioned, a believer in free enterprise, unwilling to usher in the "corporate and consolidated society" which Mr. Hofstadter takes to be the wave of the future. "Wilson's speeches," Hofstadter observes, "the best parts of which are printed in *The New Freedom,* sound like the collective wail of the American middle class." Wilson did not strike to the heart of things; he ought to have removed the causes of national antagonism: "It had always been Wilson's aim to preserve the essentials of the *status quo* by reforming it; but failing essentially to reform, he was unable in the end to preserve."

Coming from an historical determinist like Hofstadter, this complaint that Wilson did not singlehandedly turn the world inside out is amusing. But Hofstadter's indictment is thoroughgoing:

"He appealed for neutrality in thought and deed, and launched upon a diplomatic policy that is classic for its partisanship. He said that American entrance into the war would be a world calamity, and led the nation in. He said that only a peace between equals would last, and participated in the *Diktat* of Versailles. He said that the future security of the world depended on removing the economic causes of war, and did not attempt even to discuss these causes at the Peace Conference. He declared his belief in the future of government ownership, and allowed his administration to close in a riot of reaction. He wanted desperately to bring the United States into the League, and launched on a course of action that made American participation impossible. No wonder that in one of his moments of apprehension he should have confessed to George Creel: 'What I seem to see—with all my heart I hope that I am wrong—is a tragedy of disappointment.' "

This verdict on Wilson is true enough; and yet there was more to Wilson than inconsistency, ineffectuality, and failure. I think that there is something better in failing as Wilson failed than in sitting in the scorner's seat. Such judgments by Hofstadter and Hartz illustrate the realism and the destructive power of the revisionist liberal; but also they reveal the prudential liberal's inability to offer any alternative to tradition, short of totalist ideology.

Still, Wilson failed. He talked of a war to end war; but his policies, at the end of that war, had a terrible part in breaking up the old international order and precipitating our civilization into that "antagonist world" (Burke's phrase), in sundering the bands of established community "on speculations of a contingent improvement," and condemning the world to "madness, discord, vice, confusion, and unavailing sorrow." Now Wilson was a good man, a strong man, a learned man, an intelligent man, a religious man. It seems worthwhile to inquire into the causes of this consequential failure.

Hartz and Hofstadter imply that Wilson failed because he was not a radical; he did not tear up the old order by the roots and supplant it by a Grand Design. "The Conservative as Liberal," Hofstadter calls Wilson, accurately. The bent of Wilson's nature was conservative; and Hartz and Hofstadter cannot forgive him for that. But he was born into a liberal era; the political vocabulary of his time was that of the liberals; and, perhaps more than in most eras, the conservatives of the time seemed to be the Stupid Party. Wilson the natural conservative became the rhetorical liberal. A man's words can master him; phrases can intoxicate; and, uttering the slogans of liberalism that were fashionable in his generation, Wilson presently came to act upon liberal abstractions. Out of that conflict between conservative impulse and liberal phrase grew much of Wilson's inconsistency when he had practical decisions to make; and the inconsistency attained its grim culmination when the Peace was to be made.

Before recounting what Wilson lacked, we ought to recall what he possessed. He was pious and courageous, well educated, honest, devoted to duty. He knew much of history and political theory. He tried always to emulate Burke's model of a statesman, combining a disposition to preserve with an ability to reform. There was little of the demagogue in Wilson. As things are going, he may be recorded as the last of our literary statesmen, bringing to the presidential office the humane and juridical disciplines. He did not merely drift with events: he perceived some of the deeper issues of this century better than anyone else among successful politicians, and much of *The New Freedom* remains worth reading. He was the sort of leader who makes possible the existence of democratic republics.

Wilson stood in the line of two strong schools of political wisdom: the constitutional writings of the founders of the American Republic, and the Christian doctrines and English experience that found their best expression in Burke. "Ever since I had independent judgments of my own, I have been a Federalist," Wilson said once. From an early age, too, he had been a disciple of Burke. His essay on "Edmund Burke and the French Revolution" shows a better understanding of Burke's principles than was possessed by most English scholars of his generation; it is, indeed, one of the better essays ever written on Burke. "Burke was himself, and was right," Wilson says, when Burke set his face against the French Revolution. And in that essay occurs a passage which cast its shadow upon Wilson's future career: "There is often to be found in the life of a great man some point of eminence at which his powers culminate and his character stands best revealed, his characteristic gifts brought to light and illustrated with a sort of dramatic force. Generally it is a moment of success that reveals him, when his will has had its way and his genius its triumph." Wilson's own moment came with the making of the Peace, in an hour of triumph; but all of Wilson's weaknesses stood revealed in that moment, and the apparent success sank abruptly into the bitterness and frustration of his final months.

Hartz and Hofstadter believe that this failure resulted from Wilson's innate conservatism, which prevented him from getting at the real causes of national rivalry and war. But is it not more true to say that Wilson's failing was rather that he was insufficiently conservative? The political wisdom of the Federalists and Burke was diluted, in Wilson, by a dose of doctrinaire liberalism. In the hour of crisis, liberal abstraction prevailed over conservative prudence. Wilson's failure was not that he declined to reconstitute the whole complex fabric of European and American society, warp and woof. Had he undertaken any grand design of this sort, his failure would have been more catastrophic. For it was not in Wilson's power, nor in any other man's, to accomplish anything of that sort. Even supposing this undertaking to have been desirable, neither Wilson nor anyone else possessed the knowledge, the force, and the following even to contemplate such a scheme. Wilson knew that such an attempt must provoke impassioned resistance, and that this resistance could be broken only by means which would corrupt the reformers. Seeing such an attempt being made in Russia, and recognizing the Russian Revolution as the grimmer brother of the French Revolution, he strove to check that Revolution. Like Burke, he was right, though it has taken some people nearly half a century to learn to agree with him. It is silly to reproach Wilson for not undertaking what he could not even have thought of undertaking; and he would have been wicked, knowing history as he did, to have set his hand to such a task.

Wilson resigned himself to the possible: he did what he could to establish a better order among nations. His principles were confused, the times moved too fast for him (particularly in the ruins of the Austro-Hungarian system), and he proved far too thoroughly convinced of his own wisdom, too unyielding, to achieve anything which might endure. Yet the errors into which he fell were not the errors of conservative policy; they were the errors of liberalism;

they were errors of the sort which Gladstone made in diplomacy. The climate of opinion in 1918 and 1919 was liberal, and it is hard to say who might have done better in Wilson's place. It is vain to imagine John Adams or John Quincy Adams, Disraeli or Salisbury, dominating the meetings of the Big Four. Wilson, then, was no unworthy spokesman for America. His failure was the failure of the nation's political imagination in those years, a normative failure. We may have learned something since then; but often I doubt it.

Certain liberal abstractions concerning the nature of political order and the nature of man lay behind Wilson's doctrine of national self-determination, behind his assumption that leagues of nations and paper constitutions and treaties might of themselves bring peace and contentment, behind his insistence upon fitting the map of Europe into his ideal design. He had learned much from the Federalists and Burke; but he had not learned prudence, which Burke considered the highest virtue in a statesman. His attachment to Burke's politics was similar to that of the English Liberal school, best exemplified by Gladstone and Morley. That aspect of Burke's thought which defends prescription and prejudice, which perceives how dangerous it is to disturb anything that is at rest, which is prepared to tolerate an old evil lest the cure prove worse than the disease, he understood imperfectly. Burke, respecting the ancient political communities of Europe, seeing in them Gothic edifices whose grotesqueness masked a mighty strength for good, never would have thought of approving a doctrinaire and wholesale shifting of boundaries, a vast abolition of governments and substitution of new ones, an overthrow of historical and natural groupings in favor of simple language-affinity. Burke would have perceived at once the consequence of abolishing the power which held together the heart of Europe and checked German and Russian ambition, the Austrian system. But it was Bentham or Mill, not Burke, whose pupil Wilson became in the making of the Peace.

To the conservative of Burke's school, the world is at best a tolerable place, kept in order chiefly through respect for custom and precedent. It may be patched and pruned here and there; but the nature of man remains flawed, ambition always aspires to domination, and states are kept at peace only by a balancing of power, a recognition of the traditions of civility, and a concern for real interests. Parchment and declarations of the rights of man cannot restrain private or national concupiscence. To the liberal, on the other hand, the world is infinitely improvable, and so is man himself; experiment and emancipation will lead to peace; and what ought to be, shall be. So Wilson thought and acted through the War and the making of the Peace.

The idea that power may be checked only by countervailing power always has been distasteful to the liberal. Wilson's concept of national self-determination, his championship of the League, and much of the rest of his program reflected that distaste. A vague confidence in Progress, Equality, and the People overcame the cautionary precepts of Burke and the Federalists. "You are a Liberal," the Duke of Omnium says to Phineas Phinn, in one of Trollope's parliamentary novels, "because you know that it is not all as it ought to be, and because you would still march on to some nearer approach to equality; though the thing itself is so great, so glorious, so god-like,—nay so absolutely divine,—that you have been disgusted by the very promise of it, because its perfection is unattainable."

Trollope knew his Liberals. This yearning to march on toward some future universal condition of democracy and equality got the better of Wilson, when authority was his. Despite his earlier declarations that the American Republic—though a model for other states—could not be transplanted, he called upon America to make the world safe for democracy; and this same liberal universalism marked his arguments in the shaping of the evanescent Peace. They were arguments not from prudence, not from principle as Burke had described principle, but from abstraction; and the states upon which he bestowed his blessing collapsed in less than two decades, because they were constructed in defiance of history, of real interests, and of the hard facts of power.

Ortega, in the year Wilson died, already was writing of "decadent democracy," betrayed by its own fallacies and mediocrity. Wilson did not make the world safe for democracy: in Europe, he succeeded only in clearing away the old forms and loyalties which might have withstood the totalitarians. He helped to bring to a transitory ascendancy democratic governments which were modelled upon France (whatever institutions they may have borrowed superficially from Britain and America) with all the weaknesses which the abstractions of the French Revolution inflicted upon political administration and popular opinion. The task was impossible to achieve. American political features that were the peculiar products of a peculiar historical experience could not be transported to Europe. No American, probably, was better qualified for the work than Wilson, for he knew history, and he had been much abroad; yet, in the haste and confusion which preceded the Versailles conference, he made arbitrary decision after arbitrary decision which ran counter to the simple facts of European political reality. His naïve acceptance of Benes' claim that the Sudeten Germans were few and feeble is only one of many errors. And, disastrous though these decisions were in the immediate sense, they have done even greater harm in encouraging among many Americans, ever since, the notion that somehow American "experts," given rein, possess knowledge and energy sufficient to resolve happily, in short order, the quarrels which have plagued the Old World these weary centuries. That mood of optimism brooded over Yalta; it is not gone from among us yet. Like faith without works, faith without insight can work infinite mischief; and optimism without a chastening humility can undo the practical, patient accomplishment of dutiful men over many centuries.

To argue whether Wilson, in these matters, was a "true liberal" or a false liberal is to waste time and to ignore the regular progression through which the liberal creed has gone since the beginning of the nineteenth century. The germ of what liberalism affirms today was present in the theories of Bentham, and even in the orations of Charles James Fox. The augmented role of positive law, the sweeping away of prescriptive institutions, an egalitarianism progressing from equality of franchises to equality of condition: these doctrines the liberals simply have extended logically. And the triumph of their doctrine has left them feeble before the totalists, who claim the right to inherit the liberal hegemony; there is nothing surprising in the canonization of Tom Paine by the Soviets. So far as Wilson was swept along by the liberal climate of opinion in his generation, he was as true a liberal as any in that camp. Not long before he died, he uttered some kind words about socialism. But so did Acton; so did John Stuart Mill; so did even old John Bright.

It is the liberal veneer upon Wilson's mind and action which has diminished his reputation among us, and it is no longer possible to defend him successfully in his liberal aspect—those mordant latter-day liberals Hartz and Hofstadter have seen to that. Yet I think that we should remember how Wilson was more than a doctrinaire liberal. A statesman deserves to be recollected not simply for what he did, but also for what he refrained from doing. Burke and Adams lingered always at the back of Wilson's mind: if he indulged in radical political alteration abroad, still he refused to countenance radical social alteration; and it is difficult to imagine him sanctioning the blunders and fallacies of Yalta, or singing the praise of the Universal Declaration of Human Rights.

If, on speculations of a contingent improvement, he confounded abstraction with principle and unwittingly opened a way unto that antagonist world of discord and unavailing sorrow which now is ours, still he stood by his God, his country, and his civilization. Woodrow Wilson knew what was worth conserving, though unhappily he vacillated at the crisis of his fate.

But what shall we say of Professors Hofstadter and Hartz? Whither are they wending? It is so simple to be wise by hindsight, to clap Woodrow Wilson in the pillory. Hartz and Hofstadter are aware of the feebleness of the old American liberalism. To them, conservative beliefs are hopelessly antiquated, if not beneath contempt. How would they amend liberalism? Or what radicalism would they advocate? One discerns in their writings little positive recommendation except hints of a nostalgic hankering after the Grand Designs of Harry Hopkins or R. G. Tugwell—already comically old-hat. They might smile upon "democratic socialism," were it not an ideology. But a political and economic system deprived of *both* tradition and ideology is like an airplane without either propeller or jet-power. They imply the creation of some sort of elite of intellectuals and planners—how motivated?—presumably governed by the general aspirations of socialism, without the moral imperative of socialism. This would be very like an army of pacifists. Men do not live and die by the speculations of centralizing scholars, or rest their hopes in Lockianism transcended. If, in historical and political studies, revisionist liberalism has no more to offer than this—why, we may as well turn to a latter-day sociological liberal, David Riesman.

The Liberalism of Diversion

In the terminology of Eric Voegelin—which will be examined in a later chapter—Professor Riesman is a Gnostic of the extreme right wing: that is, usually a moderate and amiable liberal, disavowing ideology nearly as strongly as does Voegelin himself. Although Riesman's historical perspective never extends back beyond the middle of the nineteenth century—and rarely so far—he is no doctrinaire evangel of Progress.

"My own view, which smiles on compromise, also has nineteenth-century roots, especially in the English tradition of Burke, Morley, Bagehot, Acton," Riesman writes in *Faces in the Crowd.* "But in a way, one has to have lived through the mid-twentieth century properly to appreciate the virtues of the bourgeois age and class, and to regard the terms 'bourgeois' or 'middle class' as ones of amiable praise rather than Sorelian or Marxist epithets."

In a time when even the more enthusiastic liberals confess that intellectual initiative has passed to the conservatives—a time when the remaining unconstructed liberals of yesteryear, like Henry Steele Commager and Archibald MacLeish, sound quaintly archaic —the most influential liberal thinker in this country is Riesman; and he is influential precisely because he is not a ritualistic or doctrinaire liberal.

An eminent European economist, some years ago, asked me whether Riesman ought to be classified as a "New Conservative." I replied that he ought not; but there are conservative elements in Riesman's thought, at least if one employs "conservative" as a term of relation. Riesman observes that "the rich are a minority and have their rights, too"; he implies that much "social" legislation and the enthusiasm it inspires are quite out of date, since the nineteenth-century conundrum of want is being solved by modern productivity, rather than by egalitarian laws; he is concerned for individuality; he shies away from cant and slogan; he pokes fun at many stereotypes, the sort which obsess "intellectuals and academic people." Yet his premises unquestionably are liberal; they are almost identical with those of John Stuart Mill, whom he takes deliberately for his model in much. It is not the fact that he has tried to effect a synthesis of conservatism and liberalism which makes him one of our important modern social critics; actually, he accomplishes nothing of that sort. His achievement is to restore to American liberalism, long sunk into the condition of a quasi-ideology, a measure of candor, moderation, and perceptivity.

I do not mean that Riesman is wholly contemptuous of every King Charles's head of ritualistic liberalism. Whenever he turns to the "emancipation of woman," for instance, he is back in Harriet Taylor's parlor with John Stuart Mill; he regrets that recently women have been turning back to their old duties and status, and implies that really they ought to be emancipated, "deprivatized," and taught sexual freedom, whether they relish it or not. Yet, by and large, Riesman stands for reformed liberalism. Perhaps his ideas may be criticized adequately by examining his concept of utopia.

"I suggest that the utopian tradition has gone sour," Riesman writes in *Individualism Reconsidered,* "because of collectivist, especially Communist, abuse, and gone stale (especially in America) because so many of our earlier hopes for equality and abundance have been attained—leaving us either to try to put meaning back into outdated struggles or to find a political agenda not in planning for a better future, but in postponing a worse one."

The old Fabian and social-democratic slogans have worn thin, he continues; and the utopianism of American business enterprise, the promise of a chicken in every pot and a car in every garage, also has lost its meaning: "First, given our resources, it is not difficult to fulfill them; they are, in fact, just around the corner. Second, attainment of these goals would not make the great mass of well-fed Americans noticeably happier." Populism and the New Deal merely aped the spurious utopia of business enterprise, without gaining any concept of a fundamental change in the quality of American life.

What we require, then, Riesman says, is not an ideological enthusiasm for some vague scheme of economic abundance or "fair shares for all," but a utopia founded upon new concepts of community and individuality. He is forever recurring to Bellamy's *Looking Backward,* and he commends the Goodmans' *Communi-*

tas: Means of Livelihood and Ways of Life. But the ends and means of his own utopia remain obscure. He mentions "more spontaneous pleasures and more democratic cooperation"; he takes up town planning; he has several suggestions for "autonomous play." Still, when all this is said, Riesman leaves us groping for purpose in this utopia—supposing it really is something quite different from the social-democratic or business-enterprise pseudo-utopia.

Probably Riesman's ambiguity is the child of his pragmatism. If he were asked, "What is the end of man?" he might have difficulty in replying; one gathers from his books that he might be compelled to say, "Diversion." Man is not made for work, in Riesman's eyes, or for duty, or for high loyalties; grand hopes and ideologies are disastrous. Therefore all man may hope for is a round of small pleasures; he may experiment in consumption and sex and urban living. Although tolerant of religious belief, Riesman remains condescendingly incredulous. All theological concepts and nearly the whole body of inherited belief are repugnant to him: "A concept of original sin is typical of a view of life which makes the past an authority over the present, in which the individual is mortgaged to society, and both the individual and society are mortgaged to the preceding generations." This debt to the past and obligation to the future, which Burke called "the contract of eternal society," has been the cement of classical and Christian social order; yet Riesman heartily dislikes it. It is not easy to construct a utopia which denies the legacy of dead generations and the claims of those yet unborn; but Riesman is logical in casting off natural rights and inherent obligations when he rejects the religious understanding.

One principle does seem to govern this Riesman utopia: the motto of the Abbey of Thélème (in its truncated version), "Do as you will." Since the frowning collectivism of the modern age menaces this principle, Riesman desires to check somehow the growth of centralized political authority and—more particularly— the sheep-conformity of the modern crowd, the "other-directed" men. In the final paragraph of *The Lonely Crowd*, he writes, "The idea that men are created free and equal is both true and misleading; they lose their social freedom and their individual autonomy in seeking to become like each other." The silent and impalpable democratic despotism over opinion and conduct which Tocqueville foresaw often is in the forefront of Riesman's mind; yet when he approaches the difficulty, he leaves out of consideration Tocqueville's reverential view, which was founded upon the Christian understanding of personality and the Christian moral doctrines.

It is John Stuart Mill to whom Riesman turns, rather; and Mill's idea of individuality, as expressed in his *Liberty*, had no sanction but difference for the sake of differing. That man has an end which is more than immanent; that man finds his happiness through the performance of duties, and his freedom through the acquirement of moral character—these concepts are wanting altogether in Riesman's thought. His is a utopianism, and a liberalism, without norms.

Thus we are brought back to an unexciting concept of man, a being who finds his whole duty in the triumph of self in this world, and whose highest hope is to be "autonomous"—somehow different from dull conformists, though severed from tradition, from duty, from hope of much attainment in this world, and from expectation of reward in another realm than this. How satisfying such autonomy would be, if practical at all; how long such a utopia would gratify the longings of men and keep them from ideology and violence (after the New Left fashion); whether, indeed, even the utopia-life of small experimental pleasures and improved cities and abundant leisure and innumerable creature-comforts might endure in America for any length of time, what with the present rate of destruction of moral capital—all these questions Riesman does not take into account. Along with ideology, he has discarded theory; and he implies that human nature is merely whatever the drift of society makes it, and therefore requires no further attention.

Yet, this said, Riesman's writings represent a reformed and chastened liberalism. Prudence, at least in its lower aspect, governs this liberalism—not ideology. There is no intention of creating a classless society, or a universal state, or an egalitarian monotony. If there occurs no appreciation of human dignity, still there is understanding of the importance of individuality. Just this humdrum and compromising liberalism, conceivably, may become the common pattern of American "progressive" and secularistic thought, now that American liberals have recoiled—most of them—from collectivistic ideology. There is no crusading spirit in this liberalism; one wonders whether there is enough vigor remaining in it to resist any strong evil.

Although Riesman has won the intellectual field among liberals, by a cultural lag of sorts many intellectuals and reforming zealots continue to shout the slogans, and to sign the petitions, of a generation gone. I shall deal with some of these in the following chapter. It requires more than Riesman's complacency to give the quietus to ideology.

The liberalism of Hartz and Hofstadter is hostile toward norms and toward traditions; the liberalism of Riesman is indifferent. Therefore latter-day liberalism cannot be taken very seriously. Without standards to defend or seek, human mind and heart are starved, and human society expires of ennui, if not from violence.

The man who respects tradition prefers the devil he knows to the devil he doesn't; and he is not disposed to sweep away a body of beliefs that have served us well in exchange for some new domination to which its prophets cannot even put a name. The American political tradition has given the American people a higher degree of justice and order and freedom—with the possible exception of the British—than any other political tradition has conferred upon any other people.

Like other things, tradition may be judged empirically—though that is not the exclusive standard of judgment. Our political tradition, our social normality, has been fruitful, and the only discernible alternative to it is political abnormity. The prudent social reformer must make his amendments in consonance with this tradition, for the sake of renewing his society's vitality. His only other course is to sweep all the pieces off the board. But then he would not be playing the same game, or reforming the same nation, or, conceivably, dealing with civilized human beings.

III. THE IDEOLOGUE UNREGENERATE

The Scholar is neither Lion nor Fox

WHATEVER MAY BE SAID OF THE SHORTCOMINGS OF THE
revisionist and prudential liberals, at least such gentlemen are thinking, and have sheered away from ideology. But much as the doctrines discussed today in seminaries and schools of education may
not filter down to the typical clergyman and the typical teacher for
a generation to come, so fresh speculation among the advance-
guard of political liberalism suffers from a time-lag in penetrating
to liberal professor and liberal student. Thus ideology continues to
cramp the minds of many dwellers in the academy.

Today, perhaps more than ever before, American public opinion
needs responsible leadership in the understanding of foreign affairs.
American public policy requires close criticism in this time of up-
heaval. Of a sudden, many gentlemen in the academy volunteer
their services as molders of public opinion and critics of the State
Department and the Pentagon: challenge and response.

Yet are all these "committed" scholars really endowed with a
mastery of statecraft? Senator J. William Fulbright, in 1966, declared that our professors may be trusted to guide foreign policy
aright. At the height of the hearings of the Senate Committee on
Foreign Relations concerning the struggle in Vietnam, Mr. Fulbright stated that the men of the academy ought to become even

more active in current foreign-affairs controversies. He seemed confident that in such concerns the opinions of the professors would coincide with his own.

Conceivably Senator Fulbright was troubled by a few misgivings subsequently, once the scholars' testimony before the Foreign Relations Committee was concluded. For some of the professors upon whom Fulbright presumably relied for reinforcement of his views must have been disappointing to him—notably Dr. John K. Fairbank, of Harvard. Other witnesses must have pleased him still less.

However that may have been, the general question that Senator Fulbright raised deserves attention. Should the scholar give primacy to our present discontents? Should he issue manifestoes and fulminations on the principal issues of foreign affairs, protest and demonstrate, league himself with party and faction, offer a confident prescription for the woes of all the world?

Or should he stick to his folios, most of the time? Should he take meditation and research and the teaching of his discipline for his fundamental duties? Is he competent—collectively speaking—to ride the diplomatic whirlwind and direct the international storm?

"He that lives in a college, after his mind is sufficiently stocked with learning," wrote the young Edmund Burke, "is like a man, who having built and rigged and victualled a ship, should lock her up in a drydock." Though Burke was far from despising learned professors of arts and sciences, he meant that the man who aspires to alter public affairs should enter upon public life, not lingering within college walls. The politician must live the politician's existence, and the scholar the scholar's.

Yet not a few professors today demand the best of both worlds. Their examplar is Dr. Staughton Lynd, speechifying in Hanoi, leading marches on Washington, joining the DuBois Clubs as a gesture. They would relish mightily the role of Mr. Nelson Algren or Mr. Norman Mailer, discoursing in public of the infamy of American foreign policy—even if their discourses are blemished by remarkable exhibitions of ignorance. They aspire to enjoy simultaneously the prestige (and security) of the academy, and the excitement of the soapbox. They bring to mind C. S. Lewis' anecdote of the small boy who was solemnly informed that sexual connection is the most intense of pleasures. "Do they eat chocolate while they do it?" the eager child inquired.

So we observe afresh many of the attitudes of certain circles of professors in the thirties. Consider the virtual adulation, in some quarters, of Dr. Herbert Aptheker, a dogmatic Communist, one of the dullest speakers ever to try the patience of college audiences— who, Bourbonlike, learned nothing and forgot nothing since the days of popular fronts. Professors were eminent among the men of the Left who, in 1966, hoped to secure a seat in Congress for Aptheker. More, Dr. Aptheker was chosen to give a major address to the Organization of American Historians, on the day after a testimonial dinner in Manhattan meant to launch him on the sea of congressional politics. When a number of professors of history— themselves sufficiently liberal—objected to this part of the Organization's program, they were informed that Dr. Aptheker had been invited to speak because he had "suffered persecution." The late George Lincoln Rockwell might have been invited on the same ground.

Such muddy sentimentality, and such notions of "no enemies to the Left," recently have been so conspicuous that serious journalists have mused upon a conceivable widespread revival, among American intellectuals, of the illusions of a generation gone. For my part, I doubt that any large part of our community of scholars will worship anew the God that Failed. Yet a scattering of individuals may blight their own intellectual promise, and bring disrepute upon the academy, by pontificating on foreign and domestic policies of which they know next to nothing.

I suggest that although for the past two generations the ideological pressures within the American academy have come mainly from the Left, one may conceive of circumstances in which scholars of the Right might be equally imprudent and intemperate. Or professors with governmental subsidies may become the servants, rather than the architects, of state policies; indeed, just that already has occurred, from Harvard to Michigan State, in the dispatch of missions of professors to the far corners of the earth. ("Most of these grand Washington schemes for sending a covey of professors overseas," a very well-known sociologist remarked to me, "involve either Harvard or Michigan State. When the people in Washington wish a project to succeed, they turn to Harvard. When they wouldn't be sorry if a project were to fail, they contract with Michigan State.")

It seems worthwhile, then, to draw a line of demarcation between the scholar and the ideologue. A scholar has, of course, the right and the duty to be as much concerned with the common good as is any other citizen; but by definition, he must give most of his mind and his time to learning.

By contrast, the ideologue—a political dogmatist hotly seeking his particular utopia—has little to do with the speculative pursuit of truth; he already knows all the answers to everything, for they are contained in his simple social formula; for him, research is but a means to his political end, and his writing ought to be propaganda. No man may be at once a genuine scholar and a convinced ideologue.

Do not mistake me: I do not suggest that every scholar who publicly expresses his political convictions is an ideologue, or that a scholar may not have knowledge of high value in the conduct of foreign affairs—this latter depending, often, upon his particular scholarly discipline. Distinctions must be made.

Consider the teach-ins about the Vietnam war. Most of the professors and instructors who have taken an active part in these gatherings have given off more heat than light; and it has been remarked that the more remote their scholarly specialties seem from diplomatic and military affairs in southeastern Asia, the more such gentlemen behave as if omniscient. They are converting themselves into ideologues.

Between the mere enthusiast with a recent Ph.D., however, and the learned man who criticizes policy in Vietnam on the basis of much study, a gulf is fixed. On the one hand, we see the young instructor in philosophy (perhaps bored by his own logical positivism) who reveals in the teach-ins a burning certitude about foreign affairs which he never professes in his lectures on metaphysics and ethics; he mistakes a university post for a political prophetic afflatus. On the other hand, we find that similar practical conclusions may be drawn by scholars like Dr. Hans Morgenthau, who—whether or not one agrees with him—at least speaks with some authority about the theory and practice of diplomacy. The former professor is in process of becoming what the Greeks called a "philodoxer," a lover of private opinion and the winds of doctrine. The latter professor disdains ideology, remaining a realist; his judgments, whether sound or erroneous, are prudential, rather than ideological.

In essence, my argument is this: if the scholar deserts his realm of scholarly competence for the agora, he is liable to attain neither wisdom nor the public good. The man who has been an able professor may become an able politician. Congress has, in both parties, a fair number of useful members with such a background, and others are in the Executive Force. Very few persons, nevertheless, can be competent simultaneously in quite different vocations. For better or worse, the scholar turned politician must give up pure scholarship. If one has a taste for the hustings, one ought to abandon the pose of speaking authoritatively from a chaste, impartial love of pure learning.

When, however, scholarship and political passion are embroiled in a confusion worse confounded, both honest learning and practical politics suffer. Let me suggest first the dangers to learning which result from this admixture.

When professors and men of letters let themselves be frozen into ideological rigidity, the community of scholars is disrupted. College faculties are bitterly divided by ideological passions, so that appointment and promotion are determined, too often, by conformity to the prevalent doctrine of the hour. The classroom becomes a center for political indoctrination of the students, at the expense of free discussion and exploration. Humane and scientific studies are subordinated to political or economic prejudices. A sour, fanatic temper infects both senior scholars and students. Literature sinks into sloganizing, special pleading, and the baser sort of polemics. Before scholarship at length recovers from the merciless grip of ideology, whole generations may suffer.

This baneful academic phenomenon has been described by a number of critics. However much ideological infatuation and prejudice may have touched the American intellectual community from time to time, we may be thankful that ordinarily we have escaped the severer consequences of bundling scholarship and political dogmatism together in one extramarital bed. Contrary to the assumption of many Americans, there may be less ideological prejudice at a typical American university than at Oxford, say, or at Cambridge.

Abroad, as in this country, the scholar who has surrendered to a set of ideologues the keeping of his mind and his conscience is not a highly agreeable person; and outside his field of specialization (or even within it, sometimes) he may sink into shabby scholarship. Some years ago, for instance, I sat at high table in an Oxford college beside that college's master, a celebrated man in his scientific discipline. He had been told that I was the author of a book he had not read, *The Conservative Mind,* and so he cast a suspicious eye upon me.

"What do you think of your Senator Taft?" he inquired. I replied that I believed Robert Taft to have been a man of honesty, courage, and ability.

"Oh!" He ceased to be the courteous host. "Then I suppose you approve of Malan, in South Africa."

This *non sequitur* puzzled me, until I ascertained that he believed Ohio to be a Southern state; that all Southerners were racists; that, consequently, Robert Taft must have been an advocate of apartheid. Had this don turned to making speeches at Hyde Park Corner, I would have taken no more stock in his verdict upon American society than one ought to take stock in the perfervid utterances of his American counterparts concerning the affairs of Asia or Africa.

My Oxford host, though he was in his particular discipline a man of mark, knew next to nothing of history, politics, or geography. Nor did he perceive any necessity for informing himself: ideology, and a few partisan publications, provided him with all the approved attitudes in politics. One trusts that a kindly providence may preserve us from the shaping of foreign policy by such ignorant, if learned, ideologues.

In the academy, the scholar turned ideologue does mischief to his colleagues, his students, and the search for wisdom. And if the scholar-ideologue contrives to inflict his abstractions upon the affairs of nations, more harm is worked. The academy simply is not the place to acquire an apprehension of the complexity of public affairs, or an acquaintance with the skills and limits of diplomacy. Politics being the art of the possible, a broad knowledge of the world, the flesh, and the devil ought to be possessed by the architect of foreign policy. In the politician, prudence is the chief virtue; but the ideologue, sheltered by academic tenure and campus immunities, demands that we work instanter a radical reformation of man and society; he knows not prudence. Fancy Staughton Lynd, or a professor of the extreme opposite persuasion, as Secretary of State!

I readily acknowledge that scholars (as distinguished from ideologues) may become statesmen. In this century, Presidents Wilson and Hoover were men of real scholarship in their own fields, and also practical—if not wholly successful—politicians. In general, though, the scholar does well to stick to his original calling. Robert Taft (so misunderstood by my Oxford ideologue) said once that businessmen should stick to business, leaving politics to the politicians. This is no less true of scholars and scholarship. Quite as *some* men of business can become competent political leaders and administrators, so can *some* scholars; yet we retain a legitimate presumption that talents for making money or for writing dissertations do not, *per se*, qualify well-intentioned folk to administer justice and defend the national interest.

It is easy enough to understand the frustrations and aspirations which impel some scholars—particularly members of our "academic proletariat" of overworked, underpaid, and mass-campus-harassed young instructors and graduate assistants—to leap from the dull "survey" course to the advocacy of some political cause—nay, *any* political cause. At least a teach-in audience pays attention, unlike the typical classroom undergraduate; and it would be so very pleasant if, through direct political action, somehow one might transform Behemoth State University, or Dismal Swamp A. & M., or all America, or all the world, into a dominion of sweetness and light. It seems infinitely difficult to leaven the lump of campus smugness; but it seems so delicious to declaim about the sinfulness of war—and to be applauded.

Have scholars, then, nothing to do with public affairs? My belief is quite the contrary: the professor, in whatever discipline, does and should exert a profound influence upon the civil social order. But that power is exerted through study, teaching, and contemplation. In the comparative leisure of the academy, the minds of the rising generation are molded; and the arts and sciences alter, enduringly if imperceptibly, the world without. T. S. Eliot or Reinhold Niebuhr, say, will influence the commonwealth and the conscience long after the names of Hubert Humphrey and John Tower (with all respect to those former professors) have become names only. Perhaps true scholarship will not produce philosopher-kings; yet it works upon mind and heart to give us a better republic.

Senator Fulbright beckons the scholar into political action, now. But action uncontrolled by reflection is ungovernable and unpredictable; while "activist" professors and students have a tricky way, abruptly, of taking up other causes and commencing new actions unpalatable to the gentlemen who persuaded them to shut their books.

By his nature, the scholar is not calculated for direct action, nor is the professor endowed with the talents of either lion or fox. "In politics, the professor always plays the comic role," says Nietzsche.

Yet the professor need feel no shame at this. Practical politics is not the whole of life, nor the most important aspect of life. Socrates took the measure of the demagogue Cleon and of the oligarch Critias, and found both wanting. Would Socrates have done well to have thrust himself into one of the seats of the mighty? Had he done anything of that sort, he would mean no more to us today than do Cleon and Critias. He fulfilled, spear in hand, his duty to the state; but Socrates knew that the lover of wisdom must not drink deep from the cup of power.

Order and justice and freedom cannot be secured by professorial haranguing of mobs. The scholar truly committed is the man of learning who works honestly and tirelessly at his high duty of elevating mind and conscience.

You Can't Trust Perpetual Adolescents

Early in 1966, in the pages of a women's magazine, Mr. Edward Keating, editor of the radical journal *Ramparts*, proclaimed that today's youth knows that you can't trust anyone over thirty. Reading farther in this essay, however, one discovered that you can't trust many people under thirty, either, by Mr. Keating's admission. Indeed, Keating soon was taught that you can't trust even radicals under thirty: for he was expelled by conspiring young associates from control of the magazine he had founded, edited, and heavily subsidized.

The only trustworthy folk, Keating believed before his juniors heaped indignities upon him, are such of the rising generation as follow the *Ramparts* line—or some line farther to the Left—grow beards (if masculine), and parade in the streets their own moral superiority to those dreary dogs who enforce the laws, defend the republic, and turn the great wheel of circulation.

What a happy, just, peaceful world would be ours if only these youthful fantastics were endowed with total authority! Or so Mr. Keating believed.

But I am unable to agree, even though this nation urgently needs responsible criticism in addition to moral imagination. In the groups which Keating admires, I find little except the attitudes of prolonged adolescence—though I have talked with the "New Left" enthusiasts on dozens of campuses, and have seen them at their demonstrations.

To pose as a virtuous young rebel seems pleasant—for a while. How boring it is to turn from slogans and demonstrations to the painful labor of practical accomplishment in this imperfect world! Shouting about other people's alleged injustices is more fun than trying to establish tolerable order in one's own soul and community; demanding immediate universal peace is less risky than personally repelling aggression.

Yet the young Pharisee, declaring himself holier than his misguided elders, may be frozen into an attitude of perpetual adolescent rebelliousness. Few human types are more repellent than the smug radical who declines to assume responsibilities—who, hurling abuse at anyone stodgy enough to perform regular duties, nevertheless lives in comfort and safety provided by the very institutions and men he denounces.

Haven't we been through all this before? I remember with clarity the cult of youth which enjoyed considerable influence in the early thirties. Those were the years of "strength through joy" and "youth solidarity" in various forms: Communist youth movements, Socialist youth movements, pacifist youth movements, Fascist youth movements. One such association of young zealots attained power, for a time—a group called Hitler Youth, headed by an idealistic social revolutionary now serving a sentence in Spandau prison.

In any age, there exists much against which intelligent and conscientious young people ought to protest. But reckless protest for
the sake of protest, like revolution for the sake of revolution, can
convert a fairly tolerable society into general misery. Revolutions
do not remain peaceful, and they devour their own children.

How genuinely serious and imaginative are the youth movements
which Keating applauded? Against what evils do they contend? In
Keating's eyes, the young radicals are alarmed primarily by the
Bomb. They recognize, however, that general peace cannot be
achieved until justice becomes concrete. Then Keating and his
young friends fall into bathos. Youth must protest, according to
Keating, for the sake of "the starving child in India, the Negro who
needs dignified employment, the mother smothered in napalm in
some Vietnam village."

Well! More food in India, better employment for American Negroes, and security for civilians in Vietnam are earnestly to be
desired. These things are as much sought by people over thirty as by
those under thirty, and as much advocated by the young "con-
servators," whom Keating denounces, as they are by the young
bearded demonstrators whom he idealizes.

Yet precisely how are these goals to be achieved by sit-ins, teach-
ins, street demonstrations, burning of draft cards, or even loose
rhetoric? India will obtain more food only by a massive improvement of Indian agriculture—certainly not by breast-beating in
Berkeley, Washington, and New York. The Negro will obtain a
better job only by a complex process of improved education and
training, responsible and tolerant conduct on the part of both white
and colored people, and restoration of community and family life
among the Negroes who have poured abruptly into the big cities.
The Vietnamese mother will be saved only by military and diplomatic policies which teach the Communists of the North that their
game is not worth the candle.

What are Keating's humanitarian radicals under thirty doing to
insure the improvement of Indian agriculture? How are they bringing about better understanding between whites and Negroes, heal-
ing old wounds, helping the Negroes settle down to practical
improvement? What do they propose, after their allegedly "nonviolent" fashion, for southeastern Asia?

Far from recommending practical alternatives to present poli-

cies, the under-thirty set commended by Keating seems more interested in the ego-gratifying defiance of the malcontent adolescent.
Denounce whatever exists. Blame Daddy. Be a rebel, on any pre-
text. Form a gang, and give it a name, and adopt a gang-costume.
But never condescend to look critically at your own actions, or to
propose any rational alternative to the ways and institutions you
denounce. And sedulously avoid any strenuous personal involve-
ment—except in mass demonstrations.

The young radicals, according to Keating, regard the medical
and legal professions as "petty ambitions." Through the law, practical justice is obtained. Through medical science, suffering is alleviated. But how much more dramatic to man the barricades!
Thought and self-discipline always are exacting. Instead, sprawl on
the floor, listening to Pete Seeger records; sing along with Pete:
don't think—just drift with the rhythm. When you're in the mood,
simply act—non-violently, of course.

What are these youth groups that Keating trusts so unreservedly?
What way are they drifting? Why, they have the approbation of
Gus Hall, chief spokesman for the Communist party in America.
In the summer of 1965, Hall declared publicly that "Fronts are a
thing of the past. We don't need them. We've got the W. E. B.
DuBois Clubs, the Student Nonviolent Coordinating Committee,
and Students for a Democratic Society going for us, but they're not
'fronts' in the usual sense of the word. They're just part of the
'responsible Left'—that portion of American youth that realizes
society is sick."

Consider one of these organizations, Students for a Democratic
Society. I have encountered many members of SDS, from coast to
coast. They are sentimental, bearded, earnest, and muddled. In the
beginning, SDS members spoke of the Communists contemptu-
ously, as old fuddy-duddies, not sufficiently radical. The society
professed to be free from any rigorous ideology; it was merely seeking avenues to radical reform. In the beginning, SDS refused to
admit Communists to membership.

But since then, the society has decided that its anti-Communist
stand was "irrelevant"; anyone can join now. And anyone does.
Once it became clear that such loose-knit protest clubs could be
used to denounce American policy in Asia and elsewhere, Communist infiltration commenced—a fact remarked by the United States

Attorney General, by the director of the Federal Bureau of Investigation, and by the Internal Security Subcommittee of the Senate.

Nowadays it is somewhat painful to observe the evasions and contortions of an SDS activist when he is questioned about the presence of Communists in his organization. I wish these people would read Lionel Trilling's novel *The Middle of the Journey,* because they are involved in the grim process described by Trilling— passing through stages of self-deception and willful blindness which must lead them to totalist ideology and intellectual servitude, if not to extreme violence.

So I distrust the vagueness of these "under-thirty" organizations, easily subjugated by fanatics. I distrust, too, in many instances, their professions of non-violence on principle.

Take the Student Nonviolent Co-ordinating Committee, so active at Selma, and since then given to chanting hymns about killing Whitey. Rabbi Richard L. Rubenstein, chaplain to Jewish students at Pittsburgh universities and colleges, led some 135 students from Pittsburgh to the Alabama demonstrations. He found himself aghast at the character and tactics of the "activists and revolutionaries" who form the Student Nonviolent Coordinating Committee. The SNCC zealots, Rabbi Rubenstein declared upon his return to Pittsburgh, deliberately tried to push demonstrators into trouble— so that "martyrs" might be created and violence provoked. SNCC fanatics repeatedly lied to the Pittsburgh students in order to incite incidents with the police, illegally invaded a high school to recruit children for demonstrations, and broke through police lines. "They wanted dead bodies—our bodies," Rabbi Rubenstein said.

To put it mildly, we cannot entrust our civil social order, so laboriously developed through many centuries of trial, error, and discovery, to the mercies of people with the mentality and the temperament of adolescents. Bearded or shaven, the new radical youth seems altogether incompetent to renew the vitality of our civilization. The youthful neurotic is a symptom of our personal and social disorders, but scarcely the physician we need.

Yet I do not despair of the rising generation. The little groups of extremists are few in number, really, and generally ineffectual, obtaining far more attention in the press than their influence justifies. The political understanding of many Americans under thirty is sounder than were the opinions of most young people a generation ago. The abler students and other people under thirty are beginning to think; and reflection, not frantic action, is what our time needs. The recovery of order in the soul and order in society is the first necessity of this century. By a mere prolonged teen-age rebelliousness, a doctrinaire detestation of all authority, the world is plunged deeper into confusion and injustice.

Of this hard truth, the present excitement over the war in Vietnam is sufficient illustration. American diplomatic and military policies in southeastern Asia should be scrutinized closely—and improved. People under thirty should have a part in this scrutiny. But an hysterical "mass protest," sloganizing and almost mindless, cannot bring justice or peace to Vietnam. Flight before Communist terrorism does not abolish the Bomb. Yet such silliness can provoke a public reaction which would make more difficult any prudent criticism of foreign policy.

Edward Keating wishes youth to recast this world nearer to his heart's desire. How? Why, "just capture the feel of the music," says Keating. Like the intemperate young fantastics whom he praises, Keating reduces politics to a mood, or to a pastiche of vague humanitarian sentiments. Get into the rhythm, you glorious youths: swing it. "Trust in the music," Keating tells us, benignly.

But what if the progressive orchestra is playing a *danse macabre?* What if the music is Wagnerian? What, after all, if politics is more than a game of musical chairs? *Who* shall overcome what? Is Pete Seeger, the Marx of folk-song, a messiah who shall usher us into the Earthly Paradise to the twang of a guitar?

Defy convention: grow a beard. There's the profundity of the under-thirty radicalism. I have no objection to young beards, having sported one myself when I was a graduate student. But beard-wearing is a perilous measure of the wisdom of people under thirty. Hell's Angels, those kindly motorcyclists who are continually being involved in altercations with the police, wear beards quite as impressive as the whiskers displayed by Students for a Democratic Society. Once *youth* and *rhythm* are made the criteria for social leadership, it becomes difficult to discriminate among beards and guitars.

The appeal to emotionalism, the unqualified praise of Youth in the abstract, the contempt for old political forms, the sneering at our ancestors' wisdom, the exhortation to lose ourselves in movement, rhythm, the feel of things, confidence in a revolutionary future—some of us have encountered these notions before. German youth heard them, a generation gone—and acted upon them. When idealized youth is told repeatedly that youth must be served, theories of non-violence do not endure long.

Youthful ignorance and inexperience work much more harm than do the alleged apathy and complacency of older minds. I do not intend to entrust my dearest interests to persons suffering from senility; but I do not mean, either, to entrust them to persons still afflicted by the psychological disturbances of adolescence. Although not enamored of Mr. Lyndon Johnson, I had rather have him keep the Bomb than place our national security in the hands of the young freaks of the May 2nd Movement.

Age does not necessarily make a man clean, brave, and wise; but neither does youth. The unlikeliest person to trust, in private concerns or in public, is "the humanitarian with the guillotine," the enthusiast confident that the world lay in darkness until he, in his moral perfection, burst upon mankind. You do not have to be elderly to become a destructive fool. All you require is sufficient arrogance—and to "trust in the music," the unreasoning rhythm, of perpetual adolescence.

✾✾✾✾✾✾✾✾✾✾✾✾✾✾✾✾✾✾✾✾✾✾

IV. BEHAVIORISTS' BEHAVIOR

Social Science as Ideology

THE INTEMPERATE PROFESSOR AND THE IMMATURE STUDENT, AS
described in the preceding chapter, may be nuisances; most of
them, nevertheless, are so impulsive and unsystematic that they
become the dupes, rather than the authors, of ideology. Their passion is expended upon questions of the hour and the moment; and,
far from attracting a popular following, commonly they wake resentments against themselves among the American public, and may
even provoke an opposite extreme. Except in times of revolutionary anarchy—when, as Tocqueville says, madness may be a positive advantage to a man, and may elevate him, briefly, to power—
such people are like the grasshoppers to which Burke compared the
radicals of his day: noisy, but feeble.

For success, any ideology requires more thorough organization
and more patient advancement than the typical intemperate professor and the typical immature student are able to provide. Ideology
demands, that is, its priestly caste and its bureaucracy; also it must
present a coherent and internally consistent body of doctrine, allegedly scientific. If a new ideology is to arise in America, seriously
challenging church and state, devastating the old standards—why,
it may take the form of the academic cult called Behaviorism or
Behavioralism. More than Communism or Fascism or anarchism,
behaviorism appeals to a certain type of American mind; also it

already is well rooted in American universities and colleges, and its devotees are at work extending behaviorism's empire. This intellectual cult displays many of the symptoms of nascent ideology, particularly in its hostility toward established norms.

All ideologies claim to be sciences of society. To assert that society may be ruled on scientific principles, indeed, is to open the door to the ideologue. In this chapter, I describe the tendency of American social studies—particularly sociology and political science—to harden into an ideology which denies and assails the ancient sources of normative knowledge. Such an intellectual movement, in the long run, is a grimmer enemy to the permanent things than any amount of ritualistic-liberal demonstrating and petition-signing could be.

Sociology has become a power in this land. Since Gunnar Myrdal's *An American Dilemma* was cited as a basis for the Supreme Court's anti-segregation decisions, reforming social scientists have believed themselves to be nearing, at last, the high estate they have long claimed.

Certainly their realm has grown mushroom-like in this century. "Social studies" is a required course in nearly every public school. Teacher-training is heavily laden with social-science indoctrination, at the expense of the humanities and the natural sciences. For the past quarter of a century, the big foundations have poured hundreds of millions of dollars into the social sciences. And recently the federal government began to subsidize social-science research.

Still, the social scientists' standing is insecure. They are split into warring camps, the basis of their authority remains in question, and there lingers a certain public reluctance to grant them the respect they covet. If a professor declares roundly, "I speak as a social scientist," some other professor may mutter, "That stuff isn't science—it's only scientism."

Among themselves, the social scientists are divided and vague as to any definition of their discipline. It is "the science of society," of course; and Auguste Comte expected sociology to be the master science. But in America, the disciplines of economics and politics already were established before sociology made its appearance; so, often, the sociologist is compelled either to deal with marginal activities or to indulge in grand generalizations about society. For the typical college student, sociology consists of "introductory sociology"—mostly talk about "in-groups and out-groups," "marriage and the family," and "social problems."

This is a pity, for it is silly or baneful to expose undergraduates in college, and even high-school students, to hasty generalization about the civil social order when as yet they possess no basis for judgment. One cannot be a tolerable sociologist until he knows a good deal about humane letters, history, philosophy, politics, and theology—and has had some experience of life. Sociology ought to be the crown, rather than the foundation, of studies in the civil social order.

For there have been sociologists of strong insight and broad learning: such writers as Tocqueville, Taine, Fustel de Coulanges, Durkheim, Le Play, Simmel, and Weber, whose significance is made clear by R. A. Nisbet in his recent book *The Sociological Imagination*. But the typical American professor or instructor in sociology has been little influenced by these men of real intellect; perhaps he has not read them at all. Humane and historical learning are not his; ignorant of the classical languages, he cannot even coin words with genuine Greek or Latin roots. The representative American sociologist aspires to be "scientific"—not humane—on the pattern of the natural sciences. He asserts that his discipline, like those of the natural sciences, may describe, predict, and control phenomena; he lays down "laws" of behavior; he claims that he is "value-free"; he thinks of himself as the engineer and the architect of a new, rational social order.

He is the intellectual descendant, that is, of Comte and Saint-Simon. His opinion-polls, his analyses of out-groups, his indices of prejudice, his statistical computations of popular choice (and nowadays he is intoxicated by the computer) all are intended to convert mankind into a predictable and controllable species.

Philosophically, the representative social scientist is an empiricist of the positivistic variety; emotionally, often he is a secular evangelist. Yet despite his increasing influence in many quarters, he is less confident than was Comte that the future belongs to him and his science. Jacques Barzun suggests that the term "behavioral sciences" is supplanting the older term "social sciences" because of the sociologist's "desperate conviction that man does *not* behave and should be made to with the help of science."

About five years ago, a youngish instructor in sociology declared to me, somewhat defiantly, "I really believe that we can teach everybody the scientific approach." A touch of shrillness in his "really" suggested that even this zealot was afflicted by doubts. For today's humanitarian social scientist is discouraged by one hard fact: only in totalist states have positivistic doctrines of social reconstruction on "scientific" lines been applied thoroughly. So he is forced back upon studies in "democratic behavior patterns"; but if "democracy" is his ideal, how can he ever attain the status of priest-scientist that Comte ordained?

Thus the aims of social science remain in dispute: whether this discipline is meant to give coherence and fresh meaning to older disciplines; whether it is intended to work toward a terrestrial paradise; or whether it ought to rest content with recording group behavior. Is this branch of study, strictly speaking, a science at all? Pitirim Sorokin, probably the most widely-read of American sociologists, maintains that it is indeed a science—but a science which requires something more than the empirical method for its basis, and which ought to recognize and respect knowledge already possessed by the several intellectual disciplines, including the sociological discipline itself.

Were Sorokin listened to by his colleagues of the rising generation, American sociology would show more promise. But the typical behaviorist rejects Sorokin's ethical convictions (founded on the Golden Rule) and denies the very existence of abiding "values," or norms. He would be a scientist, pure and simple; so he makes himself into a votary of scientism.

Loosely employed, the word "science" means any orderly and reputable study, on systematic principles. But the social scientists, or most of them, have not been satisfied with so general a claim to the laurels of science: the majority assert that their discipline must be, or already is, as exact and regular a science as physics, or chemistry, or botany, or geology. (Some, indeed, have used the term "social physics.") Envying the precision of the natural sciences, they have sought to emulate the methods of their natural-science colleagues, and to assert parallel claims of certitude in prediction and control.

"The nemesis of such simulacra," Sorokin writes, "is sterility and error—and this nemesis is already walking abroad among the contemporary psychosocial sciences. . . . In spite of our narcissistic self-admiration, of the enormous energy and funds spent in pseudo-mathematical and statistical research, its achievements have been singularly modest, its sterility unexpectedly notable, and its fallacies surprisingly numerous."

One consequence of this common social-scientist passion for imitating the outward development of natural science is the development of a depressing jargon, incomprehensible even to nineteen-twentieths of the body of university graduates and, one suspects, to many sociologists themselves. This "scientific" vocabulary of the sociologist, to which every professor feels free to add at will (by way of establishing his title to originality) resembles the deliberate obscurity of the learned Marxist—an opaqueness intended to persuade the vulgar through awe of erudition.

The medical word "synergy," for instance, when redefined to convey the meaning of "the sum total of energy which any group can command and expend," obscures rather than enlightens. The word "valence" is borrowed from physics and converted to mean "attraction in society"—which is not at all like its natural-science meaning, and is severed from its linguistic root. Even a popular and comparatively lucid sociologist like David Riesman twists terms to suit his passing purpose and, perhaps, to impress his general readership—using the word "anomic," for example, to mean a condition of being cut off from the tone and temper of a society, which is an injudicious borrowing from Durkheim's *anomique*, the masterless man.

In an age which needs the restoration of clarity and of reasonable persuasion, this pedantry in terminology is a sorry tendency. Genuine science does not need to cloak itself in convoluted verbiage.

Quite as warped as this distorting of language is what Sorokin calls "quantophrenia," or infatuation with statistical surveys and nose-counting. Because the natural sciences are non-moral—they have to do, that is, only with things, not with consciences—the aspiring "behavioral scientist" endeavors to develop a methodology which will be equally indifferent to moral norms. For old normative judgments, the social scientist of this persuasion substitutes opinion-surveys and statistical compilations. The behaviorist probably has never read the words of Carlyle: "Statistics is a science which ought to be honorable, the basis of many most important sciences; but . . .

a wise head is requisite for carrying it on. Conclusive facts are inseparable from inconclusive except by a head that already understands and knows."

There have sprung up the immense behavioral-research centers, most notably the Center for Advanced Study in the Behavioral Sciences, at Stanford University: the Mecca of this sect. The University of Michigan has a whole series of such institutions, supported by fat grants from foundations and government—the Center for Research on Conflict Resolution, the Research Center for Group Dynamics, the Survey Research Center.

C. Wright Mills, a radical gadfly among sociologists, suggested once that most research-assistants in behavioral institutes are chosen from among the second-rate: "I have seldom seen one of these young men, once he is well caught up, in a condition of genuine intellectual puzzlement." Servants to the computers, emancipated from the necessity of normative judgments, these assistants are spared the pains of real thought. Deficient in imagination, they mistake fact-accumulation for wisdom. The old Greeks had one word, philodoxer, for the lover of opinion; and another word, philosopher, for the lover of wisdom. Much modern opinion-and-behavior investigation is but philodoxy.

Such behaviorists usually ignore theory and history in favor of the currents of the year or of the decade; awareness of drift is all. One young behavioral professor said to me recently, when the name of a distinguished historian of ideas was mentioned, "How does he think he knows all this? Did he make a survey?" Resentment of imaginative powers and obsession with nose-counting are the behaviorist's form of anti-intellectualism.

The consequence of such narrowness and pretentious scientism is absurdity. One behavioristic study, cited by Barzun and Graff in their *Modern Researcher*, came to the solemn conclusion that "if in a given society an aunt resides with or near the mother, and assists in giving care to the child, the latter will regard her as a mother; less so, or not so, if the aunt lives at a distance."

Thus do some sociologists establish, as brilliant new discoveries, the tiny secrets of the bassinet. Another expensive survey, financed by the federal Office of Education, proposed the analysis of "succorance and playmirth"—that is, seeking of comfort and companionship in fun—among small children. The researchers came to the enlightening conclusion, after much statistics-juggling, that little boys like to play with little boys, and little girls with little girls.

Absurdities can grow into serious errors about men and communities. If a behavioral researcher acting upon the assumptions of nineteenth-century positivism investigates religious beliefs, he is likely to discover exactly what he expected to find: that religious convictions are unscientific, irrational, absurd, and perhaps dangerous. This "value-free" prejudice extends even to many of the more distinguished sociologists, including Dr. Robert Merton, who is not devoid of humane learning. According to Dr. Merton, sociological study, through survey techniques, has found that "people who reject orthodox religious beliefs are not more apt to engage in crime than people who hold fast to such beliefs."   This wondrous oversimplification suggests the theological and historical ignorance of the American sociologist, and his provinciality. What religion? In what country? Is that religion decayed into superstition or sociability? What is the historical background of the people studied? In Catania, for instance, a thief may be a professed Christian—most thieves there do so profess; but in Aberdeenshire, almost certainly he will not be. All the influences of culture and history are ignored in such complacent "findings," and so are all distinctions between different types of religious belief.

Aye, the behaviorist is opposed to prejudice—but, unaware of his own prejudices, because he has been deliberately cut off from theological, humane, and historical disciplines, he often mistakes his petty private rationality for self-evident truth. Although the complete behaviorist may deny the existence of objective values and normative understandings, nevertheless he does not escape, in his researches, the influence of his own value-judgments, even though they are unwittingly held as vague sentiments or animosities.

In his introduction to *The Human Meaning of the Social Sciences,* one well-known behaviorist, Daniel Lerner, declares that the social sciences have shown modern man that "there are no more eternal mysteries . . . there are no more eternal verities"; man is revealed as "plastic, variable, and amendable to reshaping." The energetic social scientist intends to set to work promptly at that reshaping, free from authority, prescription, and value-judgments.

Now the trouble with this view of social studies and their purpose is that to act without any norms except vague humanitarian sentiments may bring the person and the republic into grave confusion. It may injure the institutions which shelter community and freedom at home, and lead to the most serious of blunders in foreign policy. And there is no assurance that the social scientist will be governed always even by a vague humanitarianism. Why should he be? If no norms exist for man, why should we prefer humanitarianism to the personal and social experiments of the Nazis? The latter are more exciting and innovating, and the totalists readily provide their own behaviorists with a goodly supply of human subjects for uninhibited research and control.

Whatever his ambitions, the social scientist never can be wholly value-free, never can attain the dispassionate attitude of the natural scientist—not if he has even a vestigial conscience. For the social scientist is dealing not with things soulless or inanimate or abstract, but with man, living and erratic man, in complex community. Human beings are the least controllable, verifiable, law-obeying, and predictable of subjects. If man were predictable fully, he would cease to be truly human.

Now of course there can be ascertained certain general rules concerning human behavior in community; indeed, for a long while an ample body of literature on the subject has been available— though often ignored by the novelty-seeking behavioral scientist. But the more important part of this literature is not "scientific" in the strict modern sense. This knowledge is the acquisition of poets, theologians, political theorists, moralists, jurists, and men of imagination and logical powers generally.

One may learn much about the first principles of human nature from Dante or Samuel Johnson; but this is not the sort of knowledge which fits into the calculations of the astronomer or the engineer. Plato and Cicero, Montesquieu and Burke, are the sources of much wisdom concerning the civil social order; yet they are not scientists in the sense of the natural sciences. Even when one finds a philosopher like Hume, severely logical and methodical, the zealot for behavioral methods must be dismayed by Hume's conclusion that rational accounting for morals and politics simply is impossible.

In fine, I think that the behavioral scientist has been the victim of illusion when he has attempted to remedy all the ills to which community is heir by the application of the techniques of physics and chemistry and biology. "It is this false analogy with mechanics and mathematics," says Professor S. Herbert Frankel, of Oxford, "that accounts for the facile belief that the problem involved in living and working together in a community is similar to the problem of finding, by abstract thought or logical deduction, the 'unknown' factor in an equation. In the realm of organic life there is, and can be, no final solution—other than death itself. . . . Those who arrogantly write solutions upon their political banners . . . offend the very nature of all social evolution, which rests on the slow unfolding of institutions, laws, and habit-patterns of thought and action." Amen to that.

By cutting himself off from tradition and theory, by ignoring theology and ethics and humane letters, the average behavioral scientist has deprived himself of the principal instruments for understanding human behavior—or for affecting any enduring improvement of society, let alone the "solution" of human striving which he often seeks. If a scientist at all, the behaviorist has become a scientist without reliable means for measuring and weighing. Infatuated with the empirical method, the doctrinaire social scientist omits from his calculations the higher and more enduring elements in human behavior.

As Sorokin argues, modern social science desperately needs reinvigoration of social theory and observation through the employment of reason and the recognition of poets' and philosophers' genius. Only by a return to the true sources of wisdom—which in part are the visions of genius—can the critic of society find standards by which to measure our present discontents and to propose remedies.

Neither the utopian sociologist of the old positivistic breed nor the survey-taking behaviorist of our time is prepared to confront the Gorgon's head of twentieth-century social disintegration. What social studies need more than anything else, I suspect, is the recovery of norms: a restoration of normative disciplines, a return to knowledge of standards for human personality and for the just social order. A few sociologists already have turned that way.

It is pointless, and at heart unscientific, to survey the shifting opinions of the hour unless one recognizes standards in opinion—that is, sources of truth. And it is pointless to ape the natural sciences when one has to do with whimsical and impatient and irrational mankind. Modern society needs not the short-sighted ministrations of the research-technician, but the artist's touch. Because the pure behaviorist has no imagination and no normative convictions, he soon falls victim to some energetic ideologue; and his "value-free" methods are applied to the production of ideological propaganda, masquerading as scientific objectivity.

Behaviorism in Politics

"Behavior" means the manner in which anything acts or operates. The study of how men actually behave in community is a proper part of political science, and Aristotle may be considered the first eminent practitioner of the behavioral method in politics. Mere abstract doctrine and theoretic dogma can be infinitely dangerous when divorced from an understanding of the practical conduct of the commonwealth and of popular preferences and beliefs. Political science must recognize this complexity of custom, institution, and moral conviction. In this sense, political theory always requires the check and correction of behavioral investigation.

Yet the behavioral tail may come to wag the philosophical dog. As two recent succinct definitions suggest, there is, among the exponents of behaviorism, a tendency to erect their method into scientistic dogmas. One definition of "behaviorism" occurs in the third edition (1934) of *The Concise Oxford Dictionary of Current English:* "Doctrine that, given adequate knowledge, all human actions admit of analysis into stimulus and response, and that ability to predict them depends on exhaustive study of behavior in that light." The other may be found in the Thorndike-Barnhart *Comprehensive Desk Dictionary* (1951): "Doctrine that the objective acts of persons and animals are the chief or only subject matter of scientific psychology." To chain the venerable study of politics to a quasi-scientific hypothesis of recent psychology is risky, I think; at best, the application of behavioral doctrines to political science has limitations that must be recognized.

Political science includes consideration of the form of government, the principles upon which government rests, the extent of governmental intervention in public and private affairs, the charac-

ter of laws in relation to community and individual, and the inter-
course of citizens as members of a community. Also it comprehends
ideas of order, justice, freedom, and—of increasing importance
nowadays—concepts of the comity of nations. Can behavioral
methodology suffice for all these profound matters?

So the enthusiasts for behaviorism imply, and sometimes roundly
declare. Can theories borrowed from mechanistic psychology of the
nineteenth and twentieth centuries satisfactorily supplant the political philosophy and the art of statecraft which have descended to us
from classical times? Can behavior be all? Can theory, historical
experience, prescription, jurisprudence, precept, and a nation's
constitutional usage be swept neatly into the limbo of forgotten
things, yielding to a new domination of positivistic and utilitarian
character, which recognizes only stimulus and response as clues to
political knowledge? Is a new "social science," formed in emulation
of the methods of natural science—or what are said to be natural
science's ways—altogether superior to the humane and jurisprudential methods for the governance of men in community? The
thoroughgoing behaviorists, now strong in America, answer in the
affirmative.

But I essay here to suggest certain political problems and modes
and areas in which behavioral assumptions quickly encounter severe difficulties. Because some of these realms are the primary concerns of political science, I venture to maintain that, in the long
run, the behaviorists must relinquish their claim to suzerainty, sub-
siding to the condition of partners, not masters, in the study of
politics.

Though political behaviorism has taken pride of place chiefly
since the Second World War, its popularity with American professors is not wholly surprising, for it accords well enough, superficially, with vulgarized pragmatism in these United States. American
society seemingly has contrived well enough to get along without
political philosophy since the adopting of the Constitution, except
for the era of the Civil War. Snug in the cruise-boat of American
prosperity and complacency, many political scientists have acted
upon the assumption—held half unconsciously—that nothing ever
has happened in American history, and nothing ever will: we have
only to drift with the current of events, observing our own behavior
and occasionally giving a nudge to the tiller, through "the engi-

neering of consent." Who requires compass or navigational art? That the placid voyage might end at Niagara or in the Dead Sea— why, anyone who so suggests either must lie under the dead hand of exploded religious mythology or else must suffer from an anxiety-neurosis. The fact that many of the nations, in our century, have fallen into the antagonist world of madness and despair is not permitted to disturb the behaviorist's assurance: it can't happen here, for we Americans are going to govern ourselves scientifically, without bothering about divisive and complex theories.

Upon their theory that theory is irrelevant, the American behaviorists have founded an empire. American taste for quantitative undertakings has got the behavioral scientists unlimited funds from the big foundations—and money buys departments and whole universities. As the successful little American restaurant—in this quite unlike its French or Italian or English counterpart—at once aspires to grow enormous or to become a chain, so any successful novelty in the American university conceives a passion for power, bigness, and graduate assistants. Any academic discipline that professes to prefer Fact and Practical Result to Theory may find favor with benefactors; thus universities proudly develop curricula in Trailer-Camp Management. And so, I suggest, the useful behavioral auxiliary to the intellectual discipline of politics has dignified itself and enriched itself, until its entrepreneurs claim hegemony over all social studies and refer majestically to the Behavioral Sciences—as if nothing but Behaviorism were intellectually decent in social studies nowadays.

As pragmatism is the negation of philosophy, so behaviorism, once erected into a system, is a denial of political rationality; yet only tardily do the behaviorists recognize the paradox they have created. If the estrangement of many political scientists from theory, history, and prescription endures long enough, the influence of their discipline upon the living community will dwindle—with alarming results, perhaps, for the commonwealth. For human beings are not content merely to behave, to react to stimuli: also they think. In the absence of political philosophy, they may embrace ideology.

Like any man, any scholarly discipline is the healthier for knowing the limits of its own strength. Behavior is only behavior, not first principle. "The rise of the behavioral sciences could mean the disintegration of political science," Francis Graham Wilson writes. "For, first, it may mean that the social scientists, and more particularly the Political Scientist, will cease to represent the public order which supports him. . . . In the end either the revolution of behavioral science will destroy the system of transcendent thought that is found in the life of those who cannot be classified as 'intellectuals,' or a more conservative and humanistic intellectualism will prevail. . . . In a second sense, such a science of politics is destructive because it cannot support the proof of values. In times of crisis it must either desert its position or it must become silent while lesser figures propound the truth."*

With Professor Wilson, I suggest that human action and social operation are impelled by belief, even though the believer may be aware only amorphously of his intellectual premises; and that a political science dominated by a doctrinaire "behavioral" contempt for traditional wisdom—a political science literally anti-intellectual, as it would be anti-moral—must cease to be science at all. Therefore I suggest several segments of political study which are not amenable to behavioristic treatment. Somewhat arbitrarily, because of the limits of space, I choose to touch upon the relationship of politics to religion and morals, to the principles of order, to the principles of justice, to the principles of freedom, and to the problems of international comity. If behaviorism cannot deal unaided with questions so fundamental as these to political science, it seems time for the behavioral scholars to effect some reconciliation with their theoretical and historical and institutional and jurisprudential colleagues.

Turn we first to religion and morals. Although generally the behaviorists treat with indifference or contempt any such concerns, their own predilection for molding society into a thoroughly democratic, egalitarian, strifeless unity necessarily brings them face to face—no matter how disconcerting this may be—with religious and moral influences upon politics. No longer are the behaviorists content to describe, or even to predict. Like Comte, most of them are intent upon control of the future; with Harold Lasswell, they hope

* Wilson, "The Behaviorist's Persuasion," *Modern Age*, vol. 3 (Summer, 1959), p. 316.

to efface the old order of things. Since natural science talks of prediction and control, why should not social scientists be entitled to make the course of man predictable and controllable?

Yet what would such a predictable and controllable society be like? Having disavowed all value-judgments, how can the political behaviorists demonstrate their utopia of democracy, equality of condition, and social unity to be superior to a society of autocracy, inequality, and diversity? The behaviorists lack even dogmatic atheism to fall back upon as sanction for their ideology. But they do recognize that religious faith is a formidable barrier to the attainment of their behavioral secular paradise.

Now it is not surprising that the behaviorists, in their analysis of modern American society, write as if religion scarcely existed here —despite the high records of church attendance—or as if it were no more than the refuge of the ignorant and bigoted. What have been called "the American Religion" and "the ethos of sociability" are prevalent in many American churches—a soft and dull religiosity, at best. The hot social gospellers, demonstrating against American foreign policy or identifying themselves with the more extreme forms of "civil rights" activity, do not much impress the behaviorists, either: for these are ineffectual people, these marchers to fife and drum ecclesiastic, and besides their religious convictions are submerged in their ideological proclivities.

Yet the power of faith may be much greater than the behaviorist thinks it. Churches decline throughout history—and revive as often; and, more important for the political scientist perhaps, religious assumptions about the nature of man and society continue to leaven a people and give motive to their actions long after the formal cult has decayed. We may be entering a "post-Christian era," but Christian doctrines remain the cement of social order and retain an evocative power. To ignore this enduring element of human behavior, while emphasizing voting records in obscure Tennessee districts and analyzing eccentric groups in the suburbs, surely is a curious way to go about the business of prediction and control of Brave New World. Can it be that the behaviorists shy away from religious considerations because they are almost wholly ignorant of theological and ethical doctrine? Or that they fear to touch pitch, lest they be defiled?

At any rate, religious convictions and their political influences no more can be left out of a sound political scientist's reckoning than bedrock can be omitted from the calculations of a bridge-builder. In every age, church and state must be in tension—even if the church is only the church of inverted religion, ideology. The universal mass-state which some behaviorists smile upon would be challenged repeatedly by the Christian concept of personal responsibility. Only a Jacobin or a Bolshevik persecution, or else a state monopoly of education, could break this rival power. However old-fangled the behaviorists may take religion and prescriptive morality to be, these realities form behavior. They have helped to form even the ideas of the behaviorists. And were religious conviction and the cake of moral custom to be broken altogether, what would the behaviorists put in their place, as motives to integrity and social duty?

Apparently disturbed by this problem, Harold Lasswell writes repeatedly of "the dignity of man" as object and goal of the good society. But the essence of this dignity, and its source, Lasswell does not describe. Nor can he, within the limits of behaviorism or of "positive liberalism." For the very phrase "the dignity of man" is of Christian origin. Man has dignity because he is created in the image of God, and is made for eternity, and possesses an immortal essence that marks him off from the beasts that perish. This lacking, how much dignity can be discerned in the life of the average sensual man? Pico della Mirandola, in 1486, best expressed the concept of which Lasswell employs only the ghost. By "the dignity of man," Pico meant the high nobility of disciplined reason and imagination, human nature as redeemed by Christ, the uplifting of the truly human person through an exercise of soul and mind. But Professor Lasswell and the other behaviorists mean nothing of this sort. For them, there is but one law, if any law, and man is simply the creature of stimulus and response, like all other creatures. It is hard to say what Lasswell means by his "dignity of man," except that everybody should be like everybody else.

If, then, the behaviorists cannot make anything of religion and morality, and can define no norms—not even values—as guides for the civil social order, it must suffice to suggest that they might turn to the old normative politics for assistance. Plato and St. Augustine, after all, did have something to say about the distinctions between good and evil, in the soul and in society.

Behaviorism and the Fundamental Challenges of Politics

The objects of the civil social order are the maintenance of order and justice and freedom. What has the behaviorist to say about these ends?

For both the student of politics and the statesman, order is primary: until some tolerable political order is achieved, nothing else can be. Order is the harmonious arrangement of classes and functions which guards justice and obtains willing consent to law and ensures that we shall be safe together. Order also signifies the honor or dignity of a rank in society, and it signifies those established usages which deserve veneration. Through a satisfactory order are produced political leaders, the makers of public decisions.

To the problem of order the behaviorists have given little more attention than they have to the relationship between religio-ethical beliefs and the state. It seems improbable that their methods can produce a tolerable concept of order—or even recognize and preserve an existing order.

The most learned and severe critic of behaviorism, Professor Leo Strauss, points out that this "new political science" is governed by a vague ideological democratism, provincial in its outlook, mistaking American institutions and habits for universals.

"The alleged value-free analysis of political phenomena is controlled by an unavowed commitment built into the new political science to that version of liberal democracy," Strauss writes. "That version of liberal democracy is not discussed openly and impartially, with full consideration of all relevant pros and cons. . . . The new political science looks for laws of human behavior to be discovered by means of data supplied through certain techniques of research which are believed to guarantee the maximum of objectivity; it therefore puts a premium on the study of things which occur frequently now in democratic societies: neither those in their graves nor those behind the Curtains can respond to questionnaires or to interviews. . . . Yet this same new political science came into being through the revolt against what one may call the democratic orthodoxy of the immediate past. It had learned certain lessons which were hard for that orthodoxy to swallow regarding the irrationality of the masses and the necessity of elites; if it had been wise it would have learned those lessons from the galaxy of anti-democratic thinkers of the remote past."*

Whatever the typical behaviorist may have discovered about the necessity for leadership, he makes no clear provision for virtuous leaders in his system; in fine, the behavioral view of society is disorderly. How is our society, or any political order, to arrive at sound general decisions concerning public policy? Not by elevated intellectual and political leadership, the aristocracy or the elite, it appears. Rather, the behaviorist resorts once more to a muddy democratism, in which one "value" is quite as good as any other, any one man's random opinion or inchoate desire is equipollent to any other man's. An interesting example of this attitude is "Project Aimscales," conducted by the Public Opinion Laboratory at the University of Washington. The Laboratory's director, Mr. Stuart C. Dodd, desires to measure, predict, and control American national goals, through an intricate system of polls in depth and calibration of opinions and desires.

"Aimscales can improve the *democratic* pursuit of goals," Mr. Dodd writes. "For through its representative polls-in-depth, all citizens and their leaders can take part in choosing the goals and the programs thereto. The individual's preferences and efforts and satisfactions can be taken into account in due proportion toward practicing the theory of democracy." †

Without criticizing in detail this amusing scheme—which, as explained by its author, seems almost a burlesque of behaviorist techniques and objectives—I observe merely that this "aimscale" is founded upon a transparent fallacy. Dodd takes it for granted that important national decisions are made by ascertaining what the mass of the people desire at any particular moment; and that the average man knows what he wants, and deserves to get it. Dodd's intention is merely to make it easier for the "decision-makers" (his own term) to ascertain accurately the state of popular appetites at

* Leo Strauss, "An Epilogue," in Storing, *Essays on the Scientific Study of Politics* (New York, 1962).

† Stuart C. Dodd, "Ascertaining National Goals: Project Aimscales," *The American Behavioral Scientist,* Vol. IV (March, 1961), pp. 11-15.

any given time. Then, with dispatch, the decision-makers can execute the general will, for national goals simply are what mass appetite dictates—for instance, choice among "budget categories, e.g., Defense Department operation, crop price supports, foreign aid, research, retiring the debt, and so forth."

Well! Any government that should attempt to "accelerate full and balanced progress" by such devices soon would cease to maintain any order at all. To assume that the average citizen entertains reasoned convictions, or even consistent desires, on a vast multitude of questions, grave or trivial—and to try to rule a nation according to the calculation of these appetites—is to ignore the whole business of opinion-forming. More important still, the "decision-maker" is converted into a humble follower, or rather a pander to ephemeral preferences. Such a society would be deprived of all leadership and energy—except that supplied by the behavioral scientist, at work controlling progress through his punch-card system. But progress whither? This is the behaviorist's ideology of democratism reduced to absurdity.

There exists little danger that this country might endeavor to govern itself by Project Aimscales—though the degradation of the democratic dogma is at work in other ways. I touch upon this design merely to suggest the unreality into which the behaviorist (who thinks himself supremely realistic) often falls; and to illustrate the inadequacy of behaviorism for recognizing—let alone formulating—the principles of order.

As for the principles of justice, the representative behaviorist is no clearer in this field. One might assume that the representative behaviorist would be a Benthamite in his concept of justice. For if political science is to be "value-free" and is to recognize no religious or ethical norms, no source remains for justice but the decrees of governors. Whatever is, is right; it is a behavior pattern. The "value-judgments" and distributive justice of Communist People's Courts and Nazi tribunals have as much claim to authority, on this basis, as does the Supreme Court of the United States or the King's Bench.

In defiance of his own system, nevertheless, the typical behaviorist retains a prejudice in favor of an undefined "democracy," with civil liberties attached. And he entertains, often, a concept of justice which is not Platonic or Ciceronian or Scholastic or Utilitarian, and which has nothing to do with the Corpus Juris or the decisions of the Supreme Court. His is not a *truly* behavioral view of justice (if by behaviorism we mean the scientific observation of existing phenomena), for it is in conflict with the prevailing judicial practices and established rights in the United States.

For the typical behaviorist's idea of justice seems to be a vulgarized Marxism. It assumes that equality of condition is an absolute good, and that the power of the state ought to work toward this egalitarianism. It relishes the prospect of a society from which all tensions and differences will have been eliminated, in which all individuals will be treated as identical units. Not all behaviorists would dash impetuously down the road to this brummagem utopia; but so far as one can define their theory of justice, such are its roots.

In discussion once with a professor of political science at a western university, I found that he thought the federal government should collect all school revenues through the United States and allocate them according to need. "But that's not justice," I protested.

"Why, of course it's justice; that's what justice *is!*" It became clear that he believed a central political authority ought to gather the whole income of a nation and redistribute it annually according to need and merit. This professor was not a Communist—merely an advanced behaviorist, pressing for "positive liberalism."

Like too many other behavioral scholars, this gentleman suffered from what Eric Voegelin calls "theoretical illiteracy." The whole immense complexity of the problem of justice, commutative and distributive, from Job to the International Court of Justice, quite escaped him. In this, the typical behaviorist's tendency to ignore or deny strong differences among individuals and classes and nations has its part. "To each his own" seemed to my professor mere selfishness. Innocent of jurisprudence and of the history of law, my acquaintance filled the vacuum with a notion of justice sentimental and ideological. If executed, this system of "justice" probably would have been disagreeable to this particular behaviorist, his income already being greater than the national average; he would have had to alter his own behavior-patterns considerably. And his assumption that somehow a beneficent authority at the national capital might sit forever Rhadamanthus-like, doling out to every American his proper deserts, was the reduction of politics to puerility. *No* political science would be better than such sentimentality, so divorced from the nature of things, as this.

Precisely because he disdains theory and customary usage, the average behaviorist falls into pits of this sort; and, just so, he weakens his own influence upon men of affairs. It is so with his understanding of freedom.

It seems natural that any group of political scientists should have much to say about ordered liberty nowadays. For despite the high degree of personal freedom which remains in America, more than half the world is servile now, and everywhere the dangers to real freedom are more dismaying in this mass-age than they have been for centuries: the powers and efficacy of the modern state, including the influence of propaganda, invest modern government with possibilities for repression that never before existed in any civilized society.

But what do we find upon reading the numerous, and monthly increasing, works of the behaviorists? Sensible or imaginative discussion of freedom is scanty in that quarter. What analysis of freedom and its difficulties we do encounter is amorphous and glancing, with few exceptions.

Among the behaviorists, "freedom" is confounded with "democracy"—the latter, by implication, an absolute respected by scholars who deny all absolutes; surely, we are meant to infer, we always will be free so long as we are democratic. The behaviorists suggest that we dismiss the vaticinations of Tocqueville and even of Madison. Sometimes they maintain that freedom is the ability to spend one's time as one likes; and since we are more prosperous nowadays, and have the prospect of a prosperity guaranteed by central political authority, surely we are more free.

This feebleness in apprehending the precarious state of modern liberty is produced by behaviorism's natural deficiencies. Modern freedom is the result of three principal influences. First, we derive freedom from the Christian belief in the free and responsible person, meant for eternity. Second, freedom comes from the heritage of prescriptive rights and constitutional guarantees that grew out of medieval and modern historical experience. Third, the kind of freedom we know, at least in the West, has been powerfully influenced by the framework of a free economy, developing since the beginnings of the Commercial Revolution.

But the behaviorist refuses to water these roots. Christianity he rejects as undone by the triumph of science; prescriptive law and right he despises in his neoterism; and often he entertains a mighty prejudice against "capitalism," feeling it his duty to direct behavior into non-competitive channels, leading to a society without economic challenge—or, presumably, without economic response. So, having turned his back on the roots of ordered liberty, the behaviorist strays in the desert of his own impoverished vocabulary, where "freedom" is only a semantic trick—except when it is supposed to mean the opportunity to dissent from middle-class dominations. In the discussion of freedom, as of much else, the behaviorist is cribbed within the "empirical" ideology he has created.

If behaviorism stopped here, its treatment of the principles of freedom would be shabby enough. But scientistic political thought goes farther still with Harold Lasswell and some of his disciples; it contemplates with a smile the prospect of a political order from which freedom, in the old sense of the word, will have vanished completely. Bernard Crick, the most astute foreign commentator upon American political thought in recent years, points out the "direct totalitarian implication in Lasswell's manner of thought," for Lasswell would weed out, through education, any "moral mavericks" (Lasswell's own phrase) who might object to the changeless and monotonous Lasswell utopia—such mavericks as Christians, American constitutionalists, and all who (again in Lasswell's own terms) "take a dim view of human perfectability." As Crick notes, Lasswell and his school would realize, were it in their power, precisely the democratic despotism that Tocqueville dreaded.*

Lasswell's future political order would be dominated by the social psychiatrist invested with enormous power—which he would exercise, as Lasswell admits, for his own gratification. This, as Robert Horwitz writes, "is a prospect to strike terror in the hearts of free men"—this "Free Man's Commonwealth," as Lasswell calls his utopia. With Lasswell, social control—the third function of behavioral political science—has eclipsed description and prediction, and has abolished freedom. This bureaucratic social psychiatrist of the "Free Man's Commonwealth," in Horwitz's words, is something more than the Grand Inquisitor.

* Bernard Crick, *The American Science of Politics* (London, 1959), pp. 195-196.

"Having been taught to deal with himself and others 'objectively' —and having in addition, secured unlimited power—he will be in a position," Horwitz comments, "to secure for himself a level of indulgence utterly beyond the reach of traditional political man and, *at the same time,* to free his subjects from anxiety, tension, and conflict—to indulge them in a permanent, pleasant, psychological coma. He will, in a word, make those tyrannies with which *homo politicus* has periodically tarnished the history of mankind look, literally, like child's play."*

It is unnecessary to point out the similarities between this "Free Man's Commonwealth" and the Logicalist regime of *Seven Days in New Crete,* or the Ingsoc of *1984.* To put the matter as delicately as possible, the concept of freedom is not a segment of political science conspicuously amenable to behavioristic treatment.

Behaviorism in a World of Conflict

Possibly the behaviorist himself may regard theories of order, justice, and freedom as too misty to deserve the consideration of the new political scientist. The comity of nations, nevertheless, he scarcely can ignore in our time of troubles. And from scholarly reformers of foreign policy, among them Hans Morgenthau and Robert Strausz-Hupé, comes much of the shrewdest criticism of the behaviorists.

After some unkind cuts at behaviorism in general, the director of the Foreign Policy Research Institute at the University of Pennsylvania argues that powers of introspection, in a desperately practical sense, may be much injured by reliance upon behavioral analogies.

"Thus, for example, not a few Western statesmen are prone to act on the assumption that because a Communist leader *behaves* on certain occasions as such leaders are wont to do, he will prove a predictable and manageable quantity in every world political equation. . . ." Strausz-Hupé writes. "Since the average Soviet citizen displays a well-documented interest in electrical refrigerators and

* Horwitz, "Scientific Propaganda: Harold D. Lasswell," in Storing, *Essays on the Scientific Study of Politics, op. cit.,* pp. 300-304.

cars, the Soviet rulers will seek to satisfy their demand for semi-durable goods, cut down on military hardware, and settle down to the *status quo*—just as our statesmen would do were they in the Soviets' shoes. These clichés reflect all that is most shallow in reliance on both behavioral analogy and introspective analogy. Our 'statesman,' because he has abandoned an ethical position to empiricism, is smitten with deafness to the voice of intuition and with blindness to observable facts: he understands anything except the inwardness of political conduct."*

The structure of political organization throughout the world, Strausz-Hupé continues, is in urgent need of restoration and even reconstitution, particularly in international relationships and in the national and sub-natural societies that have just emerged from long isolation. Interdependence must grow. For sympathetic development among nations, a theory of institutional synthesis is required, but the behaviorist's contempt for theory, and his preoccupation with American life, prevent him from doing his part in this work. Worse, such misconceptions prevent many American scholars and officials, affected by behavioral doctrines, from putting clearly before the nations the case of America and her allies—indeed, of Western civilization—for, when political science rejects human consciousness and reason, one falls into a habit of dealing with the leaders of other nations as if they, too, were simply behavioral specimens.

American behaviorism has many of the aspects of a "cultural lag." It is a hothouse plant, nurtured in the comparatively safe United States and taking as a condition of its existence the "givenness" of American life. This isolation from the ideas and the risks of the rest of the world now has ended: America will change, and, for intelligent change, theory and imaginative leadership are required. Behaviorism cannot suffice, for Americans no longer can be snug as guinea-pigs. International order, and our own security, require a transcending of methods applied by biologists and psychologists to the study of canine behavior. "The 'science of politics' has been a political doctrine and an intellectual movement passionately concerned to regain that original American sense of uniqueness and completeness which has been frustrated by the incalculable politics

* Strausz-Hupé, "Social Science versus the Obsession of 'Scientism,' " in Schoeck and Wiggins, *Scientism and Values* (Princeton, 1960), p. 227.

of an undeniable reinvolvement in a complicated and changing outside world," Bernard Crick says. "Such a movement could only succeed in the sense of forsaking actual politics for the abstract safety and certainty of pseudo-science."*

I agree with Crick that an understanding of the requirements for international order scarcely is a strong point of the behaviorists' persuasion.

Finally, if by behaviorism we are to understand prudent research in a practical way in well-defined political and social matters; if we mean by the word principally a branch of political science concerned with verification and investigation in partnership with theory and historical study—why, then there is no more opposition between the great tradition of politics and the practitioners of behavioral methods than there is between the theorist of quantum mechanics and the designers and operators of a cyclotron.

But the new inverted orthodoxy of Behaviorism with a capital B has disdained this amicable partnership. By a perilous analogy, the Behaviorists have transferred from zoology to psychology, and then to politics, certain theories about animal behavior which already are seriously challenged in their original biological discipline. And, thrusting aside human reason into any handy cubbyhole, they have maintained that observed behavior, minus consciousness, actually can suffice for the governance of man. Not with human nature or the character of institutions, but with irrational members of almost inexplicable groups, the dedicated Behaviorist has concerned himself.

As an explanation of the great mysterious incorporation of the human race, this doctrinaire Benthamism now is obsolete—as absurd and impractical as the phrenology of Spurzheim and Gall, in which pseudo-science Comte believed utterly. It won't wash, in American affairs or in international relations. It has turned into an ideology.

By all means, let us give empirical tools sufficient praise. But it is men with imagination and conscience who employ the tools. If a zealous Behaviorist seizes these tools, he will carve the "Free Man's Commonwealth" for us: the prison-commonwealth. The Academy of Athens was not the Academy of Lagado, and the American Republic is not a cage for white mice.

* Crick, *op. cit.,* pp. 247-248.

V. THE UNTHINKING CENTRALIZER

Federalism in Peril

THE PERMANENT THINGS IN AMERICAN POLITICS ARE BOUND UP
with the federal structure of government and with what Orestes
Brownson called "territorial democracy." With some speed, though
on no coherent design, the American political structure is being
converted into a centralized system; and if this process goes far
enough, political permanence in this country may be lost altogether, the American people being launched upon the rough sea of
uncontrollable innovation.

Although most ideologues are centralizers, not all centralizers
are ideologues. Some centralizers-on-principle are at work among
us; but most of the men who recommend or accept political
centralization in one respect or another are governed by fancied
self-interest or imagined interest of a particular group, rather than
by abstract doctrine, in this country. We slip into a totalist order in
a fit of absence of mind.

In theory and, to no small extent, in practice, the American
system remains federal today. But pressures to supplant effective
federalism by a centralized "plebiscitary democracy" are strong.
When farmers of the most remote county are supervised by Wash-
ington-appointed officials; when hot lunches in schools are subsidized and regulated by central authority; when federal courts sit in

judgment on the boundaries of state legislative districts—then the process of centralization already is well advanced.

Some intelligent men are taking alarm—among them, somewhat abruptly, such liberal Democrats as Richard Goodwin and Daniel Moynihan, both of whom now acknowledge that conservatives have been quite right in supporting the cause of state and local governments, as against central power. It is becoming clear that great modern cities cannot be administered competently by a remote central bureaucracy, for one thing. Still, centralization continues to increase, almost mindlessly; and until we refresh our understanding of the limits of central political authority, and of the merits of genuine federalism and of territorial democracy, the concentration of power in the national capital will not be arrested.

A century ago, Orestes Brownson wrote that the United States of America form a republic in which territorial democracy prevails locally. The general or federal institutions were republican, not democratic, in character: that is, the Federal Constitution deliberately erected barriers against direct popular control of the national political apparatus. But in their townships and counties, and to some extent even in their state governments, the mass of the people enjoyed strong powers and rights—"territorial democracy." This manner of democracy Brownson contrasted with "Jacobin democracy," the infatuation with an abstract, infallible People, and the concentration of "popular" power in an absolute, centralized government.

Only a generation before Brownson wrote, Tocqueville had described and praised the institutions of this peculiar political system, in which he saw a principal safeguard against democratic despotism and enervating centralization. The New England town meeting is the perfect example of territorial democracy at work; but analogous institutions existed from the first in the counties of the Southern states; and upon one pattern or another, American local government has been directly responsive to popular opinion.

The state governments, though not directly democratic, were meant to stand between the national administration and local interests, and to represent territorial convictions and carry on territorial administration in a fashion which the government at Washington could not and should not attempt. "State rights" really are state powers: the states, in theory, do not derive their authority from the general government, but are the basic political entities.

In America, centralization on principle has had few frank champions. Among the leaders of the early Republic, only one—Alexander Hamilton—would have preferred a political structure more concentrated than the present Constitution of the United States and the existing state constitutions and local establishments. Although leaders of factions so hostile toward one another as John Adams, Thomas Jefferson, and John Randolph differed greatly upon questions of national and state policy, they shared an attachment to the principle of state and local control of most political functions.

"Federalism" is not altogether a satisfactory term of politics. In the beginning, the word implied "league," rather than union; and doubtless the majority of Americans who voted to ratify the Federal Constitution believed that they were approving merely a more efficient form of the Articles of Confederation; it was sufficiently difficult, indeed, to persuade them to accept the Constitution even upon such an understanding. Yet the structure created at Philadelphia amounted to a new pattern of government, not truly federal in the old sense of that word; it was, as John Adams said, a new system, not founded upon the model of those historic confederations in which the federal council was only a diplomatic body.

Thus the success of the American Republic has altered the usage of the very word "federalism," which no longer is commonly taken to mean a simple league of sovereign states. Nowadays the signification of this term is adequately expressed by the third definition offered in *The Century Dictionary* (edition of 1904):

"Pertaining to a union of states in some essential degree constituted by and deriving its power from the people of all, considered as an entirety, and not solely by and from each of the states separately; as, a *federal* government, such as the governments of the United States, Switzerland, and some of the Spanish-American republics. A *federal* government is properly one in which the federal authority is independent of any of its component parts within the sphere of the federal action; distinguished from a *confederate* government, in which the states alone are sovereign, and which possesses no inherent power."

Yet this is not all. "Federalism" still implies a voluntary and limited union for certain defined purposes, rather than a central system of government. In his essay "Federalism and Freedom," Professor Werner Kägi, of Zurich, distinguishes five characteristics of federalism: (a) federalism is an order of "multiplicity in unity"; (b) federalism is an order that is based upon the autonomy of the narrower communities; (c) federalism is an order in which the smaller circles and communities are granted the maximum possible power to direct their own affairs; (d) federalism is an order which makes it possible for minorities to live together in freedom; (e) federalism is an order built upwards from the smaller communities, in which the conditions can, to a certain degree, be seen at a glance, and in which relationships have, to a certain degree, remained on a personal footing.*

As Kägi points out, the spirit of federalism sometimes subsists in political systems that do not bear the formal label "federal"—as in Britain, where in practice and by prescription county and town authorities retain large permanent rights and powers (not to mention the partial autonomy of Scotland, Northern Ireland, and even Wales), although in theory Parliament is supreme under the Crown. And some orders that still are called "federal" have ceased, in large part, so to operate. In general, one may say that a modern federal order divides power between a general government and territorial governments, with the aim of safeguarding local liberties while securing national interests.

When several states have joined to establish a federal union, one of their two principal aims ordinarily has been the preservation of what we now call "democracy"—that is, local representation of popular interests. The most celebrated champions of democracy, indeed, have not expected democracy ever to be expressed in a national government. "God alone can rule the *world*," says Rousseau, "and to govern great nations requires superhuman qualities." The advocates of centralization have not been practical democrats, but rather administrators (whether or not levelling in their social proclivities) like Turgot, an intendant of the Old Regime, who wrote to Dr. Price that in America the people should collect "all authority into one centre, the nation." To this, John Adams replied mordantly:

* Kägi, "Federalism and Freedom," in Hunold (ed.), *Freedom and Serfdom, an Anthology of Western Thought* (Dordrecht, 1961).

"It is easily understood how all authority may be collected into 'one centre' in a despot or monarch; but how it may be done when the centre is to be the nation, is much more difficult to comprehend. . . . If, after the pains of 'collecting all authority into one centre,' that centre is to be the nation, we shall remain exactly where we began, and no collection of authority at all will be made. The nation will be the authority, and the authority the nation. The centre will be the circle, and the circle the centre. When a number of men, women, and children, are simply congregated together, there is no political authority among them; nor any natural authority, but that of parents over their children."

To resort to a word cherished by Ambrose Bierce, truly central government and true democracy are incompossible. The American "federal" system was adopted to perpetuate and protect and improve the institutions of territorial democracy that already existed in America—even though the phrase "territorial democracy" was not then employed. If the federal character of American government decays badly, then American democracy also must decline terribly, until nothing remains of it but a name; and the new "democrats" may be economic and social levellers, indeed, but they will give popular government short shrift.

Genuine federalism, then, is the protector both of private rights and of local interests and powers of free decision. "Our organic law seeks to harmonize all government action with the talent of a truly free people for self-government," Dr. Felix Morley writes in his book *Freedom and Federalism*. "They remain free only as long as they maintain this spiritual aspiration. Without faith, the Constitution fails. Whether or not our Federal Republic will be maintained is therefore at bottom a moral issue. It depends as much on the churches and the synagogues as on the legislators and the law courts. The growth of Big Government goes hand in hand with the loss of Big Conviction."

Federalism, *modern* federalism, is a device to reconcile self-government—territorial democracy—with the great exigencies of the nation-state. If the federal character of government vanishes, it still may be possible to maintain national strength—though even here, among a people long accustomed to self-government, there are grave difficulties. But in such an eventuality, it will not be possible to retain the institutions of orderly and genuine democracy. Many of the ardent advocates of centralization being at the same time ardent democrats, they ought to confront this conundrum with something better than cries of "The people, yes!"

Centralizers' Illusions

Though not truly federal in the older sense of that word, the American constitutional system has succeeded, most of the time, in dividing power justly between the general government and the state governments, and in providing for national necessities. "When it is not necessary to change," said Falkland, "it is necessary not to change." So a heavy burden of proof rests upon the advocates of centralization in America: by imprudent alteration, we would run severe risk of an enduring constriction of freedom and an enduring injury to order.

There exist Americans who would like to convert the American political system into a *complete* national government. But even today, few practical politicians openly advocate political centralization and the removal of power from the hands of the citizenry. The notion of "plebiscitary" or Jacobin democracy, far from obtaining public sanction, remains confined to small circles of governmental administrators, professors, trade-union officers, and lobbyists for certain special-interest groups.

For all that, states' powers and territorial democracy are insecure in these United States, and the process of weakening has been observable for a century. Ever since the Civil War, with only occasional exceptions, the tendency of the Federal courts has been to exalt central governmental power above state and local claims; in the past two decades, this drift has become almost an ideological obsession in the Supreme Court. And the concentration of military and economic power in Washington that resulted from the Second World War and from the competition with the Communist powers, together with the vast increase in the proportion of federal taxation, more and more have given state and local governments an archaic appearance.

In an age of increasing economic concentration, mobility of

population, and stern military necessity, to some degree it is inevitable that the political patterns of an era more peaceful and less urban must undergo marked change. Speedways require state traffic patrolmen; the sprawl of the suburbs requires prudent reorganization of old political boundaries; the sudden rise of population in Tennessee or New Mexico because of governmental projects requires, for instance, federal subsidies in aid of local school districts directly affected.

For the man who takes long views, then, our pressing necessity seems to be the reconciliation of the principal aspects of American federalism and territorial democracy with such reform and consolidation as appear essential. But not enough people pay any attention to this problem; and some strong pressure-groups are quite ready to sweep away traditional democracy altogether, in favor of a centralized system which would surpass even Jacobin democracy in its unitary character and—if justly it could be called democracy at all—perhaps is better described as "plebiscitary democracy."

Why are some persons in positions of influence indifferent to the menace of centralization, or else reluctant to confront the difficulty? Why do certain American politicians and a good many leaders of American pressure-groups repeat, like incantations, cant phrases about "the ultimate truth of democracy" and "the fundamental wisdom of the people"—when, at the same time, they advocate legislation that would transfer power from public bodies genuinely democratic to an executive authority almost unrestrained? Why, for instance, do certain gentlemen who repeatedly and vociferously affirm their unqualified faith in "the democratic way of life" simultaneously recommend that more and more categories of cases be transferred from regular courts of law to the jurisdiction of recently-created administrative tribunals, not governed in any sense by the "democratic process"?

Well, the causes of this inconsistency are several. Logically, one can maintain such a position only if one subscribes to Turgot's notion that "the nation shall be the centre, and the centre the nation"—that is, to the doctrine that somehow the People may act as a whole, through a central government, in an abstract, infallible Democracy.

But few of the centralizers go so far or are so consistent. Most of them do not recommend, or see as immediately possible, the culmination of this movement in a total centralization of power. They are willing to allow the states and even local units of government to remain as junior partners in the system, supposing these do not presume to assert any claims to distinct powers or rights. Yet the centralizers' general assumption is that authorities in Washington should make the important decisions, and that the state and local governments should obey promptly. This may be called partnership; but in reality it would be a dissolution of the old constitutional partnership, and a gradual emerging of a new relationship: master and servants. The new master would be far more difficult to restrain, if unjust or in error, than the present state and local authorities.

Not logic, then, but a humanitarianism thrusting aside political theory, allied to the immediate advantages of a particular group, is the source of the centralizing movement. Consequences may result, nevertheless, which are infinitely disagreeable to the humanitarian and the well-intentioned member of a pressure-group.

Piecemeal, rather than by any grand design, centralization of political authority proceeds in this country. No man can predict precisely when the nation may cross the line of demarcation that distinguishes a federal system from a unitary structure. "Government is force," President Washington said. Having transferred gradually all real power from state and local authorities to "federal" authorities, the humanitarian or special-interest advocates of increased activities by the general government may find that, in a fit of absence of mind, they have created a unitary power-structure which can be resisted by no one. Only power restrains power; and impotent state and local "governments" that have been deprived, over the years, of effective decision-making must end unable to hold in check the force of the total state.

Even in the function of national defense, where the Washington authorities have constitutional responsibility and precedence, a thoroughgoing centralization might defeat the intention of its advocates. We are told, for instance, that effective preparation for national security cannot be achieved under our present constitutional structure. Yet I am unaware of any hostility by state or local governments to measures for defense and survival. If the federal government sets out a coherent plan for building shelters, creating stockpiles, relocating some industries, redesigning urban centers, and the like, it seems certain that we can count upon state and local co-operation. Surely it is unnecessary to go farther than offering federal grants-in-aid. What we have lacked in this field has not been state and local good will, but rather any general plan in Washington. If there has been negligence, the fault has lain with the very general government upon which the centralizers would load fresh responsibilities.

Something more: today one of the chief perils from atomic attack is that missiles might destroy the centers of command, so rendering resistance leaderless throughout a country. Just that would happen in centralized France, presumably, if Paris were to be destroyed, while federal Australia or Canada would be less injured. Sound preparation for such a blow requires that authority be widely diffused throughout a nation, and that state and local leaders be accustomed to decision-making, able to maintain the fabric of order even if the national capital is smashed. By concentrating powers of decision in the federal apparatus—necessarily, for the most part, in Washington—the centralizers' system seems calculated to increase, rather than diminish, risk of disruption by a single military attack. Of all times in our history, the present is the era when we need healthy and self-reliant state and local governments. The same argument applies to the maintenance of order in America's great cities, now assaulted by fanatics, terrorists, and criminal elements.

Who seeks guidance in time of crisis from the clerk of the federal district court, the handiest representative of the Department of Agriculture, or the state administrator of the National Defense Education Act? A nation cannot be led by district agents of the Federal Bureau of Investigation, or even by generals operating upon contingent orders from Washington. Obedience and sacrifice, in such circumstances, may be obtained only by men generally recognized as the expression of state and local popular will: the responsible politician, if you will, not the civil servant or the commander of troops. What, then, if the springs of territorial democracy have dried up?

But of course the primary responsibility for defense against external enemies is that of the federal government. Let us turn to a field where almost the whole work has been done, in the past, by local and state authorities, but which very recently has been entered upon by the federal government: public instruction.

In 1965, for the first time the federal government appropriated vast general subsidies for public schools. Initially, this pleased such organizations as the National Education Association, which had long lobbied for "federal aid." The consequences, nevertheless, already are unpopular in many quarters.

Why did the National Education Association and its affiliates labor so enthusiastically for federal subsidies to the schools? It is improbable that the typical superintendent of schools desires centralized, authoritarian government, or even plebiscitary democracy —if ever he has heard of the latter. So far as the average superintendent reflects upon general political considerations, probably he does not desire to be supervised from Washington, nor intend that the central government should subsidize local police forces, say, on a scale equal to that of aid for the public schools. He is a centralizer only so far as the immediate interests of his own group are involved.

But the educationists of the public schools felt, in 1965, that it would be easier to obtain ample funds for the schools through congressional appropriation than through local and state political agencies. Everybody's money is nobody's money, and the economies which citizens demand in a village or city or even a state may be forgotten when the funds come from the seemingly inexhaustible coffers of Washington. Beyond this, the transfer of school financing to a central bureaucracy would mean the transfer of effectual school control to the same hands—which hands, the officers of the NEA believed, would be the hands of their own members or their allies, what with the interlocking directorate of the NEA and the federal Office of Education. At present, a strong movement for the reform and restoration of curricula is gaining strength in America. So long as state and local control prevails, such citizen-sponsored reforms are difficult for the educationist establishment to resist. But once effective control of policy should pass from local school boards to a central bureaucracy, the friends of the present educational establishment would have little to dread from "laymen" in education—or so they thought.

With such special-interest groups as the NEA have been leagued a number of intellectuals who desire a grandiose centralization of authority of which schooling would be only a part. An example of this type of mind is Dr. Henry S. Kariel, who holds that "to put it bluntly, government must be centralized to carry out the tasks of public regulation. Virtually all our problems today are national problems, and they must be dealt with nationally." The schools are part of this consolidation, he continues: "Initially, this will require joining educational government and general government at the local level. But as we recognize that no relation obtains between the mélange of school districts and the demands of our contemporary political life, more becomes essential. We must regulate the framework of the curriculum, the subsidization of students, the salaries of the teachers and administrators, and the construction of plants in accordance with national needs and national standards arrived at publicly."*

There's candor for you. Usually the centralizers try to sweeten this dose by arguing that, after all, the federal government already has had a hand in education; and besides, we don't want educational chaos, do we? Nearly half the units of government in the United States are school boards. Why have nearly fifty thousand school boards? Why not have just one? And these school boards have no right to consider themselves distinct sovereignties.

Now of course it is quite true that school districts are not autonomous authorities: like all other divisions of local government, in theory they are agencies of the state governments, and cannot claim to exercise absolute power in their realm. No one ever held otherwise. Yet the fact remains that in the majority of states, local school boards determine the curriculum, supervise the finances, and appoint the administrators and teachers—that is, they exercise the really important functions of government. This local power tends to produce local interest in schooling, and enables the school system to raise money with less complaint than it could otherwise; it gives the population a feeling of direct representation and of making voluntary grants for the support of public schools. The boards' existence is fully justified.

The fact that we have tens of thousands of school districts in the United States does not mean that we are enduring educational chaos—any more than the existence of tens of thousands of city, county, town, and village governments means that we are enduring political chaos. On the contrary, it means that we still are experiencing territorial democracy, healthy voluntary participation in an important public function. This system is not wasteful, for the

* Kariel, *The Decline of Pluralism* (Stanford, 1961), pp. 274-275.

emoluments of school-board members are negligible—far less costly than the salaries of civil servants who would replace them under centralization. And, as Mrs. Agnes Meyer—a person whom no one has suspected of political obscurantism—said once, "If we deprive the state and local school boards of their autonomy, we undermine our whole democratic structure, since local control of education is the strongest bulwark we have left against the growing tendency in our country toward over-centralization of power in the Federal Government, in our military hierarchy, and in our industrial bureaucracy."

It was the expectation of the National Education Association that federal subsidies to the public schools would be free from federal direction; and that such a piece of legislation would provide equalizing assistance to impoverished school districts and to states with a per capita income comparatively low. Both expectations were disappointed promptly.

For the man who pays the piper necessarily calls the tune. As every experienced member of Congress knew in advance, to grant massive federal subsidies to the schools must involve a considerable degree of central control over those schools. Even during the first months of administration of the Johnson administration's school-aid bill, local school administrators and school boards—including those of such big northern cities as Chicago—found themselves in fierce controversy with the federal Office of Education, which was insisting upon drastic measures to abolish *de facto* racial segregation, the use of certain tests repugnant to local authorities, and other policies. This battle continues to rage. The chief officer of the National Education Association, on retiring in 1967, lamented to the national convention of his organization that federal educational functionaries were determined to inject political considerations into the federal subsidies. It never could have been otherwise.

The Johnson administration's school-aid measures (adopted, for the most part, as nominally part of the "war on poverty"), moreover, did next to nothing toward the achieving of equal opportunities in less affluent states and school districts. Because of a "matching funds" provision, the lion's share of the money has gone to districts and states already affluent; while really impoverished districts, or many of them, may gain nothing at all, because the intricacy of applying for federal assistance is too much for their over-worked administators.

Finally, the billions of dollars already expended by the federal government in aid of schools have not helped at all to improve the *quality* of American schooling—our real necessity. Our difficulty in public instruction has not been one of niggardliness. (The United States spends twice as much on public schooling, per pupil, as does Soviet Russia, its nearest competitor in this field, and far more than do Britain, France, or Switzerland, *per capita*; while even Mississippi spends more per pupil than do most of the countries of western Europe.) The true difficulty has been intellectual softness and lack of imagination. These afflictions are not touched by the federal appropriations; and it is quite possible to kill a school, intellectually, with financial largesse.

Many things are not bought with a price. This digression is meant to suggest that in general, as in the instance of federal subsidies to schools, the case for centralization is not proved; and that possibilities for reform through our present political structure and social institutions have not been exhausted.

Why Centralization Would Fail

What with the present rapid rate of growth in the powers of the general government, the merits of true federalism and territorial democracy ought to be re-examined. An immense centralized system of national planning and benefaction is incompatible with our old constitutional structure. If the real powers of decision are vested in professional administrators at the nation's capital, genuine democracy—that is, the making of decisions locally and freely, by the citizens, on a humane scale—soon becomes a shadow. With it there vanishes the proliferating variety which the complex American political structure has nurtured; and that is not all which disappears.

Reasons exist why such a supplanting of the old constitutional structure would present most serious dangers to American order and justice and freedom. I mention here only four of these.

The first is the problem of efficiency. The general government is designed to carry out certain responsibilities, fairly well defined: most notably, the conduct of foreign relations, the defense of the country, and the management of undertakings too widespread for any state to manage. But already the government in Washington is dismayingly oppressed by too much work and too many servants. Perhaps the most notorious case of federal inefficiency is that of the State Department, which has almost lost the power of decision-making because of its complexity, so that the Presidents resort increasingly to personal diplomacy; the State Department already has at least one-third too many employees, countermanding one another's instructions, so that Mr. George Kennan says gloomily of this system's indigestion: "Only some form of catastrophe—natural disaster, financial collapse, or the atomic bomb" could "dismantle it or reduce it to healthier dimensions." * The present State Department has made it almost impossible for the United States to conduct foreign relations, and yet reform seems distant.

Now the conduct of diplomacy is a primary function of the federal government. If it is already so difficult to fulfill primary functions in Washington, what may be expected when fresh responsibilities are added on a colossal scale—when the federal government becomes a central government? By endeavoring to do everything, the Washington government might end in doing nothing successfully. And ours is not a situation in which we can reduce our defense establishment, say, to find money enough for subsidizing the rural poor of Arkansas.

The second difficulty is the problem of scale. Measures which the provincial governors at Graz or Innsbruck would refuse to entrust to Vienna are proposed, in America, as if the governing of two hundred million people were little more difficult than the conduct of a town meeting—and quite as democratic, so long as President and Congressmen still are elected. I have heard American advocates of social-welfare measures, for instance, seriously advance the example of social-democratic legislation in Denmark as precedent for American policy—though some American counties, not to mention states, are larger than Denmark, and other counties have more people than there are Danes.

* Kennan, "America's Administrative Response to its World Problems," *Daedalus* (Spring, 1958), p. 23.

Appeals against imprudent or unjust administration become immensely difficult when they are only the faint voices of individuals or local groups, opposed to the prestige and influence of administrators at the capital; indeed, the chief administrators themselves cannot possibly look deep into such complaints. Detailed administration on such a scale would require from civil servants a wisdom and a goodness never experienced in human history. "Well, appeal to your Congressman," the centralizers say, perhaps ingenuously. But Congressmen already do not have time enough to answer their constituents' mail, let alone act as so many Don Quixotes of the mass-state; and nearly every Congressman is aghast at the prospect of becoming a redresser of grievances in every local school dispute, say.

The third difficulty I raise here is the problem of leadership. Centralized political power functions smoothly only in nations accustomed to defer to the measures and opinions of a governing class—that is, in aristocratic or autocratic lands. Soviet centralization would have failed altogether, had it not been for the long-established powers of the Old Regime at Moscow and St. Petersburg. And such a body of decision-makers, of governors, of aristocrats, must possess a high degree of self-confidence and the habit of command. They must be accustomed to dealing with deferential populations.

But these United States, accustomed to territorial democracy, have no class of leaders and administrators competent to undertake the consolidated direction which the centralizers propose. An English civil servant once told a member of the House of Commons that the nation would be more efficiently governed if only Parliament were swept away and the civil service given total charge of affairs. "No doubt," the M.P. replied, "and within a fortnight you would all be hanging from lamp-posts." Bagehot wrote of England as a deferential nation; and that element of deference to a class of leaders almost hereditary has not yet altogether vanished from Britain.

But in America we have nothing of the sort. I do not discern a class of men competent to rule wisely this immense nation, once territorial democracy and the federal framework (both principal schools of national leadership) should be undone.

Fourth, even had we a class of Winchester old-school-tie administrators, I do not know how we could expect the most expert of statists to direct paternally and justly the concerns of this nation, once local volition and private self-reliance had been seriously weakened. Any man has but twenty-four hours in his day, and can read only a limited number of papers. Such centralization defeats its own object, in persons as in departments. The man-killing job of the Presidency—to which the centralizers would add numerous fresh responsibilities—may be sufficient illustration of my meaning. The late Wilhelm Roepke put the matter succinctly:

"Our world suffers from the fatal disease of concentration, and those—the politicians, leading personalities of the economy, chief editors, and others—in whose hands the threads converge have a task which simply exceeds human nature. The constant strain is propagated through all other levels, down to the harassed foreman and his like. It is the curse of our age. It is a curse twice over because these men, who can do their duty only at the peril of angina pectoris, lack the time for calm reflection or the quiet reading of a book."*

Nor will this problem be alleviated by forming committees: for committees only waste the precious time of the men who are expected to decide everything for everybody. The cure for paralyzing concentration, the centralists seem to argue, is greater concentration of power. This is such stuff as dreams are made of.

Above, I have suggested merely four of many reasons why American political centralization could not succeed—though it might ruin our present political and social structure. By way of peroration, I cannot do better than to quote Alexis de Tocqueville, in his section on Townships and Municipal Bodies, where he puts with a high acuteness the case for a general "federalism," territorial democracy, as a permanent thing:

"The partisans of centralization in Europe are wont to maintain that the government can administer the affairs of each locality better than the citizens can do it for themselves. This may be true when the central power is enlightened and the local authorities are ignorant; when it is alert and they are slow; when it is accustomed to act and they to obey. Indeed, it is evident that this double tendency must augment with the increase of centralization, and that the readiness of the one and the incapacity of the others must be-

* Roepke, *A Humane Economy* (Chicago, 1959), p. 179.

come more and more prominent. But I deny that it is so when the people are as enlightened, as awake to their own interests, and as accustomed to reflect on them, as the Americans are. I am persuaded, on the contrary, that in this case the collective strength of the citizens will always conduce more efficaciously to the public welfare than the authority of the government. I know it is difficult to point out with certainty the means of arousing a sleeping population and of giving it passions and knowledge which it does not possess; it is, I am well aware, an arduous task to persuade men to busy themselves about their own affairs. It would frequently be easier to interest them in the punctilios of court etiquette than in the repairs of their common dwelling. But whenever a central administration affects completely to supersede the persons most interested, I believe that it is either misled or desirous to mislead. However enlightened or skillful a central power may be, it cannot of itself embrace all the details of the life of a great nation. Such vigilance exceeds the powers of man. And when it attempts unaided to create and set in motion so many complicated springs, it must submit itself to a very imperfect result or exhaust itself in bootless efforts."

To destroy territorial democracy and the federal system in America is quite possible—or to let them atrophy; but it is less easy to provide some alternative satisfactory scheme of politics. Once the principle of volition, with the sense of participation and local decision, vanishes from American life, Americans are liable to become an unmanageable people. On a grander and more catastrophic scale, we might see again the resistance to authority and resort to violence which were provoked by the Eighteenth Amendment and the Volstead Act. Both the Eighteenth Amendment and the Volstead Act were "democratically" adopted; but somehow national positive democracy is not the same thing as territorial prescriptive democracy. Indeed, already we see great American cities in anarchy, from time to time—the anarchists those people, colored and white, who feel that they have been excluded from full participation in society. What would occur when the *majority* should feel excluded from decision-making?

Within a few years, if not immediately, any "guided democracy" or "plebiscitary democracy" would meet with evasion and hostility everywhere; and among the results of this would come a diminish-

ing of the really effectual and popular authority of the general
government. The energies and loyalties of volition would have been
supplanted by the compulsions of a latter-day Jacobinism, or of the
Directory. And a great big Federal Bureau of Investigation would
not be able to enforce the decrees of such a regime: for though a
new broom sweeps clean, and an elite federal detective force aiding
the local police is one thing, a permanent national secret police
would be quite another—and possibly disagreeable to some of the
"liberal" advocates of centralization. For that matter, a garrison of
federal troops in every city might not suffice to keep order.

We need, then, to recall the general distinctions among federal,
state, and local governments, putting our emphasis upon the reten-
tion of vigor by state and local authorities. In our time there exists
no danger that our country might fall into disunion because of
"chaos" in government. (To the centralizer-on-principle, diversity
and chaos are identical.) Our peril lies altogether the other way:
the triumph of the total centralized state, with the dwindling of
local and private vitality, and the extinction of federal order and
territorial democracy.

Yet life still rises in the tree of American federalism, and territorial democracy's powers of resistance and reaction ought not to
be disregarded. It is true, as Tocqueville remarked, that men in
power generally feel impelled to augment central power, while the
opponents of centralization are either stupid or powerless. Notwithstanding this, attachment to the doctrines of division of authority
and of state and local powers remains so popular in the United
States that an intelligent plan for preserving the old system would
obtain a hearing, and stand some chance of enactment.

An enormous, unitary, omnicompetent nation-state cannot abide
the American political tradition and cake of custom. If the federal
system is obsolete, then we ought to prepare to train the leaders of a
new order, and to define the character of that domination, novel to
us. If territorial democracy deserves to live, and if the federal system has virtue still, then the constitutional structure ought to be
buttressed and helped to function. At present, most of the Americans qualified to think about such matters decline to take either of
these courses. They are willing to let the norms of politics shift for
themselves—which is not in nature.

❊❊❊❊❊❊❊❊❊❊❊❊❊❊❊❊❊❊❊❊❊❊❊

VI. ERIC VOEGELIN'S NORMATIVE LABOR

Understanding Politics through History

IN HEALTHY REACTION TO THE ENEMIES OF THE PERMANENT things in politics, a considerable body of serious political and historical scholarship has appeared in recent years. Some of these writers have been mentioned in earlier chapters. Perhaps the most systematic of them is Dr. Eric Voegelin, whose historical studies are intended to point the way toward a recovery of political normality.

"The true dividing line in the contemporary crisis," Voegelin wrote fifteen years ago, "does not run between liberals and totalitarians, but between the religious and philosophical transcendentalists on the one side, and the liberal and totalitarian immanentist sectarians on the other." This theme runs through his influential little book *The New Science of Politics,* and through his massive work *Order and History* (in four volumes, one of which, at this writing, remains to be published). The delusion that human rationality may convert the world into an earthly paradise is, in Voegelin's view, the principal source of our modern political catastrophes. For politics, like science, like art, arises out of belief in a transcendent religion; and when that faith decays, politics degenerates.

Professor Voegelin's personal experience of social disorder is considerable, extending from persecution by the Nazis to being knocked on the head by a gang of young criminals not far from the

University of Notre Dame, in Indiana. Witty, good-natured, master of classical and Christian learning, Voegelin is thoroughly familiar with English and American political philosophy. Describing himself as a "pre-Reformation Christian," he draws upon both Protestant and Catholic theologians. He sees in the United States and Britain the two nations least seriously infected by ideology and Gnosticism, and in them a hope for the regeneration of our civilization.

"On my religious 'position,'" Voegelin writes of ideologues' attacks, "I have been classified as a Protestant, a Catholic, as anti-semitic and as a typical Jew; politically, as a Liberal, a Fascist, a National Socialist, and a Conservative; and on my theoretical position, as a Platonist, a Neo-Augustinian, a Thomist, a disciple of Hegel, an existentialist, a historical relativist, and an empirical sceptic; in recent years the suspicion has frequently been voiced that I am a Christian. All these classifications have been made by university professors and people with academic degrees. They give ample food for thought regarding the state of our universities."*

Such labels wake passions, when dispassionate discourse is required. And Voegelin endeavors to restore among us an understanding of general principles, emancipated from ideology.

Gnosticism, the heresy which substitutes a dream of a perfect mundane society for the City of God, lies at the root of the clamorous ideologies which compete for the support of the modern crowd. To ideology, Voegelin opposes science, or understanding of man and society founded upon observation throughout history. In disavowing ideology, Voegelin espouses political principle. Like Burke, he draws a distinction between "abstraction" (or an *a priori* assumption unsupported by history or common experience or what we call revelation) and "principle," or a justified deduction from what we have learnt, over the ages, about men and their commonwealths. With Burke, and with Richard Hooker, he makes the virtue of prudence the means of political wisdom:

"In classic and Christian ethics the first of the moral virtues is *sophia* or *prudentia,* because without adequate understanding of the structure of society, including the *conditio humana,* moral action with rational co-ordination of means and ends is hardly possi-

---

* Voegelin, "On Readiness to Rational Discussion," in Hunold (ed.), *Freedom and Serfdom* (Dordrecht, 1961), p. 280.

ble. In the Gnostic dream world, on the other hand, non-recognition of reality is the first principle."

Recognition of a transcendent order in the universe does not make the statesman into a dreamer, but into a realist. Knowing his theology and his history, he takes it for granted that man is not a perfect nor a perfectible being, and that the prudent statist will endeavor to make life in the civil social order tolerable, not perfect. It is utopianism, the Gnostic delusion, which leads (in Voegelin's words) "with increasing theoretical illiteracy to the form of various social idealisms, such as the abolition of war, of unequal distribution of property, of fear and want. And, finally, immanentization may extend to the complete Christian symbol. The result will then be the active mysticism of a state of perfection, to be achieved through a revolutionary transfiguration of the nature of man, as, for instance, in Marxism."

By definition, human nature is a constant; knowing this, the statesman is aware that human longing never can be satisfied upon this earth. For him, politics indeed is the art of the possible, and he remains content with patching and improving society here and there; he feels he has done well if he has preserved a tolerable measure of justice and order and freedom.

In modern political action, Gnosticism has two manifestations, its left wing and its right: communism and liberalism. "If liberalism is understood as the immanent salvation of man and society, communism certainly is its most radical expression; it is an evolution that was already anticipated by John Stuart Mill's faith in the ultimate advent of communism for mankind."

In the year of the Communist Manifesto, Orestes Brownson declared that communism was a heresy from Christianity; and this view is Voegelin's, as it is that of Father Martin D'Arcy and other philosophers of our time. But liberalism is only a more moderate form of the same heresy, the notion that Progress consists in material aggrandizement. A culture which abandons knowledge of God in the expectation of creature-comforts already is far gone in decadence:

"A civilization can, indeed, advance and decline at the same time—but not forever. There is a limit toward which the ambiguous process moves; the limit is reached when an activist sect which represents the Gnostic truth organizes the civilization into an empire under its rule. Totalitarianism, defined as the existential rule of Gnostic activists, is the end form of progressive civilization."

Now this is repudiation of liberalism root and branch, whether old-style individualistic liberalism or new-style collectivistic liberalism. The premises upon which liberalism is established must lead, according to Voegelin, to a total state, soon or late; for the Gnostic passion to alter society and human nature endures no opposition; and when it can, it destroys all the institutions which impede its consolidatory advance. If the only purpose of life is material success, why should reactionaries be permitted to delay the advent of utopia? Voegelin cites Harold Laski, in *Faith, Reason, and Civilization,* to illustrate his point; as Laski put it, "It is, indeed, true in a sense to argue that the Russian principle cuts deeper than the Christian, since it seeks salvation for the masses by fulfillment in this life, and, thereby, orders anew the actual world we know."

The hour is very late, Voegelin writes; our society is terribly corrupt; and "it will require all our efforts to kindle this glimmer into a flame by repressing Gnostic corruption and restoring the forces of civilization. At present the fate is in the balance."

Voegelin's primary concern is order—which is also the first concern of jurisprudence. Now "order" means the principle and the process by which the peace and harmony of society are maintained. It is the arrangement of rights and duties in a state to ensure that people may find just leaders, may be loyal citizens, and may obtain public tranquillity. "Order" implies the obedience of a nation to the laws of God, and the obedience of individuals to just authority. Without order, justice rarely can be enforced, and freedom cannot be maintained.

Yet since the French Revolution, "order" has been an unpopular word. Order implies leadership, discipline, self-restraint, duty; and the doctrinaire ideological pamphleteers, from Tom Paine onward, have been hostile to these concepts. Emancipation from all restraints, inner or outer, has been the desire of the more extreme liberals of modern times. That this anarchic emancipation ends only in tyranny is a fact which the ritualistic liberal still refuses to recognize. The terrible events of our time of troubles have suggested to many people that we no longer can expect to obtain a free and just society merely by echoing vague slogans about "democracy," "progress," and "equality." For a high civilization to subsist, and for men to live in peace with one another, some coherent principle of order must prevail. "Without order," Richard Hooker wrote, "there is no living in public society, because the want thereof is the mother of confusion."

Such arguments, advanced or implied by Voegelin in *The New Science of Politics,* are disagreeable in the extreme to rationalistic liberals—let alone political totalists—who maintain that men have no souls, and that there exists no source from which transcendent knowledge can come; and who, besides, simply do not understand the language of poetic and religious symbol, being altogether prosy. With their master Bentham, these scholars and gentlemen tend to equate poetry with pushpin; while as for religious insight, they take it for granted that all such rubbish was discarded long ago—or should have been.

Resentments of this character against Voegelin's approach were conspicuous in various reviews of *The New Science of Politics;* one professor at a middlewestern university, who previously had confined himself to the behavioral and institutional disciplines, burst in print into a denunciation of Voegelin's theories, which (he insisted) were merely an exhortation to "repression." (Voegelin, in a passage quoted earlier, feels that evil ought to be repressed; his reviewer apparently would not discriminate against evil.) They could not understand what Voegelin was writing about, these critics implied, and so he must be up to dark mischief. Once the first three volumes of *Order and History* had been published, Professor Moses Hadas, a classicist, indulged in an assault upon Voegelin's motives fortunately rare in the pages of learned journals. Voegelin simply *can't* believe in all this talk about transcendence and the divine sanctions for order, Hadas assumed; so Voegelin must be simply a political Christian, at best, disguising his ugly Fascism (though he was removed from his Austrian professorship by the National Socialists) under the tattered cloak of old-fangled piety:

"Reduced to simple terms," Hadas wrote, "Professor Voegelin's 'order' rests upon a hoax, which is justified by attributing divine afflatus to the elite which usurps the power to work it. . . . Professor Voegelin is by no means alone in his doctrine—such eminent teachers as Karl Jaspers have spoken of 'elitarian activism'—and no one can impugn the sincerity of his convictions or his right to voice them. What is disturbing is that his pietistic coloring makes it difficult for an unwary reader to apprehend what these convictions amount to. One wonders whether the 'institution that wishes to remain unnamed' which Professor Voegelin thanks for material aid in each of his Prefaces was aware of the nature of his work, and one remembers a remark attributed to a notable patron of the institution which Professor Voegelin serves: 'Sure, we'll have fascism in this country, but of course we'll call it something else.' Leap in being?" *

The preceding academic vituperation probably did greater harm to the reputation of its author than to that of Voegelin. Nearly anyone who reads *Order and History* must perceive that Hadas' review of the three volumes was studded with gross misrepresentations and groundless imputations. The "unnamed institution" to which Hadas referred ominously was a well-known American charitable foundation. And the sinister "institution which Professor Voegelin serves" is merely Hadas' slurring reference (incorrect at the time he wrote, incidentally) to Louisiana State University, where Voegelin formerly taught (*not* in Huey Long's time, though it is Long to whom the remarks about American Fascism are attributed). Guilt by association?

Yet such quasi-scholarly abuse does serve one purpose: to illustrate how the problem of order is quite as perplexing in our time as it was in the age of Socrates and Plato. Hadas sounds very like certain antagonists of Socrates—who, unable to defeat him in reasoned argument, turned then to vituperation and menaces. Apropos of one of these, Callicles in the *Gorgias,* Voegelin himself writes: "The social conventions, which Callicles despises, are wearing thin; and the advocate of nature is brought to realize that he is a murderer face to face with his victim. The situation is fascinating for those among us who find ourselves in the Platonic position and who recognize in the men with whom we associate today the intellectual pimps for power who will connive in our murder tomorrow."

It is ideological ferocity of Hadas' sort which Voegelin's books are written to resist. Humanitarian ideologues, good though their intentions may be, can bring about a dreadful decay of order. For the order of society is merely the order of souls writ large; there

* Hadas, review of *Order and History,* vol. 19, p. 444, *Journal of the History of Ideas* (1958).

cannot be a good society without individual goodness of heart; and that goodness of heart is possible only when human beings perceive, with Socrates, that man is *not* the measure: God is the measure.

"In our time," as Voegelin puts it, "we can observe the same phenomenon in that people are shocked by the horrors of war and by Nazi atrocities but are unable to see that these horrors are no more than a translation, to the physical level, of the spiritual and intellectual horrors which characterize progressive civilization in its most 'peaceful' phase; that the physical horrors are no more than the execution of the judgment (*krisis*) passed upon the historical polity."

Historical study of this sort—works like those of Voegelin and Christopher Dawson and Herbert Butterfield and J. L. Talmon— will affect our social order within this century, I believe. At one time, poets had a strong influence upon men of law and statecraft. At present, the sociologists have their hour of ascendancy. Yet the time is not far distant when the philosophical historians will begin to alter the minds of judges and presidents. A few years ago, we were informed by enthusiastic reviewers that for many years to come, all sensible magistrates and politicians must be deeply affected by the researches of Dr. Alfred Kinsey. I think not. We begin to seek again the norm for man, not the norm for wasp or snake.

Behind the Veil of History

"History is the revelation of the way of God with man," Voegelin declares in the first volume of *Order and History,* which is entitled *Israel and Revelation.* With this sentence, he becomes perhaps the most influential historian of our century, and certainly the most provocative. His first principles go against the grain of the chief schools of historical thought since the seventeenth century.

Nothing ever has happened in history, according to one school of liberal historians of the nineteenth and twentieth centuries: that is, events simply have glided one into another without discernible purpose or significance; everything has been "evolutionary development" or mere flux. All the endeavors of famous men, and all the aspirations of great nations, have had as little influence upon the stream—or web—of history as the buzzing of the flies of a summer. As for intervention in history, or creation in history, by influences more than human—why, such notions belong to the childhood of the race. For those historians, Providence does not exist; and though the Greeks (who took a view of history somewhat similar in that they found history inscrutable) at least acknowledged the existence of Fate and Fortune, the latter-day theorists of historical flux are unwilling to admit even those vague and impersonal powers to influence upon human existence. This school of writers has taken more literally than did Hegel himself the Hegelian observation that "What experience and history teach is this—that people and governments never have learned anything from history, or acted on principles deduced from it."

Another school of historians—the positivists, attached to what Voegelin calls Gnostic assumptions—strong in influence ever since the Enlightenment, has taken a very different tack: for these scholars, history has been the record of progress toward some grand terrestrial culmination and perfection—a progress sometimes impeded, but sure of ultimate triumph. Condorcet, Comte, and Marx, whatever their differences of opinion, all represent this school; and it has milder devotees. Governed by the idea of Progress, this concept—"progressivism" or "futurism" applied to historical study—dominated the writing of popular histories for a good many years, until the fearful events of our own century disconcerted the leaders of the movement.

A third school, reviving an ancient theory in modern times, has advanced the concept of historical cycles: stages of growth, maturity, and decadence, predictable and perhaps inevitable, recurring with fair regularity throughout the ages. Such was the cast of mind of Henry and Brooks Adams; Spengler's *Decline of the West* gave this theory a popular success almost scandalous; and Toynbee's *Study of History* depends upon this interpretation, though now and again tinged with meliorism.

These three schools have dominated so thoroughly the discussion of historical problems for the past century that many people seem unaware that a fourth interpretation of history exists. That fourth interpretation, nevertheless, is a venerable theory, long known to the higher civilizations, though most thoroughly developed in Christian civilization. I mean the belief that history is the record of human existence under God, meaningful only so far as it reflects and explains and illustrates the order in the soul and in society which emanates from divine purpose. The aim of history, in the eyes of this school, is not antiquarian, nor yet programmatic: that purpose is to reveal to existing men and societies the true nature of being. Without this history, indeed, no society long endures. "The order of history," so Voegelin's first sentence in *Israel and Revelation* runs, "emerges from the history of order."

In the view of this last school of historians, history is not law, in the sense of fixed fate, foreknowledge absolute; nor does it have "meaning" in the sense of providing a Grand Design for immanent improvement. A study of history reveals the general principles to which men and societies, in all ages, are subject; but it cannot confer upon the scholar a prophetic afflatus; it cannot describe the wave of the future. "For the ray of light that penetrates from an historical present into the past," Voegelin writes, "does not produce a 'meaning of history' that could be stored away as a piece of information once for all, nor does it gather in a 'legacy' or 'heritage' on which the present could sit contentedly. It rather reveals a mankind striving for its order of existence within the world while attuning itself with the truth of being beyond the world, and gaining in the process not a substantially better order within the world but an increased understanding of the gulf that lies beyond immanent existence and the transcendent truth of being. Canaan is as far away today as it has always been in the past." We tremble "before the abysmal mystery of history as the instrument of divine revelation for ultimate purposes that are unknown equally to the men of all ages."

"Immanent" and "transcendent" are words that a reader must apprehend before he essays to fight his way into the learning of *Israel and Revelation*. The historian who espouses the cause of immanentization believes that the origin and end of everything in history, including mankind's religions, is to be found within the world of sensation, the world apprehended by the average sensual man. The historian who takes the transcendental view believes that the origin and end of everything in history must be sought, often symbolically, in realities more than human and more than terrestrial. We might call the school to which Voegelin belongs the "transcendentalist school," were there not danger of confounding the opinions of Voegelin and Emerson.

The historians of this latter school are at odds with Hegel's concept of remorseless destiny operating in history, with Marx's idea of the resolution of thesis and antithesis in a classless society, and with Toynbee's endeavor to predict the coming of a new religion and a new society formed out of a worldwide synthesis. With Gabriel Marcel, the historian of this school—let us call it, for immediate purposes, the Christian school of historical scholarship—sets his face against "this crowned ghost, the meaning of history."

For the ends of man and society are not to be found *in* history: those ends are transcendent, attaining fruition only beyond the limits of the time and the space which we know in this little world of ours. History has many meanings, but they are particular meanings for the regulation of private conduct and public polity, not a Gnostic plan for immanent regeneration before which we must abase ourselves. Who are the historians of this Christian school? To name three almost at random, St. Augustine, Bossuet, Edmund Burke. Voegelin is our present principal representative of this body of conviction, which he presents with system.

The term "Christian school" of historical scholarship is not entirely adequate, perhaps, for this theory of history is rooted in Judaic and Greek and Roman thought and experience, as well as in Christian doctrine and knowledge, and there exist parallels in other religions. But the fullest expression of this understanding of history is found among Christian thinkers. Voegelin stands for religious insight as opposed to "political religion," ideology, which, he writes, is "rebellion against God and man." Voegelin is no vulgarizer, but a scholar of such breadth and depth as the educational tendency of our age has made rare among us. His work requires interpreters, if it is to exert influence. Voegelin makes no concessions to theoretical illiteracy in our age: he takes for granted in his readers a familiarity with metaphysical terms, historical events, Biblical texts, and modes of reasoning which a pragmatic schooling neglects. Nor can he do otherwise: though he spreads his learning over several volumes, the field is so wide that he must sacrifice illustration and simplification, much of the time, to compactness and precision.

But *Order and History* cannot be ignored by anyone seriously concerned with our time of troubles. It should be read, as Voegelin recommends, "not as an attempt to explore curiosities of a dead past, but as an inquiry into the structure of the order in which we live presently."

To employ a loose and risky analogy, history is a veil upon the face of a gigantic significance. The Christian historian, though denying the existence of any simple pattern of progress or cycles running through history, nevertheless detects beneath the surface of events an intelligible structure. This, in Voegelin's words, "is not a project for human or social action, but a reality to be discerned retrospectively in a flow of events that extends, through the present of the observer, indefinitely into the future. Philosophers of history have spoken of this reality as providence, when they still lived within the orbit of Christianity, or as *List der Vernunft*, when they were affected by the trauma of enlightenment. In either case they referred to a reality beyond the plans of concrete human beings—a reality of which the origin and end is unknown and which for that reason cannot be brought within the grasp of finite action."

So history is a reality, but a veiled reality, of which our knowledge always is imperfect and upon which our mundane designs can operate only slightly. History is our tool only in the sense that we employ our knowledge of history to bring ourselves to an understanding and realization, so far as we may, of the principles of private and public order. When the first school of historians I described above—the "nothing-ever-happened" school—lifts the veil upon the face of the significance behind history, that school, like Titus' soldiery in the Temple, finds the sanctuary empty—or, at best, inhabited only by Chaos and old Night. When the second school of historians—the positivistic school—lifts that veil, there looms up the voluptuous form of the Earthly Paradise. When the third school—the cyclical school—lifts that same veil, there stands revealed a species of clockwork, Ixion's wheel, with humanity bound upon it. But when the fourth school of historians, the Christian or transcendental school, lifts the veil of history, there emerges a pattern of order, a body of enduring truth, the filtered wisdom of the species, the considered opinions and experiences of the many wise men who have preceded us in time: the normative consciousness. And this complex record is rendered intelligible by a strong and subtle thread running through it, the continuity of Providence. The significance behind the veil is not simply the corpus of worldly wisdom, but—still more important—the contract of eternal society which joins our mundane order to an abiding, transcendent order.

This is the understanding of history possessed also—with varying interpretations—by Reinhold Niebuhr, Leo Strauss, and other philosophical historians I have named already. This is a revived theory of history, transcending doctrinal barriers, which gives first consideration to religious knowledge and traditional belief and classical theories as means to the proper apprehension of history. Professor Butterfield, for instance, in his book *Man on His Past,* affirms a faith in Providence which would have been astounding and shocking—but was not Christianity always a scandal?—to the rationalist and positivist historians of the nineteenth century, and which will wake indignation in many quarters today. Butterfield writes, "And here is a Providence which does not merely act (as Ranke's Providence seemed to act) at marginal points or by remote control, but which touches all the details and the intimacies of life. . . . And we, too, need not be the slaves of our analytical methods— we may still praise God, and not merely do honor to scientific laws, at the coming of spring; and we may thank Providence rather than chance for those 'conjectures' which seem to matter so much both in life and in history."

Yes, the climate of opinion among historians is clearing; and the work which may do more to effect a general revision of learned opinion than any other historical production of this century is Voegelin's. *Israel and Revelation* treats of the order, spiritual and social, that arose among the people of Israel, in contrast with the cosmological order of the ancient empires; and it traces and analyzes the struggle between Israel as a faith and the kingdom of Judah. This is a work of original insight, sustained by a startling knowledge of the literary sources.

A young lion of political science, Mr. John Roche—an official intellectual apologist for the Johnson administration—once addressed a convention of his colleagues, and made it one of his claims to fame that he had not read *The New Science of Politics,* and did not intend to, because it seemed to be all about "someone called Saint Joachim of Flora," and therefore irrelevant to political science; he would be even more dismayed by *Israel and Revelation.*

Voegelin has his work cut out for him when he attempts to reason with minds of this cast; yet he may prevail.

Israel and Revelation, though concise and even witty, is no book for the historical dilettante. It pleases neither the social gospeller nor the Bibliolater. To criticize it properly would require a book as long as the volume itself. But possibly a very brief summary may suggest its importance. Human nature is a constant; and the same problems of order—order in the realm of spirit and order in society —arise in every civilization, from the anonymous "Dialogue on Suicide" of an Egyptian who died two thousand years before Christ, dismayed at the disorder of his age, to our own present discontents. "Every society is burdened with the task, under concrete conditions, of creating an order that will endow the fact of its existence with meanings in terms of ends divine and human. And the attempts to find the symbolic forms that will adequately express the meaning, while imperfect, do not form a senseless series of failures. For the great societies, beginning with the civilizations of the Ancient Near East, have created a sequence of orders, intelligibly connected with one another as advances toward, or recessions from, an adequate symbolization of truth concerning the order of being of which the order of society is a part." The Kingdom of Judah became dust and ashes, but the revelation of divine and human nature which Israel received lies at the foundation of our whole present order.

Israelite history, Voegelin argues, cannot be received as a literal account of the events which occurred to the Israelite people. It is, rather, a symbolic history; and the deep truths of revelation commonly are expressed in symbol, not literally. In the symbol of the voice from out the Burning Bush, there was expressed a reality the cosmological empires had not known—and which Spengler and Toynbee, toiling in "the intellectual climate in which 'religious founders' were busy with founding 'religions,' when in fact they were concerned with the ordering of human souls," still had not learnt many centuries after. What took place on Sinai was a leap in being, a revelation quite new in human experience; and any close examination of the literary sources will reveal that here commenced the historical form of existence in the present under God, with history as the symbolism of that form. Moses (as distinguished from the mythical Moses of the Deuteronomic Code) was not the "founder of a religion," but the intermediary between man and the God previously unknown, who declared, "I am who I am." The Israelites, the Chosen People, the collective Son of God, did not desire to be chosen; it is improbable that they understood the revelation when it came from the lips of Moses; indeed, throughout the history of Israel and Judah, the spiritual and temporal order was perplexed by confusion; and when the Temple fell, that misunderstanding was as baleful as ever. Here lay the difficulty: "In Israel the spirit of God, the *ruach* of Yahweh, is present with the community and with individuals in their capacity as representatives of the community, but it is not present as the ordering force in the soul of every man, as the Nous of the philosophers or the Logos of Christ is present in every member of the Mystical Body, creating by its presence the *homonoia,* the likemindedness of the community."

The soul, to the Israelites, had no destiny beyond death; therefore the hope of Israel was fixed upon a mundane realization of Yahweh's promises to Israel. Only the Remnant who followed the Prophets preferred the Spirit to the Letter, and were willing to sacrifice existential triumph to the keeping of the Covenant. But the Prophets, in their contest with the Kings, were hopelessly impractical, leaving no place to worldly wisdom; they were "torn by the conflict between spiritual universalism and patriotic parochialism that had been inherent from the beginning in the conception of a Chosen People." Judah was doomed to dissolution, whatever her kings might do by way of compromise with the Baals and Ashtaroths. Yet "from the struggle for the bare survival of order in the soul of man emerged the Jewish community victoriously, both in its own right and as the matrix of Christianity."

Emancipated from "ideological mortgages upon science," Voegelin proceeds to trace the alteration of the prophetic understanding from Isaiah to Jeremiah. Isaiah, denouncing the king's unfaithfulness to the moral ideal of Israel, refused to come to terms at all with existential circumstances; he expected faith alone to reconstitute the order of human personality and of society. This is what Voegelin calls "metastasis," the will "to transform reality into something which by essence it is not . . . the rebellion against the nature of things as ordained by God." In a much later age, this impulse expressed itself as Gnosis. "Isaiah, we may say, has tried the impossible: to make the leap in being a leap out of existence into a divinely transfigured world beyond the laws of mundane existence." But Isaiah stopped short of an attempt to realize the Terrestrial Paradise by human endeavors. "If the prophets, in their despair over Israel, indulged in metastatic dreams, in which the tension of historical order was abolished by a divine act of grace, at least they did not indulge in tetastatic nightmares, in which the *opus* was performed by human acts of revolution." Yet Jeremiah, going to his trial, passed beyond metastasis. "The great motive that had animated the prophetic criticism of conduct and commendation of the virtues had at last been traced to its source in the concern with the order of personal existence under God. In Jeremiah the human personality had broken the compactness of collective existence and recognized itself as the authoritative source of order in society."

Jeremiah "had at least a glimpse of the terrible truth: that the existence of a concrete society in a definite form will not resolve the problem of order in history, that no Chosen People in any form will be the ultimate omphalos of the true order of mankind. . . . With Isaiah's and Jeremiah's movement away from the concrete Israel begins the anguish of the third procreative act of divine order in history: the Exodus of Israel from itself." The Deutero-Isaiah, with his song of the Suffering Servant, completes this Exodus from the cosmic-divine order of empire. God becomes known successively as Creator, as Lord and Judge of history, and as Redeemer. "The Servant who suffers many a death to live, who is humiliated to be exalted, who bears the guilt of the many to see them saved as his offspring, is the King above the kings, the representative of divine above imperial order. And the history of Israel as the people under God is consummated in the vision of the unknown genius, for as the representative sufferer Israel has gone beyond itself and become the light of salvation to mankind." The Zadokite fragment and the Dead Sea scrolls prove that the symbol of the Suffering Servant was not forgotten, during the five hundred years that followed. In Israel, the prophets had shared the suffering of God; now, in Jerusalem, the greatest event in history was to be consummated: God was to share the suffering of man.

Yes, Voegelin's work of scholarship will stick in the craws of the schools of historical theory still dominant; they may receive *Israel and Revelation* much as Jehoiakim received the scroll of Jeremiah, sent by Baruch: "It was in the wintry season, and a fire was burning before him in a brazier as an attendant read the scroll to him. Whenever three or four columns had been read, the King, who had listened in stony silence, would cut them off with his knife—and then Jehoiakim, the King of Judah, dropped the words of Yahweh, the King of Israel, on the brazier until the whole scroll was consumed by fire."

This volume and its companions, the work of a man of intellectual power, boldly deny the assumptions of the hegemony of intellectuals. With Isaiah, its author seems to say,

"Thy wisdom and thy knowledge,
   It hath perverted thee;
And thou hast said in thine heart,
   I am, and none else beside me."

This dreary loneliness of the modern ego, this denial of the divine guidance which is the source of all order in personality and in society, becomes the parent of fanatic ideology. From that isolation of spirit, Voegelin's labor of historical and theoretical reconstruction is intended to redeem us.

Philosophers and Philodoxers

A philosopher aspires to teach wisdom; a philodoxer is a purveyor of *doxa*, illusory opinions and vain wishes. Out of the *doxa* comes disorder, in the soul and in the body politic. But *eunomia*, righteousness, the disciplined harmony of a man's soul, Solon said, makes "all things proper and sensible in the affairs of men." Eric Voegelin is a philosopher, as well as an historian and a professor of the *nomos*—that is, of institutions and traditions.

His knowledge of early civilizations and Old Testament scholarship, manifested in the first volume of *Order and History,* is equalled by his understanding of the Greek poets and philosophers whose thought is the subject of the two succeeding volumes, *The World of the Polis* and *Plato and Aristotle*. Yet the serious reader of these two volumes might do well to turn, before opening them, to the one twentieth-century critic whose ends and convictions seem closest to Voegelin's own: Paul Elmer More. For More was a more lucid writer, though Voegelin is the more thoroughgoing. In the concluding chapter of More's *Platonism,* indeed, occurs a summary of Voegelin's own intention clearer than any passage in the two volumes of *Order and History* concerned with the Greeks.

"It is a fact, sad and indisputable," More wrote, "that no one is more likely to call himself, or to be called by his admirers, a Platonist than the reformer with a futile scheme for the regeneration of the world, or the dreamer who has spurned the realities of human nature for some illusion of easy perfection, or the romantic visionary who has set the spontaneity of fancy above the rational imagination, or the 'fair soul' who has withdrawn from the conflict of life into the indulgence of a morbid introspection, or the votary of faith as a law abrogating the sterner law of works and retribution. Half the enthusiasts and inspired maniacs of society have shielded themselves under the aegis of the great Athenian. . . . If these are the only products of Platonism, then it is a pity the works of Plato were not lost altogether, with the books of so many other ancient philosophers, and we who busy ourselves with interpreting the Dialogues are merely adding to the sum of the world's folly. But it is not so. It is with Platonism as with Christianity and every other strong excitement of the human heart. Liberty is the noblest and at the same time the most perilous possession that can be given to mankind; and, unless we are prepared to silence the higher call of religion and philosophy altogether for the safer demands of a purely practical wisdom, we must expect, while we try to expose, the vagaries of minds made drunk with excess of enthusiasm. . . . 'Believe not every spirit, but try the spirits whether they are of God, because many false prophets are gone out into the world.' "

In this endeavor justly to distinguish between the lovers of wisdom and the devotees of illusion (and, as More says, perhaps the best definition of a true Platonist is "a lover of distinctions"), we are handicapped by our imperfect terms, tools that snap in the hand; for nowadays, in our language, the wise man is caught with the label of the persons whom Plato opposed, the Sophists; while for "philodoxer," the man whose desires override his righteousness, the perverter of the intellect, the ideologue, we have no precise equivalent in English. ("Sophist" expresses only in part the concept of the preacher of the *doxa*.) A principal portion of Voegelin's labor is to restore a sound vocabulary to philosophy and politics. Nowhere, surely, is this restoration more important than in the discussion of Plato, the central figure in these two volumes. The Serbonian bog of controversy over *The Republic,* for instance, is watered by writers and teachers who do not understand their own words; who, as Voegelin observes, repeat in our century the errors of the muddled, well-meaning Old School Tie and of the arrogant "amoral" controversalists: "The way from the well-intentioned, but philosophically no longer sensitive generation, which translated the 'good polis' as an 'ideal state,' to the generation which attacks Plato as an 'ideologue,' is the way from Cephalus to Thrasymachus."

Every serious discussion of order runs back, eventually, to Moses and Plato. Voegelin's discussion of Plato is as interesting as his examination of Moses; and the controversy which it has begun to arouse may serve here to illustrate how the problem of order has become central in men's minds once more.

Plato's theories of justice and order have been variously criticized in different ages, the critics of any period tending to see in *The Republic* and *The Laws* the reflection of opinion and event in their own time, and to commend or denounce Plato as he seemed to sympathize with, or to oppose, their own climate of opinion. At the end of the last century and the beginning of this, Plato generally was approved of as an "idealist," who commendably desired to shape this world nearer to our hearts' desire: for this interpretation suited the humanitarian and melioristic inclinations of the dominant critical school among professors of philosophy and politics.

With the coming of the ideological struggles since 1917, however, the scholarly partisans of this or that particular twentieth-century brand of politics began to convert Plato into an ideologue; and most of them denounced him as a totalist, though some Socialists ventured to welcome Plato as a forward-looking advocate of social planning. A number of writers condemned Plato as a Communist; others, as a Fascist; *The Republic* and *The Laws* were assumed to be merely embryo versions of our own ideological tracts, and so were fitted into convenient pigeon-holes to Right and Left.

The most influential criticism of this sort has been that of Karl Popper, in his book *The Open Society and its Enemies.* Professor Popper, an old-school doctrinaire liberal, rationalistic and utilitarian, bitterly opposed to "myth" (in which he includes religion), warns all true democrats and liberals that Plato was a totalitarian, a Fascist, and a racist, an inveterate enemy of freedom. Popper makes no secret of his own hostility toward any long-established principle of order; for to him, equality, competition, and emancipation from tradition seem sufficient guarantees of "the open society." What Popper never intended, his condemnation of Plato aroused a good deal of serious interest in Plato's doctrines, and attracted a number of replies.

Intemperance of Popper's sort, however, was not the only approach to Plato provoked by the troubles of this age. A temperate and learned classical scholar, David Grene, re-examined the political ideas of Thucydides and Plato as reflections upon an age of disorder remarkably similar to our own time. Mr. Grene understands clearly what Popper does not understand at all—the motive of Plato in writing *The Republic:* that is, to offer a decadent society, which had lost faith in its religion, its traditions, and its customs, a means to make possible once more the life of the soul and the life of civilization. Yet Grene, in his book *Man in His Pride,* sees two Platos, young and old, the Plato of *The Republic* and the Plato of *The Laws,* at loggerheads one with the other.

"In the *Timaeus* and *Laws* trilogy," Grene writes, "the ideal state has become historical; somewhere in the past it can be thought of as having been, and its past actions can be imagined and fitted into a scheme which will lead all the way to the 'best' state of the future. But for the earlier Plato, the Plato of the *Republic,* there could be no assertion, lightly made, that his model city had been achieved, or even that it would be, exactly as outlined, the 'best' state for the future. The possibility of its actual existence meant far too much to him."

In short, Grene believes that Plato meant his Republic to take on actuality in this world, and looks sympathetically upon Plato's design—while Popper recoils in horror from the same prospect. "In the *Laws,*" Grene continues, "the importance of the actual historical past is gone; history can become myth rich in meaning, and myth, history; and both can point to the future, which has no hopes of fulfillment and no agonies of frustration."

Now Voegelin, in his detailed analysis of Plato in the third volume of *Order and History*—possibly the most important section of his whole series—takes a position quite different from that of either Popper or Grene. Voegelin reasons, convincingly, that Plato's intention and accomplishment is to teach obedience to the incarnate Truth; not to preach some dismal set of totalist dogmas, nor yet to bring into being an "ideal" state in his own time, but rather to reveal those principles of order in the soul and order in the commonwealth which make us truly human and which keep the knife from our throats.

"The philosopher who is in possession of the Truth should consistently go the way of Plato in the *Republic;* he should issue the call for repentance and submission to the theocratic rule of the incarnate Truth." *The Republic* is an analogy or allegory of order, not a model constitution, though it will suggest reforms in the existential state; and there exists no opposition between *Republic* and *Laws,* but only a continuous development of the complex theme. Men cannot well remain pure in a corrupt society, Plato says repeatedly; nor can corrupt men maintain a high and just order. Therefore the problem of ordered soul and ordered state cannot be split into halves. Plato is seeking transcendent reality; his work is a leap in being, a glimpse of an eternal order, divinely ordained, which we must try to imitate in our souls and our institutions. "When the philosopher explores the spiritual order of the soul," Voegelin says, "he explores a realm of experiences which he can appropriately describe only in the language of symbols expressing the movement of the soul toward transcendental reality and the flooding of the soul by transcendence. At the border of transcendence the language of philosophical anthropology must become the language of religious symbolization."

Voegelin tells us, that is, with Plato, that order in society is possible only if there is true order in individual souls; and that there cannot be order in souls unless those souls, in some degree, know the author of their being and His intention for them. Plato writes in symbol, for there is no other way in which transcendent knowledge can be expressed; and, at its highest level, the truth about man and his state must be religious truth, and in some degree mystery.

From the age of Moses onward, there have been men—prophets or philosophers—who sought for the transcendent meaning in history: who groped for knowledge of the soul, and glimpsed in the record of history a divine meaning, a revelation of the way of God with man, and of the reality of the soul. Yet in Israel and in Athens, as today, there were men who, succumbing to *doxa,* endeavored to make immanent the transcendent symbols of order: to take by storm the Kingdom of Heaven, but to annex that Kingdom to an earthly realm, rather than to enter into eternity. Such were those Jews who hoped vainly that Judah would prevail in this world over her great enemies, and those Greek philodoxers who made power and success the objects of life, and those medieval Gnostics who looked for salvation and perfection in time and space, and those enthusiasts for the Enlightenment who expected the French Revolution to usher in the unending regime of universal happiness. Such are the "progressivists" and utopians of our own century, whether "liberal" or "totalitarian" in their factional affiliations. This is *doxa:* for human nature is not perfectible by human means, nor is society. And men intoxicated with *doxa,* even famous philodoxers, break up the order in personality when they blind men to the nature of the soul; and they upset the balance in any good society when they conjure up visions of desire satisfied which really are impossible of attainment.

So long as man is a mere part of nature, bound to this life and earth, impotent beneath mighty cosmological empires, he cannot tell or understand significant history: existence remains mere existence, a dog's life, full of sound and fury, perhaps, but empty of meaning as the idiot's tale; a simple bloody jumble of coronations and conquests. A leap in being is necessary for the ascent from cosmological myth to transcendent perception of the soul; and so there cannot be true history without this leap in being. Such a leap is not a mere "stage in cultural progress," though of course, once accomplished, that leap produces enduring cultural changes. The nature of the leap varies from one people to another; and it is not a single leap which is required, but a series of leaps.

In Israel, the problems of order—that is, of human existence under God—were the concern of the prophets; and through the prophets came the leap in being. In Hellas, the problems of order— that is, of an enduring justice and its sanctions—were the concern of the poets and the philosophers; and through the poets and the philosophers came the leap in being. Revelation and reason both are ways to order, and by either can a transcending leap be achieved. But that leap is not the work of narrow logic; instead, it is accomplished by the higher imagination, by the perceptions of genius, by an intuition which transcends ordinary experience—by a means, in fine, which we cannot adequately describe with those tools called words. Neither the leap of Israel nor the leap of Hellas brought full knowledge of the transcendent order; it required the fusing of Jewish and Greek genius in Christianity for a leap still higher.

Among the Greeks, the leap in being was principally the achievement of Plato; yet Plato's insight was attained only after the existential order of the polis was far sunk in decadence. Man's dreadful experience of the decay of his society, from the dawn of things, has been an impelling motive to the search for an order that is not transitory. From terror, man learns that the existential order is not real order—that mere fleshly existence is not the end of all. He awakens, Voegelin says, "to the untruth of existence." With St. Paul, man's existence before the leap in being is only "opaque existence." In Paul's words, "I once was alive without the law." The law is the *nomos,* which after the leap in being means not merely traditions and institutions, but norms, laws, that transcend things existential. Man awakens to his own nature, to his soul. Then he may "transform the succession of societies preceding in time into a past of mankind." This does not end the struggle for the knowledge of order; it only makes the search for order intelligible. Mankind becomes conscious "of the open horizon of its future."

The leaps of Israel and Hellas, roughly parallel in time and quite independent of each other, were achieved only after much travail, and the mass of men never really understood the nature of these discoveries; indeed, many of the learned and the clever sought to demolish the consciousness of the soul already acquired: such were the philodoxers. The power of the *doxa* is enormous. From early times in the Hellenic age, nevertheless, the Greek genius groped and toiled toward order: toward an apprehension of divine purpose and divine justice, toward a moral order among men. The principal expressions of this search are the writings of Homer, Hesiod, Xenophanes, Parmenides, Heraclitus, Aeschylus, Sophocles, Herodotus, the Old Oligarch, Thucydides, Plato, and Aristotle.

In Homer, the soul still is opaque; and so there can be no transcendence of the existential order. Achilles had rather be the meanest thrall in Boetia than king among the shades. But Homer is struggling toward principles of order. In the disintegrated world of the ruined Mycenaean civilization, where Whirl seems master of all, where every moral tradition is broken, Homer—the blind one who sees—"astutely observed that the disorder of a society was a disorder in the soul of its component members, and especially in the soul of the ruling class. . . . Without having a term for it, he envisaged man as having a psyche with an internal organization through a center of passions and a second center of ordering and judging knowledge. . . . And he strove valiantly for the insight that ordering action is action in conformity with transcendent divine order, while disruptive action is a fall from the divine order into the specifically human disorder. . . . But the historical process in which a society declines, as well as the infinitude of acts which in the aggregate of centuries spell destruction, had a pattern of their own that could not be described in terms of individual misdeeds. Homer had to face the problem that the day-to-day causality of human action will explain the detail of the historical process but not its configuration. His answer to this mystery of the rise and fall of civilizations was the extraordinary Olympian assembly at which Zeus and Hera agreed on their program for the destruction of Mycenaean civilization, including both Trojans and Achaeans."

Hesiod, too, tried to describe the divine justice, beneficent or retributory, which orders the universe. By mighty struggles, Zeus brought out of Chaos a precarious order. "Zeus rules the world, and with tremendous sway takes back tomorrow what he grants today." The vengeance of Zeus visits the unjust upon earth. Though still encompassed by cosmological myth, Hesiod searches for an answer to the ills to which flesh is heir—an answer that must be more than the grip of Force and Power upon Prometheus. But Hesiod can discern no relief beyond the confines of the existential order; he is driven back upon the dream of an immanent salvation, as expressed in the fable of Pandora.

"The Hesiodian dream of no work, no hunger, no sickness, no old age and death, no women, lists the negatives of the experiences which are the principal sources of anxiety in human life. The paradise in this sense, as the dream of freedom from the burden and anxiety of existence, is a constant dimension of the soul that will express itself not only in the imagery of immortal existence in the beyond but generally pervades the imaginative occupation with a desirable state of mundane existence. One does not have to insist on coarse expressions that will first come to mind, such as the 'freedom from want and fear' of the Atlantic Charter. More subtly, the dream is the dynamic component in the attempts to create an earthly paradise by reducing the hours of labor (no work), by getting a living wage (no hunger), and medical care (no sickness) for everybody, and by increasing the length of human life (no death). And even the problem that man is created both man and woman, while it can not be resolved, can be psychologically diminished to the famous 'satisfaction of biological urges.' "

It will be observed from the preceding passage that Voegelin is no mere antiquarian in ideas. Human nature, and its difficulties, are constants; and the *doxa* of immanence springs eternal among men. Though ancient, it is nevertheless an error. A strong vein of passionate awareness runs through *Order and History:* a knowledge that the disorder of the smashed Mycenaean culture, and the disorder of the disintegrating polis of the fifth century, are one with the disorder of the twentieth century. And amid such disorder, there rises the figure of the philodoxer, "realistic," sardonic, driven by *pleonexia,* discarding *peitho* (righteous persuasion) in favor of trickery or intimidation; impelled by his passions and low interests, his illusions, even at the moment he claims to speak as practical logician and champion of common sense. These are men of today —who, like their predecessors in history, would obtain in the confusion of a bent world the realization of their dream-lusts. Take this passage from *Plato and Aristotle:*

"The condition of Socrates touches upon a problem, familiar to all of us who have had experiences with rightist or leftist intellectuals. Discussion is indeed impossible with a man who is intellectually dishonest, who misuses the rules of the game, who by irrelevant profuseness seeks to avoid being nailed down on a point, and who gains the semblance of victory by exhausting the time which sets an inevitable limit to a discussion."

Truly, it is history which teaches us the principles of order. It is the decay of men's apprehension of transcendent order that brings on *hybris* and *nemesis:* that is, the collapse of existential order. The philodoxers are the precursors of the atrocity-men.

Those truths of reason and revelation which men painfully have obtained over many centuries, the philodoxer endeavors to demol-

ish in a generation. Voegelin traces with care the ascent of Greek
thought toward the leap in being which came with Plato: a long
story, full of interest, full of tribulation. Xenophanes, breaking with
the myth, declared that "One God is greatest among gods and men,
not like mortals in body or thought." Heraclitus set against "much-
knowing" (*polys*) his "deep-knowing" (*bathys*); and if he did not
attain to the height of transcendence, still he penetrated to the
luminous depths of the soul: the mystic-philosophers had taken a
leap in being, for they knew what Homer and Hesiod had not
known, the soul as a source of knowledge. Solon taught the Athenians *eunomia*, righteousness, ordained by *Dike*, Justice. *Doxa*,
Solon discovered, is the source of disorder; the passion of life, the
doxa, must be disciplined for the sake of order, *eunomia*. "He passionately loves the magnificence and exuberance of life; but he
experiences it as a gift of the gods, not as an aim to be realized by
crooked means against the divine order."

From Heraclitus onward, the Greek philosophers—though not
the philodoxers—apprehended the life of the soul. The men of
Homer's time had known only the *psyche*, the life-force that departs
with death, never to live after but in dreams. To Homer, a dead
man was but a *soma*, a corpse. But the mystic-philosophers penetrated beyond the bounds of flesh. Their search for truth was continued in the tragedy: "The newly discovered humanity of the soul
expands into the realm of action." Aristotle, living in the decadence
of tragedy, thought of the tragic art only as *katharsis*, purging of
emotions, a kind of group-therapy. But for Aeschylus and Sophocles, Voegelin writes, tragedy was the opening of the soul to the
conflicting demands of Dike: not, it is true, a leap to the revelation
of God, but a descent to the depths of the soul where Dike may be
found. The tragic hero cannot merely weigh utilitarian consequences, or seek practical advice from gods and men: he must
search his soul. Only an audience capable at least of appreciating
heroic action, if not of participating in it, could understand and
support the tragic drama—and by Aristotle's time, that audience
was gone. But in the grand hour of Athens, Aeschylus and Sophocles spoke to men who still understood:

"The heroic soul-searching and suffering of consequences must
be experienced as the cult of Dike, and the fate of the hero must
arouse the shudder of his own fate in the soul of the spectator—

even if he himself should succumb to his weakness in a similar situation. The binding of the soul to its own fate through representative suffering, rather than the Aristotelian catharsis through pity and fear, is the function of tragedy."

At the moment when the tragic drama towered over Athens, nevertheless, the Sophists already were at their work: and among them, in politics at least, the greatest was Protagoras. Man is the measure of all things, Protagoras taught. He was by no means wholly a philodoxer, for Protagoras declared that reverence and justice must live in the soul of every man, or else the polis would perish; for Protagoras a man with a diseased soul brought disease to the polis, and ought to be put to death if, after five years of reformatory education, he should turn out incorrigible. Yet the general ethical tendency of the Sophists is sufficiently suggested in our word "sophistry"; and out of the struggles of Socrates and Plato against sophistry came the definitions of the Platonic virtues: justice, wisdom, fortitude, and temperance.

Against Protagoras, Socrates and Plato affirmed that God is the measure of all things. Here was the supreme Greek leap in being. Gorgias, another powerful Sophist, assailed Parmenides' concept of Being; and Gorgias' *On Being* is "one of the earliest, if not the very first, instance of the perennial type of enlightened philosophizing. Its arguments could be directed against all the symbols of transcendence." For Voegelin, "enlightenment, with its eighteenth-century rationalistic associations, is no term of commendation." Of the time of the Sophists, he writes, "We may say that the age indeed has a streak of enlightenment in so far as its representative thinkers show the same kind of insensitiveness toward experiences of transcendence that was characteristic of the Enlightenment of the eighteenth century A.D., and in so far as this sensitiveness has the same result of destroying philosophy—for philosophy by definition has its center in the experiences of transcendence."

Gomperz, in his *Greek Thinkers,* made Socrates the leader of a rationalistic Enlightenment. As Paul Elmer More says, this description is totally inadequate. Voegelin puts an end, probably forever, to the attempt of positivists and rationalists to claim Socrates for their own. "Whatever the formulations of the 'historic' Socrates may have been, the 'essence' of his identification of virtue with knowledge, as a principle in opposition to the Sophists, makes sense only if the distortions of time were meant to be corrected by the love of the measure that is out of time." Socrates and Plato set to work restoring and elaborating the problems of order. *Physis,* nature, was not their light, but *nomos,* divine law.

David Grene calls Plato "the man in the duststorm." He alludes to a passage in *The Republic.* Socrates is speaking of the philosopher in a decadent and violent age:

"He is like one who, in the storm of dust and sleet which the driving wind hurries along, retires under the shelter of a wall; and seeing the rest of mankind full of wickedness, he is content, if only he can live his own life and be pure from evil or unrighteousness, and depart in peace and good-will, with bright hopes."

Yet Plato, like Socrates, did not sit perpetually in the shelter of a wall. His expeditions to Syracuse were only the most conspicuous examples of his endeavor to regenerate Greek civilization by a reform at once internal and external. Socrates died for the sake of speaking the truth; Plato came near to dying like his teacher. As the glory of Greece had gone down to ruin in the quarries of Syracuse, Plato aspired sternly to raise up that glory again, even with Syracuse as its center. In that existential effort, he failed; but in his transcendent effort—his erection of the symbols of transcendence, with God as the measure—he triumphed; and all his detractors, ancient or modern, have not wholly undone his work. His leap in being occurred in a society much corrupted; his science of order was preached amidst existential disorder. The recovery of order in the soul cannot be separated from the restoration of order in the body politic, Plato knew, for even the philosopher may be seduced by the degeneracy of his age; and the average sensual man finds it next to impossible to maintain the order of his soul if he dwells in a corrupt community.

"Society can destroy a man's soul," Voegelin observes, "because the disorder of society is a disease in the psyche of its members. The troubles which the philosopher experiences in his own soul are the troubles in the psyche of the surrounding society which press on him. And the diagnosis of health and disease in the soul is, therefore, at the same time a diagnosis of order and disorder in society. On the level of conceptual symbols, Plato expressed his insight through the principle that society is man written in larger letters."

Plato was not an "idealist" in the sense that he entertained any notion of forcing upon a reluctant world some social trauma of his fancy. His *Republic* is a paradigm of the individual soul in harmony, not a scheme to be given actuality in positive law; Socrates says that the Republic, so far as it can be adapted to the world we know, can—nay, must—be modified. The *Republic* is a *zetema,* an inquiry, into the real nature of spiritual and social harmony. In Voegelin's phrases, "It should be clear that the inquiry is concerned with the reality of order in soul and society, not with 'ideals.' "

Plato was an inveterate foe to *doxa*—that is, to illusory social opinions, which attempt to force reality into a pattern that has no sanction in the nature of things. We moderns live in a political Babel, distorting Plato along with much else, Voegelin tells us:

"Within a few generations the Plato of the 'ideal state' has been transformed into a 'political ideologue.' This astounding transformation will be intelligible if we see it in the light of Plato's own analysis of social corruption. The generation which attributed to Plato the creation of an 'ideal state' had no evil intentions. Ideals were quite respectable at the time, and to ascribe them to Plato was praise. But even at that time the evil was lurking, for in common parlance an idealist was an impractical person who indulged his subjective valuations in opposition to reality; and the connotation of subjectivity in 'ideal' undermined the objectivity of Plato's inquiry into the nature of reality."

Thus the passionate and confused modern critic Karl Popper—as the silliest example—ascribes to Plato precisely the *doxa* entertained by Plato's sophistical adversaries. Perhaps this is not surprising: after all, the Athenian jury did just this in the trial of Socrates. But the Athenian jurors did not set up as professors of logic.

Voegelin's close analysis of all the important Platonic dialogues, in scholarship the most valuable portion of these two volumes, cannot be examined here. It must suffice to quote from his concluding remarks, which serve to summarize both the purpose of his own study and the achievement of Plato: "Truth is not a body of propositions about a world-immanent object; it is the world-transcendent *summum bonum,* experienced as an orienting force in the soul, about which we can speak only in analogical symbols."

This was the endeavor and the method of Plato. It was the error —and perhaps even the malice—of Aristotle to treat Plato's Ideas, in part, as if they were world-immanent data. But in a time that requires most urgently the restoration of the theory and the vocabulary of order, we cannot afford to misunderstand and misinterpret Plato's end and method for the sake of a scholastic wrangle.

Aristotle's partial immanentizing of Platonic Ideas resulted in an "intellectual thinning-out. . . . The mystical *via negativa* by which the soul ascends to the vision of the Idea in the *Symposium* is thinned out to rise toward the dianoetic virtues and the *bios theoretikos*." When symbols are treated as if they were objects of sensory experience, order is in imminent danger. "When the Christian idea of supernatural perfection through grace in death was immanentized to become the idea of perfection of mankind in history through individual and collective mass action, the foundation was laid for the mass creeds of modern Gnosis."

The leap in being of the Hellenic philosophers was a great stride toward the apprehension of order; but, in this, unlike the Mosaic and prophetic leap in being, it did not disengage the order of history from cosmological myth. Both Israel and Hellas were to wait some centuries for the next leap in human consciousness of the soul and the order the soul dictates. They were to wait for the truth of perfection through grace in death, which idea Socrates foreshadowed, but did not fully express.

The philodoxers are with us still, and their name is legion; while our philosophers are few. Even among our professors of philosophy, there are not many who can understand Eric Voegelin, and fewer who will sympathize: for most of them, too, are philodoxers. We dwell in the disordered world of metaphysical madness that the fourth and fifth centuries knew; and for us, as for the Greeks, spiritual disorder brings on political anarchy. Yet *Order and History* will restore to some modern minds an understanding of transcendence. And some few may speak out, as did Socrates and Plato, in the teeth of the dust-storm.

❋❋❋❋❋❋❋❋❋❋❋❋❋❋❋❋❋❋❋❋❋❋

VII. AUTHORITY, JUST GOVERNMENT, AND ORDERED FREEDOM

Our Necessity for Authority

CIVILIZED MAN LIVES BY AUTHORITY; WITHOUT SOME REFERENCE to authority, indeed, no form of truly human existence is possible. Also man lives by prescription—that is, by ancient custom and usage, and the rights which usage and custom have established. Without just authority and respected prescription, the pillars of any tolerable social order, genuine freedom is not conceivable.

For some time it has been fashionable to deride authority and prescription—though some folk have been experiencing a change of heart recently. "Authority," in the vocabulary of what has been called "the Freudian ethic," has implied arbitrary restraint; and prescription has been equated with cultural lag and superstition. But the consequences of these emancipated notions have been unpalatable. A generation of young people reared according to "permissive" tenets has grown up bored, sullen, and in revolt against the very lack of order which was supposed to ensure the full development of their personalities. And a world lulled by slogans about absolute liberty and perpetual peace has found itself devoured by thoroughgoing tyranny and increasing violence. If men are to associate at all, some authority must govern them; if they throw off traditional authority, the authority of church and precept and old educational disciplines and parents, then very soon they find themselves subjected to some new and merciless authority. Authority and prescription lacking, order cannot subsist. If the authority is unjust, and the prescription merely the decree of some new domination, then the social order will have small place for freedom. Genuinely ordered freedom is the only sort of liberty worth having: freedom made possible by order within the soul and order within the state. Anarchic freedom, liberty defiant of authority and prescription, is merely the subhuman state of the wolf and the shark, or the punishment of Cain, with his hand against every man's, and every man's against his.

So if people really desire genuine freedom, they need to know genuine authority. "Authority" is not the policeman's stick. "Conscience is an authority," John Henry Newman wrote in his essay on John Keble; "the Bible is an authority; such is the Church; such is Antiquity; such are legal saws and state maxims; such are proverbs, such are sentiments, presages, and prepossessions." Authority, then, is the ground upon which prudent action must be performed.

Political authority, the claims and powers of a legitimate state, though an important part of this complex of authority which rules our lives, is no more than a part. Sometimes authorities conflict; most of the great disputes in history have been, at bottom, controversies over the higher source of authority. And such debates never are wholly and finally resolved. Now and again, for instance, the authoritative claims of church and state cannot well be reconciled, and then trouble results. Similarly, the authority of faith and the authority of reason collide from age to age. In such clashes, the conscientious man endeavors, according to what light is given him, to determine which representatives of authority have claimed too much; but he is foolish if, despairing, he forsakes authority altogether.

Human nature being flawed, so that all of us in some degree rebel against the people and the institutions to which we owe most, there is in every man a certain impulse to make himself God: that is, to cast off all authority but his own lust and whim. From this vice, this hankering for abnormality, comes the corrupting influence of total power upon even the best of natures. The rebellion of Lucifer is the symbol of this ancient anarchic impulse—the passion for overthrowing the authority of God, that upon the vacant throne of authority the rebel may make himself absolute. Yet the doom of all such risings is as sure as Lucifer's. For a grown man to rebel against all authority is as ludicrous as for a three-year-old child to defy his parents: whether they are good parents or bad, he can live scarcely a day without them.

From its beginnings, the liberal movement of the nineteenth century had within it this fatuous yearning for the destruction of all authority. Liberalism also possessed some good qualities; but it never has recovered from this congenital defiance of authority and prescription. The early liberals were convinced that once they should overthrow established governments and churches, supplanting them by rational and egalitarian and purely secular institutions, the principal difficulties of the human condition would be nearly terminated. Poverty, ignorance, disease, and war might then cease, once enlightened self-interest, popular suffrage, and utilitarian public policies had triumphed. One had only to fight clear of the Bad Old Days and the dead weight of superstition. Abolish the old Authorities, and sweetness and light must reign.

Yet the triumph of liberalism endured little more than half a century; by the 1880's, the individualism of the early liberals was being transmuted into socialism. Liberalism had begun, defying authority and prescription, by breaking all sorts of ancient ties and obligations. But increasingly, though implicitly, as the decades passed, liberals came to accept a new authority, that of the omnicompetent welfare state; they continued to repudiate authority only in the sphere of private life.

Just how archaic and unreal, politically, latter-day liberalism has become is sufficiently illustrated by a conference of the English Liberal Party in the summer of 1961. Three principal resolutions were proposed: to abolish the monarchy, to abolish the hereditary element in the House of Lords, and to expand the welfare state. Though the first proposal was defeated after discussion, the other two were adopted enthusiastically; and so the conference adjourned, its members satisfied that they had shown the English nation how to solve its problems. To anyone but a Liberal ideologue, it is clear enough that abolition of the British monarchy would accomplish nothing but injury to the symbols of justice and order in Britain; that to destroy the hereditary element in the House of Lords would only damage the most serious—though not the most powerful—deliberative body in the world; and that to extend the

British welfare state would do no less than to finish Liberalism altogether, since that would mean complete socialism, and probably the end of the British constitution and of British prosperity.

At a later Liberal conference, it was earnestly proposed by one faction that most public parks be abolished, the trees cut down, and low-rent housing erected on such sites. The party leadership put down this resolution with some difficulty. So much for the eccentricities of a dying party. One may as well laugh as cry. To such an intellectual and moral bankruptcy have come even the more intelligent of twentieth-century liberals. Having denied the very existence of sound and just authority, having scoffed at the wisdom of our ancestors, liberalism is cut loose from such moorings as once it had. Without some principle of authority, life becomes meaningless, and intellectual factions slip into the dust-bin of history.

If authority, then—however unfashionable in recent years—remains ineluctable for civilization and for any truly human existence, how do men find such authority? They find it ordinarily through tradition, prescription, custom, a body of normative literature, and those sources of norms described in the first section of this book.

Even the most gifted of men, and always the mass of humanity, must fall back upon normative knowledge, upon tradition and prescription, if they are to act at all in this world. At very least, it saves much time. It is conceivable that, if I set myself to it, I might calculate privately the circumference of the earth, quite independently of previous calculations. But since I possess no strong mathematical gifts, it seems improbable that my calculations would be more accurate than those of the present authorities; and it seems almost certain that my result would be quite the same as the present calculation of the earth's circumference, if I should proceed rationally; so I would have spent months or years of a brief life in trying to gain what I could have had for the asking. If we are to accomplish anything in this life, we must take much for granted and settled. In the matter of the earth's circumference, nearly all of us are better off if we simply accept the "traditional" or "authoritative" calculation.

This is even more true of moral and social first principles. Only through prescription and tradition, only by habitual acceptance of just and sound authority, only by conformity to norms, can men acquire knowledge of the permanent things. Authority tells us that murder is wrong; prescription immemorially has visited severe punishments upon murderers; tradition presents us with an ancient complex of tales of the evil consequences of murder. Now a man who thinks his private petty rationality superior to the wisdom of our ancestors may undertake experiments in murder, with a view to testing these old irrational scruples; but the results of such experiments are sure to be disagreeable for everyone concerned, including the researcher; and that experimenter has no right to be surprised if we hang him by the neck until he is quite dead. For if men flout norm and convention, life becomes intolerable. It is through respect for tradition and prescription, and recourse to those sources of normative understanding, that the mass of human beings acquire a tolerable knowledge of the rules by which private and social existence is made tolerable.

Now it does not follow that an unquestioning acceptance of received opinions and long-established usage will suffice of itself to guide us always and in everything. The world does change; a certain sloughing off of tradition and prescription is at work in any vigorous society, and a certain adding to the bulk of received opinion goes on from age to age. We cannot live precisely by the lesser rules of our distant forefathers, in all matters. But the fact that a belief or institution has long been accepted by men, and seems to have exerted a benign influence, establishes in its favor a legitimate presumption. If we feel inclined to depart from old ways, we ought to do so only after sober consideration of ultimate consequences. Authority, prescription, and tradition undergo in every generation a filtering process, by which the really archaic is discarded; yet we ought to be sure that we actually are filtering, and not merely letting our heritage run down the drain.

Similarly, the general principles and tested institutions which we have inherited from past generations must be applied and utilized with prudence; here the exercise of right reason by the leaders of any society is necessary. In politics, the way in which we apply normative knowledge necessarily varies with circumstance: the statesman tries to reconcile enduring standard and passing exigency. Prescription and tradition cannot stand forever if the living do not sustain them by vigorous application and prudent reform. But it is equally true that lively action and ingenious reform are mere ropes of sand, unless undertaken in the light of the wisdom of the ages.

We may take the idea of justice, to illustrate my meaning here. There exists a norm of justice, best expressed by Plato and Cicero. This norm has its origin in the experience of men in community over many centuries, and also in the insights of men of genius. The great classical philosophers of politics argued that justice amounts to this: "to each his own." Every man, ideally, ought to obtain the things which best suit his own nature; he ought to do the work for which he is fiitted, and to receive the rewards of that work. Men's talents and desires vary conspicuously from individual to individual; therefore a society is unjust which treats all men as if they were uniform beings, or which allots to one sort of nature the rights and the duties which properly belong to other sorts of human beings.

This concept of justice has entered deeply into the ethics, the jurisprudence, and even the imaginative literature of what we call "Western civilization." It remains a strong influence upon men who never have read Cicero or Plato. It creates a wise prejudice against radical egalitarianism, which would reduce all men to a single mode of existence. It has inculcated a sound respect for order: that is, for a society marked by a variety of rewards and duties, a commonwealth in which, as Burke said, all men "have equal rights; but not to equal things." This theory of justice underlies the American and British constitutions, and the framework of order in many other countries.

Nowadays this classical idea of justice is challenged by the Marxist doctrine that order should be abolished: all human beings, the Marxist says, should be treated as identical units, and compulsory equality of condition enforced. When the average American or Englishman is brought face to face with Marxist demands for the overthrow of authority everywhere, that Marxist "justice" may triumph, he may not be able to meet the Marxist propaganda with a privately reasoned defense of constitutionalism and social diversity; but he does resist the Marxist doctrine out of a feeling that what the Communist proposes is fundamentally unjust. The average American or Englishman remains a law-abiding traditionalist to a large degree, even in this day of bewildering technological and industrial alteration; he takes it for granted that we were not born yesterday; that we have no right to cast away our tested civil social order; that monotonous uniformity of condition is contrary to fundamental human aspirations; that Communism flies in the face of the nature of things. And because he is heir to a tradition and a body of institutions, he knows something of the true character of justice, and he sets his face against the radical ideologue.

The norm of justice never is perfectly attained, nor can it be: we have to redress the balance of the scales of justice in every age. That redressing is part of the art of political prudence. But if we did not know the norm of justice, we would have no scales at all. To understand such norms, and to apply them, we turn to sound authority.

The Norms of Tolerable Government

Through recognition of authority, we know something of what constitutes a reasonably good government. I suggest here the first principles of a decent political order—principles assailed by the modern ideologue.

Government is instituted to secure justice, order, and freedom, through respect for legitimate authority; and if we ask from government more than government can provide, we imperil government's primary functions. The notion that mere political manipulation can make all men happy is one of the sorriest illusions of the liberal era. But some forms of government can make men miserable. So I describe here the general lineaments of the kind of government which seems consonant with the general welfare.

I think that we need to refer to two norms or principles. The first principle is that a good government allows the more energetic natures among a people to fulfill their promise, while ensuring that these persons shall not tyrannize over the mass of men. (For my expression of this norm, I am indebted, in part, to Eric Voegelin.) The second principle is that in every state the best possible—or least baneful—form of government is one in accord with the traditions and prescriptive ways of its people. Beyond these two general norms, there is no invariable rule of politics which may be applied, uniformly, universally, and without qualification, to all societies in all ages.

Even Mr. David Riesman has rediscovered the old truth that men are not created equal, literally: they are created different. Variety, not uniformity, gives any nation vigor and hope. Thus my first principle of good government has a hearing once more, though the overmastering tendency of the past century and a half has been social egalitarianism. "One man is as good as another, or maybe a little better": this secular dogma has done mischief to the modern world. Equality in political power has tended to lead toward equality of condition. But everybody does not belong to everybody else, and one man really is not as good as another. The first fallacy is the denial of Christian morals, the second the denial of the Christian doctrine of the person.

Aye, men are created different, and a government which ignores this law becomes an unjust domination, for it sacrifices talents to mediocrity; it pulls down the energetic natures to gratify the unaspiring natures. This degradation injures humanity in two ways. First, it frustrates the natural longing of talented men to realize their abilities; it leaves the abler men dissatisfied with themselves and their nation, and they sink into boredom; it impedes any improvement, qualitatively, of the moral, intellectual, and material condition of mankind. Second, this degradation adversely affects the well-being, in the long run, of the mass of men: for, deprived of responsible leadership and example, the innumerable men and women who live by routine suffer in the tone of their culture, and in their material condition. A government which converts into a secular dogma the Christian mystery of moral equality must be hostile toward civilization.

Remember that there exist two parts to this political principle: not only should a tolerable government recognize the rights of the more talented natures, but it should recognize the right of the majority of men not to be bullied and troubled by these aspiring talents. The prudent politician endeavors to maintain a balance between these two claims. There have been ages in which aristocracy —natural or hereditary—has usurped the whole governance of life, demanding of the average man a tribute and an obedience which deprive the majority of their desire to live quietly, and which often damage their material well-being. Such a regime, indifferent to the welfare of the majority, is as bad a government as a domination indifferent to the claims of the talented minority. But today in the West, at least, the immediate danger is not the rule of an oligarchy; rather, the curse of our time and country is "the revolt of the masses," the threat that mediocrity may submerge any elevation of mind and character. Therefore the discerning statist of our time must be more acutely concerned with the preservation of the rights of the uncommon man than with the extension of the claims of the crowd.

A domination which confounds popular government with equality of moral worth, equality of intellect, or equality of condition is a bad government. For a good government respects the claims of extraordinary ability. It respects the right of the contemplative to his solitude. It respects the right of the practical leader to take an honest initiative in the affairs of the commonwealth. It respects the right of the inventor to his ingenuity's rewards, the right of the manufacturer or the merchant to his decent gains, the right of the thrifty man to keep his savings and bequeath them to his heirs. It respects such rights and claims, this good government, because in the enjoyment of these rights, and in the performance of the duties to which these rights are joined, men fulfill themselves; and thus a considerable measure of justice—"to each his own"—is attained.

Today the balance between the claims of the uncommon man and the common man, in some ages overthrown to the advantage of aspiring talents, is injured rather by the extortionate demands of a doctrinaire egalitarianism. Communist states are the most thorough examples of this triumph of envy. I am aware that Soviet Russia, for instance, is governed by a clique of party intriguers and successful administrators, paying little more than lip-service to their own secular dogma of egalitarianism; yet this does not alter the fact that, obedient to the ideology of dialectical materialism, the Soviets have suppressed the claims of the better and the gentler natures. What we see in the new elite of Communism is not a predominance of the higher natures, but a domination of hard fanatics, devoid of high moral endowments. This is the regime of a host of squalid oligarchs. Among them are no prophets, and no poets; the only qualification for entry into this elite is ruthless cunning in the struggle for power. Not the better natures, but the lower—in terms of moral attainment and independence of mind—are recognized and re-warded by the Soviets.

Now it is not American "democracy," as such, which stands at the antipodes from the Soviet undertaking. The real forces of resist-ance, rather, are American moral and political tradition, and American constitutionalism. A political democracy may attain a tolerable balance between the rights of ability and the rights of ordinariness. But also it is possible for a monarchy to achieve that balance, or an aristocracy, or some other frame of government. Respect for natural and prescriptive rights is peculiar to no single set of political institutions.

Yet the kind of government which seems best calculated to ap-preciate and defend the claims of either interest in the common-wealth is what Aristotle called a "polity," a balancing and checking of classes in society. The United States remains, substantially, a polity; *pure* democracy was not relished by the founders of this Republic, and it has not yet triumphed among us. It ought not to triumph. For the tolerable government does not grow up from mere protection of entrenched property, nor yet from the victory of the proletariat.

A liberal professor of politics, Dr. R. M. MacIver, writing a few years ago, expressed his disquietude at the misunderstanding of the term "democracy" in America. The word has been associated, he remarked, "with a kind of loose egalitarianism, a leveling of stand-ards to the measure of the 'common man.' " This is a false premise, he continued, doing much harm; yet there is another illusion con-cerning the nature of democracy which is still worse: "the assump-tion that democracy means the rule of the many over all the affairs of men." *

Here MacIver touched on the immense dull threat of mediocrity to all the nobler achievements of humankind. A regime which iden-tifies popular government with equality of moral worth, equality of intellect, and equality of condition is a bad government, inimical to justice and order.

A prudent government, within the bounds set by decency and good order, leaves every man to consult his own humor. It does not attempt to force the happiness of the statistical Bentham upon the

* MacIver, *Academic Freedom in Our Time* (New York, 1955), pp. 250-251.

romantic Coleridge; for one man's happiness, even among the strongest personalities, is another man's misery. By a salutary neglect, this government allows private happiness to take care of itself. One may call this prudent and tolerant government "democracy," if one wishes, although I think that would be twisting the word. I call it simply a government which prefers principle to ideology, diversity to uniformity, balance to omnipotence.

The Deep Roots of Tolerable Government

Now for my second principle of good government: that a government should be in harmony with the historical experience, the traditions, and the prescriptive ways of a people. This is the view of Montesquieu and of Burke. A prudent government is no artificial contrivance, no invention of coffeehouse intellectuals, got up abstractly to suit the intellectual whim of an hour. Governments hastily designed upon theories of pure reason ordinarily are wretched and short-lived dominations. Consider the poor reeling government of France, which never has recovered from the hacking and chopping that the constitution of French society suffered at the hands of rigorous metaphysicians from 1789 onward. Much more evanescent, because they had smaller reservoirs of tradition to exhaust, were the artificial governments set up in central and southern and eastern Europe after the First World War. Now the good government, very different from these, is the tree that grows slowly from centuries of social experience. It has been called organic; I prefer the analogy "spiritual," despite my tree-simile. This political order puts its faith in precedent, prescription, historical trial and error, and consensus of opinion over many generations. Not infatuated with neatness, it prefers the strength and majesty of the Gothic style. The government of Britain, because of its age and success, has been our best example of this type. And the government of the United States is nearly as good an instance of the triumph of this principle that society is a continuity and essence, nurtured by veneration, prescription, custom, and tradition.

Nominally, we Americans created our federal Constitution by

deliberate action, within a few months. But in actuality that formal Constitution, and our state constitutions, chiefly were formalized expressions of what already existed institutionally and was widely accepted by the people: beliefs and institutions long established in the colonies, and drawn from centuries of European experience with parliaments, the common law, and the balancing of orders and interests in a realm. Respect for precedent and prescription governed the minds of the founders of the Republic. We appealed to the prescriptive liberties of Englishmen, not to *liberté, egalité, fraternité;* and the philosophical and moral structure of our civil order was rooted in the Christian faith, not in the worship of Reason.

The success of the American and British governments, I am suggesting, is produced by their preference for growth, experience, tradition, and prescription—their respect for ancient authority, indeed—over any closet-metaphysician's grand design. The lessons of politics are taught a people through their historical experience; no nation may sever itself from its past and still prosper, for the dead alone give us energy; and whatever constitution has been long accepted in a nation, that constitution—amended, perhaps, but essentially the same—is as good as a people can expect. True, that constitution may be improved, or restored; but if it is discarded altogether, like so much wastepaper, every order in society pays the penalty for generations to come.

With truth, Dr. Daniel Boorstin observes that the American Constitution is not for export. The American and British constitutions (referring, in both cases, to the underlying fundamental constitutions of society, rather than to formal documents) have worked well; but being very like living essences, they cannot be transplanted with much more success than one experiences when trying to transplant a ladyslipper or any flowering plant that prefers its native state to the tidy garden. One of the worst errors of the French revolutionaries was their endeavor to remake France upon the model of what they took English politics to be. Though any people have something to learn from the experiences of any other nation, still there exists no single constitution calculated to work wonders everywhere. For the political institutions of a people grow out of their religion, their moral habits, their economy, their literature; political ways are but part of an intricate bed of civilization, into which the roots of the social order are turned deep. Attempts to impose borrowed institutions upon an alien culture, however well intentioned, generally are disastrous—though sometimes decades, or even generations, may be required for the experiment to run its unlucky course.

True, a natural law for mankind exists—although man cannot know or obey that law until he is civilized; true, there are certain general norms of order and justice toward which all well-intentioned dominations strive; true, there may be discerned at least two general principles common to all tolerable governments, that I already have suggested. Yet beyond this, the particular institutions of any people must be of their own slow creation, over generations or centuries. The norms of order and justice and freedom are attained in an interesting variety of ways.

Notwithstanding this ineluctable diversity of political forms—notwithstanding the fact that even God is three distinct Persons—the ideologue and the well-meaning internationalist continue to demand that a single form of government will be best for all the world. They confound normality with standardization in the sense of monotony. American public opinion (or a part of it) and American foreign policy still are plagued by the delusion that some domination of American institutions and manners and aspirations will be established in every land—the American liberal's conviction, in Santayana's phrases, that the nun must not remain a nun, and China shall not keep its wall. Perennially we Americans seek for liberal, gradualist, middle-of-the-road, temperate, rational, parliamentary-minded political factions and leaders—almost identical with forward-looking Americans, though perhaps not quite so well-adjusted—in Vietnam, or the Congo, or Algeria, or Yugoslavia: people who will disavow both "feudalism" and Marxism, and behave as if they had been graduated from some American state university, if not from Princeton or Chicago. Yet somehow we fail to find these precious people, in Asia or Africa or Europe or Latin America; and we are vexed. But our hope springs eternal. Generalissimo Chiang Kai-shek, Marshal Tito, President Diem, Bung Sukarno, and other men of mark successively fall from our favor: they have strayed from the paths of righteousness; they have not been good Americans! We never are, but always are to be, blessed with some statesman or party, east of Suez, endowed with sufficient common sense to install the American Way instanter.

This fond hope of political universalism never will be realized. For individuals, as Chesterton said, are happy only when they are their own potty little selves; and this is as true of nations. The imposition of the American Way upon all the world would not make all the world cheerful; on the contrary, our institutions would function tolerably in few lands. States, like men, must find their own paths to order and justice and freedom; and those paths ordinarily are ancient and twisting routes, upon which the signposts are Tradition and Prescription and Authority. Without the legal institutions, rooted in common and Roman law, from which it arose, the American constitutional system would be unworkable; without the American economy, it is vain to impose American material aspirations upon a people.

Political universalists in either American political party, like certain people high in the American industrial system and like other people active in the American labor movement, expect to Americanize all cultures. Ambassador Chester Bowles is an adequate specimen of this mentality. By an American-sponsored industrialization of "underdeveloped regions," under forced draft, such gentlemen as Bowles would have Americans out-materialize the Soviet materialists. The world should become one immense copy of American society, repeating the phrases of Jefferson and F.D.R., adopting American technology, imitating our manners and establishments, and presumably inheriting our problems and afflictions. The Bowles brand of one-hundred-per-cent Americanism—so runs the argument—may be imposed quite simply, and with equal facility, upon the ancient cultures of Vietnam and the primitive peoples of southern Africa.

But here I interject a general proposition of mine bearing some relation to American foreign policy. It seems to be a law governing all life, from the unicellular inanimate forms to the highest human cultures, that every living organism endeavors, above all else, to preserve its identity. Whatever lives, tries to make itself the center of the universe; and it resists with the whole of its power the endeavors of competing forms of life to assimilate it to their substance and mode. Every living thing prefers even death, as an individual, to extinction as a species by absorption into other species. So if the lowliest alga struggles fatally against a threat to its peculiar identity, we ought not to be surprised that men and nations resist desperately —often unreasoningly—any attempt to assimilate their character to that of some other body social. This resistance is the first law of their being, extending below the level of consciousness. There is one sure way to make a deadly enemy; and that is to propose to anyone, "Submit yourself to me, and I will improve your condition by relieving you from the burden of your peculiar identity and reconstituting your substance in my image."

Yet this is precisely what Mr. Bowles and Americans of like mind, with good will and innocence, proclaim as a rallying-cry for American policy-makers in a revolutionary world. To be sure, they do not use precisely these phrases, and they seem to be unaware of the arrogant assumption behind their own humanitarian projects; yet naiveté does not alter the character of the first principles upon which the design is erected.

Take up the American Way, abstractly, and set it down, as an exotic plant, in Iran or Guinea or Bolivia, where the common law (English style) is unknown, and where the literature and the customs by which we have been nurtured are quite unknown—why, the thing cannot succeed. We will not create new Congresses and White Houses in Morocco or Botswana, where the bed of justice rests upon the Koran, or upon hereditary chieftainship. Such an undertaking may disrupt the old system of justice, and may even supplant it, temporarily; but in the long run, the traditional morals, habits, and establishments of a people, confirmed by their historical experience, will reassert themselves, and the innovation will be undone—if that culture is to survive at all.

We Americans tend to assume that the states which we condescend to call "underdeveloped countries" are mere primitive aggregations of population, lacking only our political practices and assumptions for the building of a regime of sweetness and light. But this is to ignore history; and it is we, not the "underdeveloped," who are fools in this matter. That many states of Asia and Africa and Latin America and even Europe, suddenly exposed to the revolutionary influences of modern technology and modern ideology, now must do something more than simply conform to old routine and custom, certainly is undeniable. But I am suggesting that these nations, for the most part, must work out their own reforms; and that their reforms must be in the line of the prescriptive ways and the traditions of a country. In many matters, they already possess their own authorities. The Asiatic or African who attempts to convert himself and his nation, abruptly and thoroughly, to Western ways must end disillusioned. We will be fortunate if he does not turn to violent reaction. Like the Arab in Cunninghame Graham's story "Sidi bu Zibbula," he will crouch resentful upon his dunghill, saying, "I have seen your cities, and the dung is better."

Good government is no mass-produced article. Order and justice and freedom are found in divers ways, but they cannot be divorced from the historical experience of a people. Theory parted from experience is infinitely dangerous, the plaything of the ideologue, the whetted dagger of the energumen. Though their social functions may be similar, the justice of the peace cannot supplant the cadi; and no James Mill, however learned, can rightfully make laws for India.

EPILOGUE

✸✸✸✸✸✸✸✸✸✸✸✸✸✸✸✸✸✸✸✸✸✸✸

Life without principle, in letters or in politics, soon becomes insufferably boring; also it cannot long endure. Nothing is sillier than the concept of an "amoral" society; for human beings may be moral, or immoral, but they cannot be neutral. The norms of morals and literature and politics are rules for the game of life, or principles for the realization of true human nature. If those norms are ignored, the game soon is over, and genuine humanity ceases to exist.

We are not made for perfect things; and if ever we found ourselves under the domination of the "perfect" government, we would make mincemeat of it, from sheer boredom. Therefore Utopia never will be discovered. Before this century is out, nevertheless, many people will discover the truth of certain old platitudes, the vexatious saws of Kipling's Gods of the Copybook Headings—such as "stick to the Devil you know" and "the Wages of Sin is Death." These Gods of the Copybook Headings, as Kipling says, outlast all the Gods of the Market-Place:

"We were living in trees when they met us.
They showed us each in turn
That Water would certainly wet us, as Fire would
certainly burn:
But we found them lacking in Uplift, Vision and
Breadth of Mind,
So we left them to teach the Gorillas while we
followed the March of Mankind."

The Gods of the Copybook Headings are Normative Authority. From just authority, from respect for our cultural and moral patrimony, comes civil freedom, and much more. It was this, I suppose, that St. Paul meant when he said, "The powers that be are ordained of God." Accepting authority, prescription, and tradition, a people may find true liberty—which, as Milton knew, consists well with order. Without such recognition of norms, a people are afflicted by the devastating "freedom" of the Congo.

"It is fashionable nowadays," Gustave Thibon wrote more than twenty years ago, "to put the blame for everything on Morality, and either heap invective upon it or treat it as a joke. Morality is thus taken to be something factitious, superficial, and 'passé,' fitted to a man like a strait-jacket or a mask. One of the rules of the psychological-literary game of our time is to oppose 'life' to 'morality.' I say again that this dichotomy will make our descendants laugh."

But the enemies of norms, Thibon continues, are conventional in their attack upon conventionality. "Nothing could be more commonplace, less original, than their caprices, or less fanciful than their fancies. They are conventionally spontaneous and artificially natural."

The enemies of the permanent things, therefore, soon promulgate their own dogmas of negation. "The decline of moral habit," as Thibon puts it, "produces, in its first stage, a rigid and exalted moralism; and in its second, an immoralism raised to the level of doctrine; sooner or later, it invariably gives birth to the lowest kind of morality."

It is not surprising to find that the advocate of private immorality embraces the literature of violence and the politics of totalism; that he rejects culture root and branch. A systematic example of this negation is a book by an Everett Knight, published a few years ago, *The Objective Society*. Having denounced the moral servitude of traditional civilization, Knight took a post at a university in Ghana, then ruled by an egomaniac tyrant—an action sufficiently symbolic of how the enemies of the permanent things progress from personal anarchy to public tyranny.

Knight's book is suffused by hatred; it denounces objectivity, religion, absolutes, the bourgeoisie, positivism, T. S. Eliot, Salvador Dali, intellectuals, variety, humanism, leadership, and culture—

especially culture. Although Knight has praise for few, he does admire inordinately the Marquis de Sade.

"The adolescent fortunate enough to be able to give free rein to his sexual appetites," Knight says, "is reacting to an evidence which society, out of a mixture of gratuitous cruelty and cowardice, does its best to obscure."

Here one need only comment that the appetites for destruction and violence and ruthless power are no less congenital than the appetite for sexual gratification; so society must obscure and repress and divert the extreme form of such appetites, that men may live at peace with one another. But for Knight and his kind, freedom consists of gratification after the visions of Sade: "No one who has passed a Sunday in a protestant community, or tried, apart from matrimony, to give to fornication the exalted and time-consuming place in his life which it so richly deserves, or dared, if he is an academic, to say exactly what he thought to his students, no such person can suppose for a moment that he is a free agent rather than a damned object."

Such a "free agent" finds his liberator in Kwame Nkrumah, the Redeemer. Knight demands that we follow "men of few ideas," but of ideas which can be "implemented." In a "truly humane communism," Knight declares, perfect freedom will be attained. He would extirpate the monkish caste of pure scholars. The wave of the future will sweep away the traditional Academy, as it already has inundated aristocratic and bourgeois institutions. In the terrestrial paradise of perfected Marxism, a few ideas "in some elemental form will be the property of every literate reasonably informed person, *because it is only this kind of idea that one can hope to implement,* and the man unconcerned about implementing his thought is not a thinker, he is a mere collector of ideas." (The italics are Knight's.) The professor should become an ideologue— Marxist variety, of course. Down with those Absolutes after which the intellectual still hankers!

"The revolt of the workers is preferable to the elegant sulking of the intellectual deprived of an Absolute. The hunger for food may be satisfied, not that for the Truth, because there is none; and it is probable that the real revolution of our time is the discovery that while something can be done about hunger, nothing can be done about spiritual hunger. This is what the intellectuals failed to understand. They thought Marxism was a religion; but it is simply, in its present form, the answer to hunger, and they are better advised to turn to Catholicism as many of them have."

The solitary merit of Knight's fulminations—which are sufficiently characteristic of the American and international "New Left"—is their candor. By "Absolutes" and "Truth," Knight means normality. Abnormity is his passion. Here one encounters the "immoralism raised to a doctrine" to which Thibon refers. In the order of the soul, as in the order of society, this brand of "freedom" means servitude to the sadistic appetite; right reason is its arch-enemy.

"When the ideal cannot become incarnate," Thibon observes, "the flesh turns to self-idealization, and then there arises a new type of decadence—that of the corrupt deifying their corruption. A new 'morality' appears, justifying theoretically the fundamental amoralism of the sick moral habits—the fallen Icarus enjoying the rest in the mire promised to all who allow themselves to be tempted by the impossible."

In such writers as Knight, then, ideology attains its final stage of corruption. Everything permanent must be destroyed, because even the permanent is imperfect; thought itself must be effaced; all men will be perfectly equal in their servitude to physical appetite. The service of Baal, we are told, is perfect freedom.

"And after all this is accomplished, and the
      brave new world begins
When all men are paid for existing and no man
      must pay for his sins,
As surely as Water will wet us, as surely as
      fire will burn,
The Gods of the Copybook Headings with fire
      and slaughter return!"

In Rudyard Kipling, as T. S. Eliot says, "the conscience of the 'fabulist' and the consciousness of the political and historical imagination are always at work." The moral imagination of the man of letters, combining with the political and historical imagination of the talented statist, may yet lead us back from the fleshpots of abnormity to the altar of the permanent things. The Gods of the Market promise us the Fuller Life, in every age—and most men have worshipped them, "till our women had no more children and the men lost reason and faith." Today Kipling's lines ring truer than they did in 1919.

During the half-century which has elapsed since Kipling wrote "The Gods of the Copybook Headings," those grim retributive deities have returned to much of the world. They take vengeance for the degradation of literature and the corruption of politics, which are the two faces of the decadent Janus. Yet though the enemies of the permanent things are arrogant in our time, still normality has its champions in arms. If we yield up our normative weapons, the Gods of the Market deliver us bound to the foe. Of those weapons, the moral imagination is keenest; and the anarch fears its edge.

Index